The Thornish Path

'The Lords of the Mound did not leave this world because they were afraid of the sons of Abraham. They never left at all but rather, stepped aside to watch the doctrine of the mad manifest itself on the land. They did this as a lesson, so that the true folk of the Earth would eventually re-awaken to a deeper appreciation of the old ways.'

- Björn Hammarson

Dedication

To Tom Shoopman
— a true friend, gifted smith and brother of the spear.

The Thornish Path

An Introduction to a Neo-Tribal Tradition

Jack Wolf

By Jack Wolf
All materials herein are © Jack Wolf 2017

Also by Jack Wolf
The Way of the Odin Brotherhood

Contents

'From the time of the Founders, not all that long ago, we have walked a tribal way, yet ours is a unique path through the wood. We are the awakened, the enduring; those sanctified in the fires of ordeal and deep trial. We have known pride in our work and joy in our undertakings yet we have walked in deepest humility. We bear the marks of the Thornwood upon our skin, our very souls. We hold close the discomforts of truly knowing the dark realities of the world. Such things keep us vigilant. We are, by our ways, trials, and our codes, nothing if not knights. We are the dark wardens of the Balance and a new form of nobility in training.

We are the Knights of the Thornwood and since the founding this has been so, even if we have never before declared it as such.'

- Björn Hammarson

Introduction

In the summer of 1987 there was a gathering of initiates at the home of the man who had started much of what you will read here in this short volume. He was a teacher, a mentor and most of all a friend to every single person who had come — some from long distances away — to gather in that place. His name was Ari, a person of mixed descent. His mother had been Cree and his father hailed from Norway and he had been walking a powerful, deeply pagan and Earth-centered path for many of the sixty-seven years he had spent here in the Middle World.

Ari had originally been an initiate of a much older order. As a young man he had been inducted into a world of powerful lore and even more powerful magic as a member of the Ghost Bear Lodge, an appendant lodge of the enigmatic Black Talon Society. During his time in this brotherhood he grew exponentially on many personal levels and became a kind of medicine-person. He was an expert woodsman, a traditional healer, and a very potent seer.

Ari became greatly respected as the green-adept that he was, and it was because of this that when the elders of the Old Lodges decreed that they would fade from the world of men that Ari would be permitted to form a Lodge of his own. They did this out of deep respect for him and because despite their embrace of what they were certain was their own destiny, they wished to leave behind a seed of knowledge and spirit that would live on and grow into a mighty new tree. Elders of the Old Lodges had foreseen greatness in the endeavor to which Ari had been trusted and they gave him their full blessing as he went out to follow his destiny.

Ari put a great deal of his heart and soul into the creation of the new lodge and when he performed this undertaking he was not alone. Again with the blessing of the fading elders he took with him several brothers of the Old Lodges (such as the respected elders Alfred Red-Tail and Jeremy Black as well as the much-respected hunter Michael Grey) and was gifted with the counsel of still others – some from the world of men and others from the realms of spirit. These included the enigmatic Augustus Schmidt, a Germanic sorcerer, and his student, Agnarr Björn, along with Walker Kale, a spirit-worker of Finnish descent.

The elder known by his tribal name as Black Coyote of the Old Lodges made himself available from time to time during the creation of the new lodge as well. Ari considered himself fortunate to have such great men available to him during this time.

The new lodge, which was named the Raven Lodge, was officially formed in the late autumn of the year 1958 and over the next few years the founders forged together new traditions that, when melded with the ways of the Old Lodges, created a unique tradition of forest Warriors the likes of which had never been seen before. The way of the Thornwood was crafted through mind, deed, and spirit and unlike the way of the Old Lodges, which had been reclusive and focused upon the retention of lore and wisdom, it took a new approach: To go outward into the world and teach the old way to those who were ready for it. Also in a fashion differing from that of the Old Lodges, the Raven Lodge actively sought out opportunities to teach female apprentices. Though the Old Lodges honored women and considered them to be deeply sacred, they had never admitted womenfolk into their tribal circles.

Like the Old Lodges before it, the way of the Thornwood, of the Raven Lodge of the Black Talon Society, would be a deep-Earth tradition, a tradition where mystical learning was combined with warrior skill forged through rite and ordeal. Through these methods would be forged a new culture of pagan folk, folk who were connected through powerful oaths and experiences and who would go forth into the world as guardians and teachers for the natural world.

Nearly thirty years passed from the time of the founding and during that time new students were taken on by those who were by now Masters and Elders of the Raven Lodge. The numbers were never great but the quality of the individuals trained to walk in this sacred way was very high indeed. Many new things were discovered, many new trails blazed, and many deep insights gathered and in the end the Thornish Warriors of the Black Talon Society had become a gleaming new tool in the arsenal of the Old Powers, just as the elders of the Old Lodges had foreseen.

As time passed some of the original Elders and Founders passed on to the spirit world, leaving others to take their places by the tribal fires. Like a great circle of understanding and power the wheel turned.

By the time of the gathering in 1987 Ari Torinsson had been walking the elder path, the path of the Lodge, for a good many years. He had taught numerous students, many of whom had come to see him and learn from him once again. There had been numerous gatherings like this before and initiates welcomed the opportunity to see old friends once again. His message this time, however, was potent and unexpected. As one who throughout his entire life had been gifted with powerful prescient abilities, he had now been given a particularly significant one: He had been given a Vision of his impending demise.

Ari, or as he was better known and loved by this time, Master Raven, or more plainly, Raven, was very calm and collected as he informed the assembled Hearth-kin of the details of his spirit-message. He told them that he would expect certain signs to come in the not-so-distant future and when those signs had manifested themselves he would be taking the long-walk back to the land of his ancestors. He estimated that he would be in the Middle World for a couple of years yet, but as always, each day was a gift: he planned to use his time well and wisely.

Also during this time, he told his students that he wanted to take another step forward in his plans to make the tradition more widely available to the rest of the world, for those who were interested. He said that while much of the previous two decades had been spent in evolving the tradition he wanted the coming times to include getting the Thornish message out into the world.

Many years earlier Raven had experienced what was now widely known in the tradition as the Black Spiral Prophecy*, a prophecy in which he saw numbers of previously hidden secret societies and other such orders, those who had walked the older ways and retained much of the old knowledge, coming forward ever so gradually and making contact with the outer world.

The reason for this was fairly obvious. The world was (and is) approaching deep crisis and in order to assist in regaining the balance the knowledge which had been hidden for years would again come forth to be of help. The Black Spiral Prophecy had come at about the time Ari and his fellows were engaged in the creation of the Raven Lodge and of course this was seen as no coincidence. Ari and his brothers had known from the early days that the way they were forging was a manifestation of the Old Ones and of the Earth herself. The tradition was being created so that its members might be an implement of balance – tools to affect change in the world and within human societies.

Raven dreamed of the tradition being made available to a wider circle, beyond the intimate, somewhat secretive gatherings which had up until 1987 largely been the entirety of the order. He and his founding brothers had foreseen a time when those awakening folk who so desired could find out about the way of the Thornwood and could, if they wished, seek to learn more.

For a time there was considerable internal dialogue concerning this. Some suggested that to make this information more widely available was to court disaster. It was thought that cultural theft, already a hallmark of the so-called new age community, especially with respect to Native and other tribal cultures, was rampant and should be avoided at all costs. Some said that their concerns went deeper, that cultural theft might be insignificant compared to what might happen if the wrong sorts of people came into possession of some of the more powerful Thornish lore. Others wondered if the outer world was ready for what those of the Thornwood had to teach.

And these dialogues went on, albeit always in a respectful fashion, for a considerable time until the gathering of 1987. Thus it was during that historic moot, especially given the news of Raven's death-Vision, that the initiates again discussed the matter and came to a decision. As a result of their decision a formal moot was set for the autumn of that year, where all initiates would have a say and a vote on the matter. The decision was unanimous: The tradition would finally be opened more to the outer world and the mechanism by which that would be accomplished would be designed.

Ari's Vision eventually came to pass and by spring of 1990 the great man was no more. His sword was taken to the mountains and his Shar, his sacred ritual spear, was returned to the river spirits from whom he had originally received it. Raven's passing was not mourned so much as celebrated, as he had gone to the next world with the satisfaction that he had accomplished much and that his students would carry on the traditions into the future. He had known that this would be a future where the wisdom of the old ways would be needed the most, just as had been foretold.

What the reader will find revealed here in the pages of this book is a very basic introduction to the world that was built not only by Raven and the brothers who founded the first Lodge of the Thornish tradition, but also by the sages of the Black Talon Society's Old Lodges, those of the way that had gone before.

The world which was woven together though these efforts is not what the average person might expect. It is the world of a gathering of Earth-Warriors; of sages, mystics and mages, all striving to do their part in the saving of our sacred Middle World. They were and still are working each day to embrace their sacred roles as stewards of the Earth, as knights of the Thornwood.

The stories shared here are in no particular chronological order. Some are told in the first person and others are conveyed in the sense of the third person, as this is the way they were originally presented or recorded. They are intended to convey an image of various aspects of the tradition and come from the experiences of various people who have been involved with our culture. Some of the stories deal with people in early stages of learning and others come from the experiences of more advanced initiates. Again, the idea here is to share various aspects of the ways of the tradition with the reader, who may have had no prior contact with the tribal tradition we call the Thornish way.

This book is divided into nine chapters. It would be a rare thing indeed to find any book of Thornish origin that has more than nine chapters in fact, as in the tradition the number nine is considered especially sacred. This volume should be considered not so much as a book of dry details but as a series of stories placed here to illustrate to the reader the rich tapestry in which people of the Thornish tradition live their lives.

Thornish folk, it should be noted for the reader who may be unfamiliar with such nuances, are very fond of stories. Often lessons are told within the tradition by way of stories and sometimes even songs. The use of metaphor and kennings are also quite common in Thornish culture. As a result, it is a very commonplace thing to find information about the Thornish traditions disseminated by way of the narrative tradition.

The first chapter contains the story entitled *Temple of the Black Root*. This tale comes to us from the time when some of the original founders of the Raven Lodge of the Black Talon Society were still living. It is presented to offer a form of introduction to the ideals and structure of the tradition. The tradition, true to the intentions of the founders, has evolved over the decades; swaying flexibly in the winds of time and societal change, yet the core principles have remained the same: To act as authentic tribal people of the Earth and to continue to seek out the wisdom of the primal powers.

The stories which follow this are offered as illustrations of various aspects of the Thornish culture – especially from those early years - which may be of educational value to those outside the tradition.

The primary purpose of this book is to provide information that might serve as a foundation for potential further reading as more works appear and to inspire those who wish to seek deeper understandings of the tradition we walk.

It has been my experience, over the years of my life and especially during my years as a Thornish initiate, that the world is indeed darkening and we are rushing to the edge of an abyss, a headlong surge that will likely end in the extinction of every living thing here on Earth. Over the past twenty years, especially, I have seen this dark flow in action and as the information age brings more and more to light a large portion of the human population is finally coming to the stark realization of what damage has been done.

It is not too late to stop the approaching maelstrom that Ari Torinsson so accurately described in decades past. More and more people are waking up to the various possibilities for change and are educating themselves about these things. People have been waking up and doing something about the state of the world and they are doing this on many levels.

In Thornish belief it is held that not only is everything in nature alive but that nature is quite capable of creating whatever she needs to deal with any given situation. Nature is highly intelligent: The Earth herself is also highly intelligent. To Thornish folk there is absolutely no doubt of this and to that end it is believed that Thornish people were forged into an implement of balance just as many other gatherings of Earth defenders also are. This world, after generations of abuse, has slowly moved towards action to defend herself and to rid herself of the vermin who have been destroying her for so long.

The Black Spiral Prophecy has begun to unfold as numerous other gatherings of people, once hidden in the black folds of time, have begun to come forward to teach, to lead and to fight. Human kind was never meant to be a plague upon the sacred Middle World; we were meant to be stewards of the land, not the despoilers of it.

The way of the Thornwood is one way in which human beings might return to that sacred role.

The need is great..
The time is upon us.

Jack Wolf
Vancouver, British Columbia
Blood Moon/November, 2014

*   A copy of the Black Spiral Prophecy may be found
    at the end of this book

1

Temple of the Black Root

'Deeper...darker....and so you must go until the nature of the Black Root is revealed to you. And when this occurs don't be so foolish as to imagine that the enormity of comprehension will not bring you pain. To those who so delve, knowledge will always come at a steep price, yet is this not why we are here in the Middle World? That we might fully experience...and truly KNOW?'

- Agnarr Björn, a founder of the first Thornish lodge

Master Talon waited for his student at the banks of the river. The water made a very soothing sound as it splashed along in its course, which only added to the delight the elder felt out there on that bright spring morning. The previous week had been very rainy and he had spent a good deal of time working around his home and in meditation. Now well into his 60's, Master Talon was one of the older initiates in his tradition. Only Masters Hawk and Tiva were older, and Tiva was his senior only by a couple of years. He had not spent a lot of time teaching over the previous handful of years and was quite pleased to be able to pass on something of what he knew to a younger person.

His brother from the Old Lodge had specifically asked him to spend

time with this particular student, who was his Lodge-brother's grandson. It was believed that due to the close relations between Black Coyote and his grandson there might be a clearer transmission of knowledge if the young man engaged with other teachers from time to time.
Talon had agreed to spend time with the young one because he agreed
that young minds need variety, but also as a favor to his dear friend.

The student's name was Russell, who was barely a Learner in the
tradition. He had not received a tribal name yet.

At last the young man appeared from the trail as it opened from
the forest onto the riverbank. As soon as he saw Talon sitting there,
clad in his usual uniform of blue jeans and worn flannel shirt, he smiled
and waved.

Talon motioned for him to come over and the young man complied.

'Come on, sit down here on the sand with me, Russell,' the old
Master requested.

Russell sat down across from him on the sand. They were now
both seated in such a fashion as they could view the river as it bent
around on its snake-like course.

Talon had been re-braiding his long grey-white hair as he waited
for Russell to arrive. Now he finished the job and tossed the braid over
his shoulder. He reached over and shook Russell's hand. As the sleeves
of his shirt were rolled up to the elbow Russell could see the many
tattoos that covered his forearms. They were not what one might expect
to see on an old man of First Nations ancestry – in fact they looked
much to Russell as though they might be symbols from some kind of
ritual magical tradition. Russell had been interested in such things at an
earlier time and read much about various sorcerous traditions. The
symbols intrigued him quite a lot, but he restrained his curiosity and
didn't ask about them.

Russell also noted the beautiful bracelet which the old man wore
on his left wrist. It was made of what looked like alternating red and
black beads and coiled around the elder's wrist like a slim coral snake.
Seeing it sent a slight chill up his spine as he realized his grandfather
had very recently gifted him one just like it.

'Your grandfather tells me you want to learn our ways,' Talon said
after a moment. 'And by this I mean the ways of the Thornwood, not
the Native ways which you already know.'

'Yes sir, I would like that,' Russell said. 'I mean, I have been learning the traditional ways, the Indian ways, from him for years and I had no idea that he was also involved with this society. Once he told me about it I was eager to know more.'

Talon nodded and sat back slightly.

'You know that although this other tradition of ours was born partly from the Native ways it has other roots as well? You know that it is unique and while you can walk in the Indian way and be happy with that, you can also walk in this way if you choose to. The two aren't really exclusive of one another.'

'I was told that, yes. That's why I am so intrigued.'

The Master grinned. It was a bright, warm expression that caused Russell to smile in return.

'You know a very, very long time ago I was in the army,' the old man said. 'Everybody was calling people sir. I didn't really like that then and am not too fond of it even now. While I appreciate the respect I'd prefer it if you called me Alfred.'

'Grandpa mentioned that you had a traditional name as well,' Russell said, nodding. 'Was it Master Talon?'

The elder chuckled on hearing that. 'You know, when you get to be my age you end up collecting more than a few names. Sure, I have a number of these. I've got my family tribal name from my people and I have a few nicknames that for now I won't make you laugh over. And yes, from the tradition you now want to learn I also have a name. The man who taught me this tradition gave it to me because of my spirit-animal, which is the hawk. So yeah, you can call me Talon. The word Master, in this case, really means that I have learned one or two things that might be of some minor use to my fellow human beings, or to spirit people or to the sacred balance in general. In our tradition we are not big on such titles. They are more used as guidelines for those we are teaching than as any kind of crutches to hold onto. But you know, I am simply me in the end; Alfred, so make of it what you will.'

'Alfred then,' Russell said at last, lightly bowing.

The elder took a stick from the grass beside him and on the sand drew a symbol which Russell had never seen before.

The drawing appeared to Russell like an oval with another, smaller oval inside of it. Bisecting this oval was a wiggling line that looked like either a snake or possibly a river of water. On either side of the wiggling line there was a simple circle. Russell's imagination made an attempt to interpret the symbol and he came up with the idea that maybe it was two holes on either side of a stream.

'Have you seen this before?' Alfred asked.

Russell told him that he had not, but that to him it looked like two holes on either side of a river.

Alfred laughed again. It was a light, pleasant sound.

'You aren't too far off,' he replied. 'It is a very special Thornish symbol. You know what I am talking about when I use the word Thornish now, don't you?'

Russell nodded. When his grandfather had told him about the tradition he also filled him in on certain aspects of the thing.

'It's the term used to describe people who have taken the Thornish path that started back in the 50's. He told me that the word Thornish comes from the idea that wisdom has to be earned, sometimes painfully, and the thorn-tree is a symbol of that.'

Alfred nodded.

'What else did he tell you?'

'That the Thornish people who were initiated were called Shar and that they had a sacred spear which was also called a Shar. He told me that the main purpose of the Shar was to work towards gaining an understanding of the laws of nature. That and working to protect the Earth. He told me that you and he were once members of a much older lodge and at one point some of the members of the old lodge started the new lodge – and that new lodge was the beginning of the Thornish ways.'

'Very good,' Alfred commented. 'Which brings me back to this symbol. It is a Thornish symbol that illustrates the quest for understanding. The two things you saw as holes are actually supposed to represent people; two people on either side of a great river of knowledge.'

'I wasn't too far off after all,' Russell said, smiling.

'On the surface at least,' the old man said. 'However there are more depths to this symbol. There are two people indicated there and they are sitting on either side of that snake-like line. They are not really separated, but rather studying the wiggling line together. They could be brothers or they could be student and teacher. What really matters is that they are studying the snake-like line in between them.'

'The line is a river?' Russell asked.

'Close… in a matter of speaking,' Alfred said. 'It is what we call the Black Root. Has your grandfather ever told you about that?'

'No.'

Alfred let out a large, mock sigh of relief and then looked at the student again, grinning.

'Well at least the old coyote has left me some of the work to do,' he chuckled. 'I was starting to wonder why he had sent you to me if he had taught you everything.'

'Actually he taught me just enough to be curious for more,' Russell admitted.

'That's his way, as I am sure you know. He is and always has been a coyote-teacher. They give just enough so the student becomes eager to learn more…then he lets them go after the truth for themselves.'

'Knowledge always sticks better when a person earns it for themselves,' Russell said, paraphrasing his grandfather's own words.

'Yes,' Alfred said.

Russell spent a long moment looking at the symbol in the sand. Finally he looked up at Alfred.

'So, can you tell me what this Black Root is?' he asked.

Alfred got up for a moment to stretch his legs. He had been sitting cross-legged for some time and wanted to get the blood flowing. When Russell moved to get up also, out of respect, the old man gently waved him down.

'After awhile the old bones complain,' he explained, smiling. Moments later Alfred sat back down again, in the exact same place he had been sitting before.

'So you want to learn and you haven't been given much more than the basics,' he continued after he was settled. 'Well, I guess I had better give you a bit of a beginner's lecture then.' He grinned.

Russell had noticed that Alfred was a very congenial kind of fellow. He smiled and grinned a lot and it was not the fake kind of smiles he had seen so often from people; his smiles were genuine. Russell found himself liking this old man very much. He was very comfortable to be around, kind of like his grandfather.

'Okay, here's a foundation for you,' Alfred began. 'Long ago there was a gathering of men who were a mixed bunch. Some were of the Indian nations and some were white. Most of the white fellas were of northern European ancestry and the ones I am talking about here weren't the typical Christian colonialists. They secretly held to the older pagan ways of their ancestors. They were a rare bunch in those days. Anyways, at some point they got together with a group of Native fellas and formed a kind of society. It was a hunter's society, a warrior society and most importantly it was a society that was kept secret. The original idea was that the members of this society could help each other. The white guys were of use to the Indians because they had some influence on the other colonial types who were swarming the traditional lands. The Native guys were of use to the white guys because of the lore and wisdom they had concerning the ways of the land. Don't forget, a lot had already been lost to these guys over in Europe and because they were secret pagans they wanted to keep what they had alive and learn more – kinda fill in the gaps.'

'Was this a long time ago?' Russell asked.

'That's what we are told, yes,' Alfred replied. 'So for these reasons, and others, these men in this hidden society were like a kind of hunters and warriors support group. They helped each other during some pretty bad times. If you know any history you will know the kinds of things that were going on against our Native relations in those times so we did what we had to to get through them. So yes, while no one really knows how long ago exactly this all happened, we do know that it was long ago.'

'How long? Does anybody actually know?'

'You are really attached to the idea that time goes only in a straight line, aren't you?'

Russell reddened a little. 'Just curious,' he replied somewhat meekly.

'As I say, nobody really knows,' Alfred said. 'But it was before my time and before anybody else's time that I know, including Old Joe, who taught me and your grandpa back in the old days. So if you figure the numbers it was a long time ago.'

'So it was a secret society,' Russell prompted.

'Yes, and like many such things it was born out of need,' Alfred said. 'We have never been apologetic about who we are or more importantly…what we are. There was a certain need in those days and men came together to fill the need. This was done as a group and on the individual level. As you know…or as you should know, we are in a constant process of inventing ourselves.'

'People would gather and have meetings,' Alfred continued after a pause. 'They would share their knowledge and help each other out. A lot of these guys were hunters and trappers which gave them a fair bit of common ground. Native guys would share stories and skills and the white guys would do the same. When there was a threat of any kind they would work together to help each other out. That's how it started. Later others heard about it and wanted to join, but the ones who were already in were always very careful about who they allowed to join.'

'Rough times,' Russell added.

'Don't forget these were times when it was illegal to be a traditionalist on either side of the ocean. Christianity was all over the place, enforcing its doctrines in very nasty ways. The colonialists figured that their god had made everything for them and they could do whatever they wanted to do. Our white brothers told us horrific stories of old days when their old religions had been attacked and how their pagan people had been slaughtered. They told us that while the times had softened somewhat on them they could see what was still being done to the Indian people and they saw this as proof that the insanity could come back onto everyone at any time. Our original white brothers were right too. The Indians were getting many brutal things happening to them. Back in those days it was illegal for Native people even to speak their language or perform their ceremonies. A lot of this kind of thing has gone on right up to very recent times.'

'I have heard about some of that,' Russell said.

'So there was a lot riding on those guys keeping things below boards so to speak,' Alfred said. 'To be found out could have resulted in people getting thrown in the jails or worse, not to mention government retaliation. There were a lot of dark and twisted things going on and let's not even get me going about those sick government schools that they would take kids away to. It was a very black time, young Russell, a very nasty time. Secrecy was very important to those original fellas.'

'And this was the original Black Talon Society?'

'Has you grandfather told you the story of Raven's Gift? And by that I mean the Thornish story, not the Native one.'

'No, he hasn't.'

Alfred nodded and paused for a moment before continuing.

'Yes, in answer to your question, they were the founders of the

Black Talon Society. The society was named in honor of Raven. Get your grandpa to tell you the story and it will fit together for you.' *

'I will.'

'So we have the hidden society there,' Alfred continued. 'They existed like this for a long time, really quiet and careful so that nobody knew what they were doing. As I say, more people wanted to come in to this and eventually more lodges were formed. I learned about it from a friend. It wasn't quite as much of a guarded secret by then, but people still kept a low profile.'

'And I get the impression that the society eventually changed,' Russell said.

'Well, time changes everything,' Alfred said. 'Even linear time as most common people see it. So yes, things changed.'

'Linear time?' Russell interrupted.

'Linear time, yes,' Alfred answered, undisturbed by the interruption. 'Most human beings see time as going in a straight line; a beginning, a middle and an end. That sort of thing. The problem is that this couldn't be further from the reality of things. Traditional people, those who are close to the Earth and to the spirits of the land, know that time is circular. Everything in nature is cyclical. In the Thornish tradition we think of time as spherical actually, because everything that has ever happened has the potential to happen again and is happening simultaneously at various points in the scheme of things. Nothing is static. Everything is subject to flow.'

After a moment Alfred said, 'Did that answer your question about time?'

'Yes.'

Now Alfred was grinning slyly at Russell, as though he was holding on to a secret joke or something.

'May I continue with what I was saying a few minutes back?'

'Sure,' Russell said, grinning back.

'We were talking about changes in the old lodges,' Alfred continued. 'Finally, after many years, lodges started disappearing and at first people thought there were some dirty tricks being played by the Christians or their government. But it turned out that this was not the case. What was happening was that a lot of the old timers were really getting sick of the modern world, a world that seemed to be getting worse and worse and they just wanted to vanish into the wild places and get away from all civilization. While the society was never really all that big it made an impact when entire lodges of guys wanted to go what one guy called *Deep Traditional* and fade out of the view of history altogether.'

'Indian traditional or white traditional?' Russell asked, curiously.

'Neither, really,' Alfred answered. 'Because, like I say, the society had been around for a while and by this time had developed this unique subculture. People remained on the outside as they always had been, with their outward traditions, families and jobs and such…well, most of them anyway…but the lodge traditions were fading from the outer world and the secrecy was coming back even more than before. Some people became very protective of the tradition and wanted to lock it away so it could never be discovered and possibly destroyed. Others were weary of the outside world and wanted to go off and live a pure life in the deepest woods they could find. There were many debates about this. Some people didn't want that to happen and so they asked permission to form a new lodge that could carry on the old ways somewhat more openly. Eventually some of them got permission to do that and this is where the actual Thornish tradition came into the world.'

'So what was different about this new lodge, besides the fact that these guys didn't want to fade away?'

'The fellas who started it believed that in order to survive everything has to be flexible, to bend in the wind, so to speak,' Alfred said. 'They wanted to eventually be able to come out of the shadows and teach people because there were more than a few Visions that the world was going to need help. They believed that one of the best ways to help was to educate people in the reality of what was being done to harm our world and what could be done to help fix it. The old guys were tired, for the most part. Don't forget they had been through a lot back in those old times and were beaten down by it. They wanted to fade away and disappear into the wild places like I said earlier. And that's exactly what most of them did.'

'So there was nobody left but these younger guys in the end?'

'Well, one of the older lodges stayed around a bit more than the others. It was called the Ghost-Bear Lodge, named after the sacred white spirit bear. The old guys in that one agreed to help the younger guys with their new idea but once this decision was made they would accept very few new members into the Ghost-Bear Lodge. They would help the younger guys and see how that went.'

'And guys like you and my grandpa are all that's left of this lodge?' Alfred smiled.

'Your mother is English,' Alfred said, 'and your father is Native, so that makes you a Métis, a mixed blood person who stands between two worlds. Well, in my own case I was raised in the Indian way by my late uncle, actually, and later in life I came to the Black Talon Society so when I accepted that way I also became a walker-in-two worlds. Many of the members are walkers-in-two-worlds on one level or another, whether that is in spirit or race or culture. What we must understand is that when we do this we are not ever half of anything, but rather more like double of something. The responsibility is much greater but so are the rewards.'

Russell nodded. He had heard similar things from his grandfather and he believed them to be true.

'So yes, there are a few others who hung around to help,' Alfred said in answer to Russell's original question. ' Some up and faded off; they went to retire in the woods. Some stayed.'

'So the old lodges are gone forever?'

'No such thing as forever, my young friend,' Alfred said. 'Spherical time, remember? The old lodges didn't go off to die, they went away to get out of the modern, mundane world. They became very secretive and selective and those who could took off to the wildest places they could find. Who's to say that there aren't one or two of them still out there, hidden in the wilderness; up north maybe? Whatever the case I do know that those who wanted to disappear did a pretty good job of it. Other than those of us who remained behind there has been no sign of our former lodge brothers for a long time.'

Alfred stood up again, stretching his legs.

'Okay, young Russ, my old body has had enough of sitting for awhile. Let's walk a bit.'

Russell got up and as he did the old man gently obscured the symbol he had drawn with his foot. After that they began to walk east along the river bank.

'So the new lodge was called the Raven Lodge after the member who had gotten permission to build it. His tribal name was Raven so it was decided that the lodge would be named after his spirit-teacher, Raven. Since the primordial spirit of Raven is also credited with the creation of the Black Talon Society, in the beginning it was thought that this new lodge, since it was also a beginning, should be named to honor him.'

'And the new lodge was still of the Black Talon Society?' Russell asked.

'Of course,' Alfred answered. 'It's part of the reason that permission was given for it to be created, so that there would be a legacy left of the old ways. The people of the Raven Lodge are very definitely also members of the Black Talon Society. It could not really be otherwise; we carry the gift forward.'

'But the new lodge was different,' Russell again prompted.

'Different, yes, but not ever abandoning the original core values and understandings of the original lodges,' the old man replied. 'There is much in the new lodge that has remained true to the original plan. This you will see if you choose to go further and learn more.'

'I see...' Russell said.

The two walked along in silence for awhile, enjoying the sights and sounds of the river valley. Alfred, for his part, seemed pleased that his student had the wisdom to know when silence served better than words.

'The core of the lodge is the understanding of the sacred balance,' Alfred said at last. 'This has not changed at all since the founding of the original lodges. That, and the respect we hold for the First Law.'

'The First Law?' Russell asked.

'We see four sets of rules in the world,' Alfred explained. 'The Fourth Law is the law of human societies, basically the rules humans set up to control other humans. It is the one which is of least importance to anyone who is truly awake and sees what is going on in the world. The so-called Fourth Law is the tool of those who have lost their way and never want to wake up. Then there is the Third Law: This is the Law of tribal societies and consists of whatever rules that traditional people hold to themselves. The Second Law is what we call the Law of the Old Ones; it is the rule-set held by those beings who are vastly older and wiser than we human beings are. Then we get to the one we see as the most important law and that is the First Law. The First Law is quite literally the law of the cosmos, the law of nature. We see that as the supreme law and it is more important than any of the other ones below it.'

Russell though about what Alfred had said for a moment. 'That's pretty profound,' he said. 'I never thought about it that way.'

'Everything in nature is organized in one way or another,' Alfred said. 'Whether we humans know it or understand it, there is always some kind of design behind things. The First Law commands balance and whatever we see out there we know that in the end it will always come back to balance. Here on Earth the humans are responsible for un-balancing things. Nature will correct this eventually and whether we survive the correction will depend on whether we can all wake up in time to start doing our parts.'

'Human beings were put here to be stewards of the land, not the destroyers of it,' Russell added. He had heard his grandfather say this enough times to have memorized it.

'Yes, that is the idea,' Alfred said. 'The sacred balance is everything. A large scale human awakening is required and the key to becoming fully awake and aware is understanding. Understanding can be kindled through good deeds and education; living by example. We who walk the ways of the Thornish lodges know that this understanding can be deepened and strengthened through the knowledge of the Black Root.'

'Yes, you mentioned that,' Russell said.

'The Black Root is something that has a very similar idea in Native thought when you think about it,' Alfred said. 'Some people call it the first wisdom or the first teachings. In the Thornish perspective it is also called the First Knowledge. The Black Root symbolizes the original knowledge that we believe was imparted to human beings when we were created. It is the knowledge of the cosmos and it is thought that at one time or another all humans had access to it in some way, shape or form. However man has been around for a long time, much longer than most people think, and a lot has been lost – at least on the surface of our minds.'

'So it's original knowledge…kind of like race memory?'

'More like species-memory,' Alfred replied. 'The theory is that at one time, when humans were much more in tune with the Earth, they had greater access to this knowledge but now as we have become decadent and give into material lusts the knowledge has faded from our consciousness. Some traditions held on to it and others lost it. It is thought that when people can get their heads back in the game and understand that we are supposed to be the caretakers and helpers of the world, not the rapers and killers of her, then we will have greater access to the First Knowledge.'

'And what will the First Knowledge do for us?' Russell asked, innocently enough.

Alfred's face lost its grin and he looked at Russell for a long, uncomfortable moment.

'It is the key to our enlightenment,' he said. 'It is the key to us becoming…more…as has been programmed into us for as long as there have been human beings. We are evolving but we have reached a kind of road block over the past thousand years or so. Organized agriculture was the original culprit even farther in the past and later revealed religions, like the ones of Abraham, came along and started poisoning the very soul of our people. It's all been pretty much downhill from there.'

'Yes, that seems to be the case.'

'Russ, everything each human being needs to survive and thrive, both on the physical level and as well, emotionally and spiritually, comes from inside us. In Thornish belief and in many others, the road to true understanding lies within. All a true teacher can do is help you to find your own trail and encourage you to cultivate wisdom along that path. The rest are just helping tools and props that are discarded once the learner reaches a certain level of understanding. So everything you will find in our tradition here is geared toward that.'

'The tendrils of the Black Root are inside the spirit of every living being,' Alfred continued. 'They are the clues which lead us back to deeper understandings and greater, more primal knowledge. It might seem complicated to some people but at the end of the day it's very simple.'

'And you say this Black Root is the way to the old knowledge? So where does that come from? Spirits? Gods?'

Alfred nodded.

'Good question,' he replied. 'Here's a quote you might hear around the lodge one day: *Everyone brings their own meat to the table.* What that means is that in this tradition you have people from various walks of life and even various cultures. The Thornish way isn't a religious doctrine. It's a tradition that teaches one to find the tools to deeper understanding of the First Law and the sacred balance. As far as I know there has ever only been one restriction on religious beliefs here and that is that people from Abrahamic worldviews are not welcome. Any belief system that sees nature as subservient to man is considered to be fundamentally flawed and so it is incompatible with our ways. Other than that there are only a few core things.'

'I like that thing about bringing your own meat to the table.' Russell grinned.

'It's been around for a long time,' Alfred said, smiling.

'So no gods then?'

'I didn't say that, Russ,' Alfred said. 'Remember that quote you like so much? There have been various initiates here who have indeed honored various gods or goddesses because those ones came from their original culture or the culture most deeply drawn to their hearts. Every Thornish person I have ever met who has a cultural preference in these older, greater beings has been either Nordic or Celtic in orientation, and of course there are those who honor the spirits in the Indian fashion. However, Thornish belief considers these gods and goddesses not as omnipotent, immortal beings, but as Elder Kin. What's an Elder Kin, you might ask?'

'Okay, I'm asking,' Russell said.

'Among Thornsmen Elder Kin is a term we use to describe the really old, ancient beings who are very far advanced. Far beyond our current abilities,' Alfred replied. 'In the past humans have seen them as some kind of magical immortals. We see the cosmos as different from that, though. We see it like this: At the beginning of everything, way back further in the cosmos than any of us can fathom, there was a spark of intelligence. This spark of intelligence we call the Great Essence. The Great Essence is the intelligence behind everything in our belief, but it is not a person or a specific deity or anything like that.'

'Kind of like the idea of the Great Mystery?'

'Like that, only we don't think of it as a godlike being. We only know that somehow it is there and that it is responsible for us existing, for all life existing. Thornish people don't get a kick out of bashing our heads against the wall trying to figure out things that are so far beyond us. We just go with the flow and this is what the Old Lodges came up with. Yes, it is much like the Indian Great Mystery concept. It is great and it is mysterious. From the Great Essence the possibility for life came. Life is essentially energy; doesn't have to be material to be alive. Life is everywhere and each life is connected to every other life in the multiplicities of the cosmos. We are all connected to it.'

'Like a great web.'

'Yes, exactly like that,' Alfred replied. 'For many years we called this life force by many different names. Names borrowed from other cultures and some various ones of our own, but it got confusing to some people. As a result, with the coming of the new lodge it was decided to simply call it Önd or even Qaa. Önd is a Germanic word that we use essentially the same way as people might use the Chinese word *Chi* or the East-Indian word *Prana*…and so on. Qaa is a uniquely Thornish word. It came from the spirit world.'

'Önd is the life-force then? That's what you call it?'

'It's just a label in the end,' Alfred replied. 'Remember what I said about the use of tools and helper things?'

Russell nodded. Indeed, he had that part figured out.

'So we have this intelligence of the cosmos here and because of it the possibility occurred for life to exist. From that life, which is everywhere, came beings who were also intelligent but maybe not so intelligent as the Great Essence. These came into existence a very long time ago and are what we refer to as the Ancient Ones. From these, eventually, were descended the beings that helped human beings come to this material world we call Earth.'

'So they created us?'

Alfred made a kind of curious expression for a moment before he answered.

'This is the subject of debate,' he answered. 'Some people have suggested that human beings were made from scratch, so to speak, and put here to be useful helpers to the Elder Kin who lived here. Others suggest that we may have already been here, perhaps as more primitive creatures who were modified by the Elder Kin. Most people I know believe the second theory, but in the end it is but a curiosity. We are here in the now and that is what counts.'

'So are these Elder Kin still here or did they go away?'

'Well, it is said that some of them who were fond of us stayed around to watch over us. Don't forget these people are powerful and are not limited to this dimension. For these guys going to and from various worlds is quite easy. The belief is that there are many of these elder ones out there. Some of them are fond of us, some aren't so fond of us and others, probably the more ancient ones, are so much beyond us that they don't even know of our existence…or wouldn't care if they did.'

'Kind of like ants in the garden?' Russell suggested. 'How many do the gardeners notice at all?'

'Yes, kind of like that.'

'So,' Alfred went on, 'Thornish people believe that there are no such things as gods or goddesses in the commonly accepted sense, only that there are indeed vastly more advanced beings out there, some of whom were probably responsible for our development here.'

'So no one worships these Elder Kin then?'

'No one in our tradition does,' Alfred replied.

'It makes an interesting kind of sense and yeah, it does remind me in some ways of the traditional Native ways,' Russell said.

'Remember what I told you about this tradition, where it all came from?' Alfred said. 'People of like mind gathering together regardless of race, and working for mutual growth. I'm not saying it's the only way by any stretch of the imagination. It's just the way that works for us. However, we will have an opinion on any people who, regardless of their beliefs, cause harm to the sacred Earth or the balance of nature. So yeah, it's our way. We make no claim to being better than anyone else.'

'But there is a spiritual connection there?'

Alfred chuckled.

'Spirit people are the main beings that Thornish people interact with when it comes down to that,' he said. 'The Thornish word we use to describe spirit-people in general is *Shaeda*. Spirit folk are all around us on a daily basis, where usually the Elder Kin present themselves only occasionally or rarely in the life of the average person. It is usually an arrogant person who assumes they have the complete attention or even friendship of one of these elder beings. We generally stick with what we know. Grass roots and all that.'

'More of an Earth-based orientation then?'

'Yes, young fella,' Alfred replied. 'A very deep one. We deal with spirit people and our many other relations here on a daily basis. The common realm we see here is the tiniest tip of the iceberg, son; there are uncountable dimensions beyond this one and even here in what we call the Middle-World there is so much going on that probably 95% of all humans have no idea about. Being a Thornsman is all about being one with nature and being balanced. It's about being in the now, being present and working to grow wise and understanding so that we can be even better at what we do.'

'Caretakers of the Earth,' Russell said.

Alfred patted Russell on the shoulder.

'Yes,' he replied. 'All humans are supposed to be stewards of the Earth. Most have no idea that it is our purpose and a large number live in the fantasy world that tells them the world was put here for their use. We were put here so we could be a part of the life-circle here and be good helpers. Most people have become the opposite of that, sadly.'

'And the way of the Black Root can help more people to awaken then?'

'Those who are worthy,' Alfred said quite sternly.

His change in attitude startled Russell slightly. He thought for a second he had said something to upset the older man. Yet after a second or so Alfred's demeanor returned to its usual light hearted self.

'Let me explain that, Russell,' the old man continued. 'There are those who *do not* treat the world with deep honor and respect. They are well aware of what they are doing and they could care less about anything but their own ridiculous perceptions. They are obsessed with power or money or material gains. Thornish people see these twisted ones as being at the root of most of the problems on the Middle World. They are sick in the spirit and, indeed, in their minds. We should actually pity them for their illness but at times this is difficult because of the damage they do.'

'I understand what you are saying,' Russell said, nodding.

'Add to this that there are great numbers of people who are blissfully ignorant, like herd animals, who are concerned only with the most base mundane things; things like material possessions, comforts, safety and pleasure,' Alfred said. 'Many of these will also never awaken, so when I say those who are worthy I mean those whose destiny it is to come back into the real human family and work to re-establish the balance.'

'I understand,' Russell said calmly. 'I agree with you on that too. The world is suffering greatly because of the greed of a relative few who are misguiding the masses of the ignorant.'

'You already know much then,' Alfred said. 'Your grandfather is probably in no small measure responsible for that.'

'Grandpa is way harsher than you are, Alfred,' Russell said. 'He is a very dark kind of Medicine person as you probably know. To him the sacredness of the Earth is so powerful and important that I think he figures a little spilled blood might not be a bad idea from time to time.'

'I know this.' The older man smiled.

'There are people who are afraid of my grandfather,' Russell said, as if he was imparting some form of highly secret information.

'Why do you think his tribal name in the lodges here is Black Coyote?' Alfred asked. 'What counts is that he has very real power and that he uses his skills for the betterment of his people and for the sacred Earth. Your grandfather has a very special gift and yes, many kinds of spirit people hang around him. It's good to have a person like that around. He is primal and close to the black Earth. He doesn't pull any punches.'

'Grandpa thinks that there are already too many people in the world, like cattle or deer who have over grazed and left everything desolate. He sees nothing wrong with a mass die off of human beings. He says it would be better for the world.'

'Many do think that way,' Alfred said. 'We understand though that in the end it all comes back to balance. Balance is the key and those of our tradition think the very best way to get people to wake up is to educate them. Whether this is by word or example the result is what we look for. Thornish people are certainly not what you would consider to be non-violent. We are instruments of the balance and implements of nature, so just like any other animal that is of use to the First Law, we may occasionally have to use aggressive means to do fulfill our role. Violence is never the preferred method, however.'

Alfred stopped walking and turned to face Russell.

'If a farmer discovers he has rats in his house, what does he do?'

'He gets rat traps?'

'Maybe he will,' Alfred suggested. 'Perhaps he will hire a pest control guy to come and poison the rats. However, if he is Thornish he will probably get a cat. A cat will kill some of the rats, yes, but the presence of the cat will likely also drive the rest of the rats away. No poisons are used, no mass slaughter is undertaken, but examples are made and hopefully, the rats learn and stay away after awhile. The cat is a natural hunter but like any sane creature it prefers peace to war. If our world is like the farmer's house I described then there are a lot of rats here right now and they are wrecking the place.'

'Time to get a cat?' Russell asked.

'Our ways are just one form of cat, yes,' Alfred replied. 'Nature creates the tools necessary to maintain balance and we are one of those tools.'

'We will always prefer the balance in any situation, be that a physical one, or an emotional or spiritual one,' Alfred continued. 'A Thornish person prefers defense to attack even in a situation where the going might get rough, and in fulfilling our role as stewards of the land are we not these days almost always on the defensive? Is there not always some sick asshole out there causing damage to the world or to someone who lives in the world? A wise man once said 'What's the point in even considering attack when you have your hands full with defense all the time?"

'I know what you mean,' Russell said. 'It's all about getting more stuff and this drives the greed further. Then people aren't responsible with their breeding and now there are too many people all wanting stuff. The world is a limited resource.'

'Well, you know in the reality of things most of us dislike that word resource,' Alfred said. 'People who are takers and ruiners use that word to take all the emotion out of the bad things they do. By using the word resource they try to hide from the fact that they are harming other living things. When they smash the Earth, rip down entire forests and poke gaping holes in the ground they are not collecting so-called resources, they are killing our relations, little brother. It's as simple as that.'

'I guess it's a loaded term, resources,' Russell said.

'Loaded like a 12 gauge to the head,' Alfred said. 'And like the shotgun, a lot of damage can result if a crazy person is pulling that trigger.'

Alfred began to walk along the trail again. Russell continued along with him.

'What tears balance apart is human beings getting addicted to things, becoming deeply attached to the idea of stuff. They live in a fantasy world of ownership which is really absurd because a truly awake person realizes that no one can ever own anything. Period. We don't even own our own bodies so how on Earth could we claim to own anything else? It's ridiculous, yet almost everyone believes it. They want to get more stuff or find more pleasure and they want it all from the environment. They haven't and probably never will learn that the only true satisfaction comes from within.'

Alfred gestured to the land all around them, to the mountains and the woods and the river flowing through the meadow.

'No one owns this, though a lot of idiots pretend to,' he said softly.

'Pretending to own something is the first step to believing the delusion that we now have some kind of power over things. When that happens abuses begin. It's a dirty cycle. Shar, the initiates of the Thornish lodges, believe exactly as Indians do that the land is sacred and is its own keeper. We don't believe in ownership but rather we believe in sacred stewardship and keeping the promises that we represent when we were put here to serve the balance.'

After a while they came to a rough-hewn wooden bridge that crossed over the river at a narrow point. The trail forked just beyond it with one trail leading into the mountains and the other continuing straight along. Alfred gestured toward the bridge and they crossed its sun-warmed, creaking planks to the other side.

'There is a lot to absorb, Alfred,' Russell said at last. 'It's very close to the Indian ways yet subtly different too. That might take a bit of getting used to.'

'Your choice, lad,' Alfred replied. 'Nothing wrong with walking the Native road at all and I walk between multiple worlds as well.'

'I am not surprised to find out that my grandfather has walked this way for so long. He has never been what you would call a strict traditionalist.'

At that Alfred laughed.

'No, you could certainly never call him that. He is not called Black Coyote for nothing, you know.'

'Well, he sent me to see you, which I think is a pretty good thing.'

'I am glad you think so,' Alfred said. 'I hope I have been of some assistance so far.'

'I still have questions,' Russell said.

'The man who runs out of questions has either stopped paying attention to the world or he has run out of life,' Alfred said. 'Never stop questing for knowledge; never stop asking questions and you will never stop learning. That is the key. Never stop learning.'

'You spoke of the Shar, the initiates of the Thornish ways,' Russell asked. 'Can you tell me more about that?'

'Shar is the name we have for people who are initiated,' Alfred said casually. 'We have several layers of association. There are people who are friends of the Thornwood and people who want to learn from us. Nowadays these folk are called either Allies or Fellows. An Ally is someone who knows about us and is our friend but does not necessarily walk in our ways. A Fellow is a person who has declared that they are walking according to what they know of our traditions. Usually a Fellow is a declared person who has no direct access to a Thornish teacher.'

'Direct access?'

'There is a hard and fast rule here, young Russ,' Alfred replied. 'It goes that *only a Shar can forge a Shar*. What that means is that if you honor the Thornish way and want to live on that good road then you are welcome to do that. Anyone who wants to live according to our traditions in that respect can do this. However, if they want to learn the deeper teachings and such they need to learn it directly, in person, from someone who has been fully initiated.'

'So if the tradition is secret how would anyone outside learn about it and want to take on the lifestyle?'

'The old society lodges were secret, yes, but nowadays we are much more open – at least some of our ways are more open,' Alfred said. 'Weren't you paying attention when I spoke about the founding of the new lodges?'

'I just wanted to clarify that,' Russell said sheepishly. 'Sorry.'

'Never be sorry for being curious,' the old man said.

'So as I was saying, there are layers of association,' Alfred continued. 'A person who wishes to live in the Thornish way but who does not have direct access to a teacher may still declare themselves Thornish if they wish. Their actions will speak to whether they actually are Thornish or not after that point. Word gets out about us these days, even if it is a slow process. The world is changing and we need to change with it. Like a tree in the wind, Russell; we bend and flow or else we might snap off in a storm.'

Alfred made a sound that to Russell sounded like he was musing something inside his head for a moment.

'There is actually one young lady amongst us who is writing a book,' Alfred continued. 'Your grandfather tells me that you are an aspiring writer too. Maybe once you learn more you could also write about our outer teachings.'

'I have been taking notes for years about my grandpa's ways,' Russell said. 'Maybe I could do that here too?'

'Be my guest,' Alfred said. 'Though you will later have oaths to keep regarding the inner ways.'

'And you were going to tell me about some of that before I interrupted you.'

'Indeed I was,' Alfred said with a grin. 'So you have Allies and Fellows. Then you have people who get taken on as a kind of probationer student I guess you could call them. These are called Learners in the tradition. They have one job and that is as you might have guessed, to learn.'

'That makes sense.'

'I think so too,' Alfred replied. 'Learners are learning and while they are learning we are watching them to see if they will make a good match for us. But the truth be told, by that point if someone has accepted them as a student we already think they are a good match. Even though you are very new to this your grandfather has vouched for you which is why I am telling you all of this stuff now rather than later. You are what could be considered a Learner right now, but we will leave it up to your grandfather to make a final decision on that.'

'He told me about Learners, yes,' Russell said. 'He told me that if this was what I wanted then I should consider myself a Learner in the tradition.'

'Did he give you anything when he said that?'

'He gave me a bracelet quite a bit like that one you are wearing.'

Alfred reflexively looked at his wrist and smiled.

'This thing is probably older than you,' he chuckled. 'And this bracelet; was it the same pattern and color as this one?'

Russell nodded.

'Why aren't you wearing it then?'

'I left it at the house.'

'You should wear it,' Alfred suggested. 'We call it a Maal. It is not something that is easily gotten in this day and age. It's a very old tradition that comes from the old lodges. It's one of the signs of the Learner.'

'I will remember that,' Russell said.

'Now, in the tradition we have what we call levels of learning and responsibility,' Alfred said. 'We have Allies and Fellows and now I have told you a bit about Learners, which it seems your grandpa has been covering too. What the Learner is trying to do is to get to the point where he or she can be considered for initiation. Usually it takes awhile. The minimum time is about a year from the time a person gets taken on as a Learner. After that, when their teacher thinks they are ready they are sent off on a Deepening. Do you know what that is?'

Russell nodded. 'Grandpa mentioned it. He said it was a sitting-out but not in the Native way.'

'Yes,' Alfred nodded. 'I will tell you more about that later, then. Let's just say that it's a pretty powerful experience and it changes people when they go out to do that for the first time. If they succeed at it they are ready to be initiated. Once a person is initiated they become a part of the inner circle of the Thornwood. They learn the inner traditions. They become what we call Shakai or Seekers. Seekers are the apprentices of Masters and they have a lot of learning ahead of them. Eventually an initiate can become a Master and so on. These are not really ranks or anything so restrictive as that. They are more like symbolic names that show that a person has learned a certain amount and has a certain level of responsibilities in the tradition.'

'It's a long way from Learner to Master then, I take it?'

'Yes it is, but how long it actually takes should be of less importance than the quality of the things one learns and the quality of the things one does while learning.'

They turned down a smaller path that led from the main pathway and in a moment more came into view of a small house set into the bush. It was quite old but had obviously been well maintained. A small lawn filled with bright yellow buttercups and dandelions led up to a sunny veranda with a sleeping dog on it. As they approached the house the dog lifted its head and wagged lazily at them.

'This is Ginger,' Alfred said, petting the dog fondly behind the ears. 'She's a golden Lab who has had a lot of summers under her old feet. Sometimes she goes with me when I walk and other times she just hangs around the house. Maybe she wanted to give us privacy while we talked today. You can never tell with dogs.'

He turned to Russell and winked.

'And as to your many other questions, maybe they can wait till we get a coffee and a piece of pie in front of us?'

Russell nodded and chuckled. He was only too happy to do that.

*   The story of Raven's Gift can be found in the book *Tales of the Red Moon Lodge* by Jack and Cassandra Wolf.

2

The Thornish Way

'There is darkness in the world and you will find it in the natural places where balance reigns. The common folk view darkness as bad or somehow evil yet if they look deeply enough they will see that this is not so. Rather, they will find evil quite readily in sicknesses of the minds of men and in organized religion.' - *Master Vala*

Allison walked up to her teacher Agnes as she was working in her vegetable garden. It was a very bright summer day, not a cloud in the sky. A gentle breeze brought the scents of flowers and especially of rosemary to her senses as she approached. Agnes had let her hens out of their pen earlier this morning and they were scattered all over the yard, just outside the garden fence, clucking and hunting bugs. Allison had to step around the busy birds as she walked, gently shooing them out of the way.

As she got closer, Agnes looked up and waved from her place by a tall stand of sunflowers. She was wearing her usual uniform of blue jeans and light cotton shirt topped off with a bright red bandana tied around her blonde hair. Allison could see that she was a bit sweaty too, there in the midday heat, and the bucket at her feet, now full of recently pulled weeds, gave evidence to the work she had been doing.

'Darn weeds anyway,' Agnes mock-complained as Allison came into the garden, closing the wooden gate behind her. 'If you don't want to spray poison to keep 'em down you've gotta companion plant and when that's not good enough you're back to plain old fashioned pulling.'

'And how are you doing today, Wataan?' Allison asked with a semi-formal Thornish bow.

Agnes straightened up and mopped her forehead with another bandana, this time a yellow one, pulled from her pants pocket.

'So, we have something special to discuss then do we?' she said with a smile, returning the light semi-bow of the Thornish tradition.

In answer Allison held up the item which she had brought to show her teacher. It was a beautiful pendant made of simple ceramic with a hole centered in the middle of it which made it look somewhat like a small doughnut. Yet this one was far from being a simple sculpture tied onto a braided leather thong: It was a true work of art. Allison proudly held up her pendant and then passed it to her teacher for inspection.

'It's only been out of the kiln for a very short time,' she said.

'It's very beautiful, Allison,' Agnes said. 'And if I might say so, it suits you.'

The glaze on the small, holed pendant gleamed in the sunlight. It had been crafted from plain river clay but Allison had added a beautiful deep green glaze that had very faint veins of gold running through it.

'I have never heard of a student actually making one like this in quite this way,' Agnes said. 'Very original.'

The object was a Lore-Stone, which is a special symbol to those who are learning the Thornish ways, representing a step in the path when the student is ready to begin seeking the deeper teachings of the traditions. In most cases the stone itself was actually fashioned from an existing stone. The student would find a suitable stone which spoke to them and after having asked for permission from said stone they would commence boring a hole in it by whatever means they had available. After they had finished this and had completed polishing the stone they would hang it on a cord passed through the center and wear it as an amulet. The Lore-Stone would represent the student's understanding of the basic Thornish worldview and demonstrate, both to the student and the teacher, that they were ready to proceed to the first of the primary Thornish rituals; the Hollowing.

'I'm glad that I was able to create this in the way I wanted to,' Allison said. 'It really speaks to me.'

'With your talent in ceramics I shouldn't doubt it,' Agnes replied in a soft English accent that despite many years in Canada had not faded overly much.

Indeed the making of a Lore-Stone from clay was something that Agnes had never heard of. Yet when her student had come to her with the idea she had seen no reason why it could not be done. Thornish tradition was usually very clear about specifics when such were required, but in this instance Agnes knew there was no hard and fast rule forbidding it. The custom required that the Lore-Stone be fashioned from natural materials which were harvested in a respectful, meditative fashion and crafted with equal respect. As a result, when Allison had come to her with the idea she had also suggested that she try to find some natural local river clay for her project.

Agnes had thought it a great idea and her student had eagerly set out on her quest. It did not take long. After a day of walking the banks of one of the local rivers Allison had returned to the house with a bucket of really nice looking river clay.

Agnes left her to it, not wanting to interfere in the process, and now, a couple of days later, held the results of that process in her hand. The subtle golden veins running through the material fascinated Agnes and she made a point later, when she was in the studio, to see what materials Allison had used in that particular glaze.

'Why am I not surprised that it's green?' she said at last, smiling and handing the pendant back.

Allison loved the color green. This had been made evident from the first time Allison had ever met her teacher. She had been wearing green colored running shoes and a beautiful top of deepest jade green Chinese silk. Since Allison had become her student and had been around much more often Agnes noted that her young student had even managed to procure for herself a pair of deep green jeans. Yes, there could be little doubt that Allison was passionate about the color.

Allison smiled and accepted her Lore-Stone back.

'Yeah, I have a bit of fondness for it, I'll admit,' she replied. 'What can I say? Ever since I was a little girl green has made me feel good.'

'Then stay with it, I say,' Agnes chuckled. 'I guess it's break time. We should go in and get something to eat.'

An hour later, after lunch, the two found themselves sitting at the patio table on the deck behind the house. A big jug of homemade iced tea sweated droplets in the middle of the table while frosted glasses sat before each of them.

'You know I haven't had the pleasure of knowing you for a long time, Allison, yet I think I have come to know you pretty well,' Agnes said. 'And during that time you have impressed me with your integrity, your closeness to the Earth and your willingness to learn. On top of that I am more than impressed with your artistic talents. The fact that you are ready to move forward this soon comes as little surprise to me.'

In Thornish tradition there are a number of levels of learning and responsibility. These areas of knowledge are signified through various customs and the bestowing of certain titles on those who have earned them. As the worldview of the Thornish people is symbolized by a thorn tree hedge surrounding a sacral core, the cultural structure consists primarily of three rings of interaction. In the core of the design, often referred to as a Glade, one finds those people who have been initiated into the inner traditions.

There are only two ranks, if one feels comfortable using such a term, and those are the Seekers (also known as Shakai) and the Masters. Beyond that there are more honorary indicators of accomplishment and wisdom, such as the Elderfolk and the Vardyr, however there are only two official core designators of tribal rank as mentioned earlier.

The next level of interaction, that which lies outside the ring of the initiates, is the area of the Learners and the Fellows. A Fellow is a person who knows of the Thornish traditions to some extent and wishes to learn them and follow their teachings. At some point, though they may not initially have access to an initiated teacher, some people may wish to declare themselves Thornish and these folk are then considered to be Fellows. Fellows are held in great respect and are often encouraged to seek the deeper mysteries of the tradition as they are able. It follows that the Thornish term for a Fellow is Kona'ri. Kona'ri means *sharp knife* and this name was given to show that the rest of the Thornwood holds much respect for the Fellows.

A Learner is a person who has sought out a teacher and who has been accepted for training by that initiate. In the Thornish dialect the term for this is Auga'ri, or *sharp-eyes*. This indicates the expectation that Learners will pay attention to their lessons. Both Fellows and Learners are permitted to fashion a Lore-Stone and to perform the Hollowing ritual, however the ways in which the Hollowing ritual are performed will be somewhat different for a Learner under the supervision of a Master.

Outside the second ring is what is considered to be the Outworld, the place where the rest of humanity dwells. In the Outworld there may be found both friends and foes and everyone in-between. Folk who are aware of the Thornish ways and in support of them are termed Allies. Allies may or may not ever seek to delve deeper into Thornish culture, yet as they are friends they are held in high esteem.

Allison had come into the picture as somewhat of a Fellow. She had learned of the Thornish ways from her friend Carolyn and had been eager to learn more. From what basics Allison had been able to learn from Carolyn, Allison began undertaking deeper explorations on her own. Finally she told Carolyn that she considered herself to be a Thornish person because she agreed with and was in sync with everything she had discovered about the Thornish way. This made her what was termed a *Declared Person* in Thornish tradition. She had become a Fellow even though at the time she was not aware of that term.

Eventually she had been introduced to Agnes and over time a friendly relationship had been formed. Finally Agnes had offered to teach Allison and as Allison had not yet created a Lore-Stone or performed the Hollowing ritual, Agnes was happy to guide her in this.

Over the six months in which Agnes had known Allison the young woman had shown her talents and proved her dedication more and more. This led eventually to the offer of teaching and Agnes honored Allison by giving her the Maal, or the traditional red and black beaded bracelet that represents the explorer of the Thornish learning path.

'So now you want to go out and perform the Hollowing, do you?' Agnes asked from over the rim of her glass. 'It is a serious matter, you know.'

'I am aware of this,' Allison replied. 'I have known about it for some time. Carolyn told me about it.'

Agnes put her glass back down after taking a sip. 'Ah, Carolyn. Have you seen her lately?'

'Not in awhile,' Allison said. 'Last I heard from her she was going to go down to the coast for a while to visit a friend.'

'She was and is an excellent student,' Agnes said. 'Kind of reminds me of you in some ways.'

'You know she was very secretive about a lot of things,' Allison said. 'I could tell she was eager to share things with me because I was so enthusiastic but I also know she was keeping a lot of it back. Now that I know she was your last Learner there are a lot of things that make sense.'

Agnes leaned back somewhat in her chair. 'Carolyn is quite a private person to begin with,' she said. 'And also, she probably wasn't too sure what she was able to tell an outsider at the time.'

'I understand,' Allison said. 'But I envy her in a way. She has gone so much further in this than I have.'

'That's because she has been walking the path for a lot longer than you have my friend.' Agnes grinned. 'Years longer in fact. If I think on it, it was probably about six years or so ago that Carolyn came along, all bright-eyed and bushy-tailed. Not too different from you.'

'And now she's a Master, I hear.'

'And who told you that?'

'Russell.'

Agnes rolled her eyes as she thought of her tribally-oathed kinsman.

'Always the stirrer of curiosity that one is,' she said. 'He's so much like his grandfather it isn't even funny.'

'Why? Isn't he supposed to tell me certain things?' Allison asked with a look of concern growing on her face.

Agnes reached across the table and patted Alison's hand in a friendly way.

'No, that's okay,' she said. 'He knows exactly what is and what isn't allowed to be told to non-initiates. He's been an initiate for more than long enough to know that. It's just that he's so much like my own teacher: He wants to teach others and he is very enthusiastic about our ways. I guess I am more like Carolyn in that regard than I am like Russell.'

'He is a coyote-person, isn't he?'

Agnes laughed out loud at that one.

'Yes he really is,' Agnes replied. 'Like his grandfather in that way even more than my old teacher is too. A consummate trickster. Watch out for that one I tell you.'

Allison grinned back.

'I know,' she said.

'Shall we talk about your Hollowing then?' Agnes asked.

The Hollowing is a form of pre-initiatory ritual that is open to non-initiated Fellows and to those who have been accepted as Learners. Named for ancient trees which have been lightning-struck and hollowed by fire, the ritual is one in which a person goes out into the green spaces and contemplates their place in the world. The idea behind the ritual is that during our lives we often accumulate a great deal of preconceptions about the world and our place in it. We also, often unknowingly, accede to many of the fictions perpetrated by mainstream society and this too colors our perception of reality.

The Hollowing is a method by which one deeply analyzes themselves and systematically strips away the veneer of fictions and other people's perceptions from our own. We try to peel away the layers until what we have left is ourselves as a person, alone before the multiverse, in contemplation of our deeds.

Very often the Hollowing is a deeply emotional experience. It is deeply magical and deeply therapeutic in nature as well. Those who have undergone the process report that potent feelings emerge which quite often can catch one off guard when they appear. Thus, it is always recommended that when one goes into the ritual they are adequately prepared for the ordeal that it most often triggers.

'You now have your Lore-Stone and I have pretty well instructed you in the best way I can concerning the process,' Agnes said. 'The Lore-Stone for me, when I did my first Hollowing, was like an anchor. It was a connection to the Old Ones and to the Ancestors as well as to my own will when I went out there that first time.'

'Yes, I remember you telling me that,' Allison said. 'I have meditated on this kind of thing already. I took this Lore-Stone down by the river earlier today when you were in town.'

'Good stuff,' Agnes said. 'Remember that as Thornish people we see everything in creation as having spirit. The wild clay that went into the making of your stone as well as all of the elements used have created a new kind of being. This new spirit will take time to adjust to you and you to it. With luck you will be together for the rest of your life, so form a good relation with it now.'

'I will,' Allison smiled. 'Just as you have with yours.'

Agnes smiled and then asked if Allison had chosen a place to perform her Hollowing ritual. Allison told her that indeed she had and she described the location she had in mind.

Agnes' brows furrowed for a moment and then the only visible sign of any form of tension vanished from her face.

'That's quite a power spot, Allie,' Agnes said after a moment. 'Have you thought this through very carefully?'

Allison told her that she had.

Allison had chosen a place along one of the numerous rivers which ran in the valley. This was no surprise to her teacher as Allison was as drawn to water as it seemed she was drawn to the color green. Agnes' concern came from the fact that the specific place she had picked was known to be a particularly potent place of power.

'You've heard about the big fire that went through there once,' Agnes said, repeating a tale she had told her student before. 'It was a long time ago, before either of us were born, but as I mentioned, lives were lost and a lot of damage was done. There is an echo of that there still and most people try to avoid that for various reasons.'

'Angry trees,' Allison said, nodding grimly. 'Yes, I know about that.'

'You have been talking to Russell about this?' Agnes intuited.

'Guilty as charged. He reacted about the same way as you are right now.'

Agnes picked up her glass of tea and sipped again.

'He's right, you know,' she said at last. 'The trees that burned in there were powerful and old and it is said that the local people had a very powerful relationship with them. Then along came loggers and the fight began. Nobody knows who started that fire or even if it was an accident but the trees know and they are still upset about it all these years later. Trees have a much longer memory than humans do.'

'I understand,' Allison said. 'I feel the need to go there because of the spirit of that place. It's like it needs more healing and I think I can help.'

'You might get dead,' Agnes warned. 'The Hollowing opens a person up to a very vulnerable place as you know…and even long dead trees can kill. You know they are not big fans of human beings up there.'

Allison remained true to her decision, and told her teacher that she had made up her mind. Agnes relented and gave her permission.

'Well, at least it will be a unique Hollowing,' Agnes said at last. 'As far as I know no one has ever used that place for the ritual before.'

And so it was that Allison, with the blessing of her teacher, made her way to the place where she had planned to sit her ritual. Agnes drove her to a place on the road where the trail began and sent her on her way.

'I will meet you back here at this spot by day's end,' she told her student. 'Good luck.'

Allison hoisted her light backpack and walked into the woods. The nature of the light changed from the open, sunny state of the gravel road into a deep, cool green that was alive with the scents and sounds of the deep green. She walked along in her soft boots, breathing it all in and mentally preparing herself for the ritual that was to come.

It was the dark of the moon. Allison had waited specifically for this time to arrive before setting out on her quest. Thornish customs often coincide with the dark phase of the moon because of its connection to the initiation of new growth and new beginnings. Even though the Hollowing ritual is commonly undertaken during the daylight hours Allison could feel the potency of the moon-time as her own energies coursed in synchronization with the lunar phase. She remembered discussing this particular time with Agnes early on in her training and had remarked that it must have been women who decided upon the custom of utilizing the dark of the moon for ritual times. Only women would have been able to intuit the extra potency to be had during such a confluence of dark and light.

Agnes had smiled at that and told her that while she might hold certain assumptions regarding the men of the mundane world she should not underestimate the connectedness of the Thornish male. In the Thornwood, Agnes explained, that while the differences between men and women were revered and celebrated, there was also a deep feeling of kinship and equality held between those who had sworn oaths to one another over sacred fires.

'We are not the same as many people in the outlands are, my young friend,' she said. 'It will take you a while to truly see that, but we are far more connected than many other human beings are.'

After about a half an hour of walking the feel of the forest began to change around Allison. This was not a subtle change that occurred in the background and took time to recognize; it was rather abrupt, as though at some point along the soft loamy trail she had crossed an invisible borderline. Once she had crossed beyond it, Allison felt the resistance to her presence. It was almost physically tangible, as though somehow the air had become thicker in an attempt to stop her from going any further. On the mental and spiritual level Allison felt the resistance as well. She had experienced this exact sort of thing the first time she had gone through this place. She had come with Russell, who had warned her beforehand but had not told her specifically when she would feel the push-back, as he had termed it.

And it was well described. Allison could feel the entire nature of the place pushing her back, trying to get her to turn around and leave this place.

Humans were not welcome here. This was quite obvious to her as it probably would be to anyone who ventured there.

Allison did not turn around and go back, but she did stop and hold her ground in a small widening of the trail between two huge Douglas fir trees. She had been strongly drawn to this place quite early on and while she could not fully fathom the reasons for this she had decided to follow her instincts.

She set her pack down at her feet and extracted a small bag from an outer pouch. In this was a mixture of seeds and sage that she had blended together at Agnes' house. In Thornish tradition there are many such mixtures made for offerings. Usually they were designed so that everyone, from the small seed eating animals of the wild, to the spirit people in any given area, could be served. White sage is a powerful spiritual cleanser and is thought to be pleasing to most spirit people when burned or simply laid out as an offering. The seeds consisted of sunflower and pumpkin seeds mixed in with various wildflower and bird seed.

Allison took some of the seed mixture from her bag and placed some at the base of each tree. She did this in a very reverent manner and opened her thoughts up to images of peace and tranquility. To her these great trees on either side of the trail were like a kind of sacred doorway and she was respectfully requesting permission to move beyond them.

She spoke to them and to the many spirit people she knew instinctively were nearby in that place. She identified herself by name and spoke a little bit about herself and why she wished to be allowed to enter the darker woods ahead. She was completely earnest in her words and she spoke as though she was at the foot of very wise and sagely elders – and in fact she considered this to be so whether the elders in question were human or otherwise.

Words from her teacher entered her mind.

'When you speak to the spirit people it is always wise to go with the deepest respect. Even if a particular spirit may not like you very much it is important to remember that manners can carry the day.'

And thoughts of Agnes' words triggered memories of something that Russell had told her when they last spoke.

'We should always treat the worlds of spirit as though we were in the presence of a human tribal elder. When you think of all these ones as respected grandmas and grandpas it's really difficult to go wrong.'

And for a long period of time Allison stood there in silence in that great, green and largely silent place. She waited after she had spoken her words. She waited for a sign, fully prepared to turn around and go back if she perceived a strong 'no' to her request for entry.

'Intent is everything,' Agnes had said. *'In this world or in any other world, some beings out there can read your intent as easily as you can read a newspaper so it is always good to be true to your word and your intent.'*

At last Allison perceived that there was a slight 'lessening' in the oppressive feel to the air around her. It felt as though someone had opened a window in a stuffy room to let fresh air come inside. But this imaginary window had only been opened a tiny, tentative crack, a minor concession to her honest application for admittance.

Allison took her backpack and, nodding in the slightly inclined way of the Thornish bow, she spoke her thanks to the spirits around her and continued down the trail.

The forest around her was deep and dark here. There were animal and bird sounds in the distance and indeed she could hear the sound of a small creek making its way through the woods somewhere in the near distance. Yet in this place it all seemed muted somehow, as though a great woolen blanket of sorrow had been cast over the area.

Sadness in this place was tangible even though evidence of what had transpired here so long ago was hardly to be seen. A massive burned out and now moss covered stump here and a few great green piles which had once been burned tree parts, now also coated with new growth; these were faint evidence in the physical realm at least. The spiritual echo of the deed long since done was another matter however. That and the memory of the surviving trees of the loss of their kin.

Agnes had been right. Allison held no illusion at all that even the spirits of dead trees could maim or kill if they were so inclined to do so. Yet what she sensed was far more into the spectrum of sorrow than anger.

At last she arrived at the place she had decided to use for her Hollowing. It was a soft, green space in between the great decaying trunks of two long dead fir trees. These two giants seemed to have been felled no doubt through great age and now served a secondary purpose as nursery logs. Numerous tiny trees grew from their boles, along with thick layers of moss and fungus. At the far end of this clearing stood a vertical reminder of a long ago lightning strike, a massive old cedar which had been almost completely hollowed out by sky-fire and yet still stood some ten meters or so in height, jaggedly pointing upwards.

In the rough rectangle of space between the nurse-trees and the lightning killed giant, Allison set her pack down and once again silently offered her thanks and respects to the spirits of that place. The feeling of unwelcome, which had begun to withdraw ever so slightly at the gate-trees, had continued to do so as she had come forward. Though it had never completely dissipated it seemed to her almost as though she was being carefully watched from many angles, scrutinized to see if she was going to be good to her word.

Allison then went to the fallen trees around her and once more offered handfuls from her sacred seed mix. She spoke aloud to anyone who wished to hear her, and she offered her thanks and her open-hearted respects to the tree people and their ancestors.

At last she made herself comfortable sitting in the center of that clearing. The moss was very deep there, very soft and very thick. There was no difficulty at all for Allison to find a perfect, comfortable sitting position.

Sitting cross-legged she removed from the main part of her pack a thick cotton pull-over jacket, which she immediately shrugged into. A deep forest green, the hoodie blended in quite well with the surrounding verdure.

Allison sat silently for a moment, breathing in the air and feeling the peace that it seemed to her had slept dormant for so long beneath the moss. She opened herself up to it and offered her love to the land.

She pulled the deep hood over her head and settled herself into a position which she often used to meditate. The process came easily to

Allison as she had been an eager student. Agnes, who was well known among her people for being an excellent meditation teacher, had no difficulties in helping her latest student fall deeply into relaxed meditative states.

In a very short time Allison had come to the place in her mind and spirit where she was relaxed, silent and in deep harmony with everything around her. She simply become one with the place in which she found herself.

For a long time, she sat there in stillness; just another green-colored feature in a soft sea of silent green.

And then she began the work of the Hollowing.

She began to contemplate her place in the world, from the earliest memories she could remember to the present day. She looked upon her life in as much detail as she could and she pondered the things she had done and the things she had learned; the things she had wrought in her time in the Middle World.

And she asked herself why.

Why had she done the things she had done? Had these things been in keeping with the sacred balance of the world? Had it been enough? Could she do more?

And Allison felt a deep sadness overcome her as she pondered the way of the world and all of the things that had been done to our sacred planet. She could feel the spirit of the Earth Mother crying out to her, as she cried out to all of her true children, asking them to awaken and care for her, to care for her other children, the non-human ones who did not speak the language of men. She asked for help from her awakened children, help to save not only the life on her surface and otherwise, but also to help in the preservation of her human children.

It was a sorrowful message and to Allison it was almost as though she was hearing the deathbed lament of a very old and venerable grandmother, one who had been cast aside by her arrogant children as though she was merely trash to be tossed to the side of the road.

This was HER grandma to whom this was happening, HER kinfolk of many species to whom this was happening!

Allison felt sorrow and then anger and then rage…but the rage subsided and became weeping waves of sorrow once again.

What had Allison done to prevent the harm being done to her

grandmother? What had Allison learned that would help to heal her grandmother and, more importantly, could her grandmother be saved?

Sudden guilt overwhelmed her. She was hammered by the deepest pangs of guilt and even deeper shame at being a member of the species whose twisted depraved acts of rape were threatening everything she knew.

Hate simmered and grew out of the ashes of her disgust. She wanted to lash out and kill everyone and everything that had ever raised its hand against the sacredness of the land. She wanted to lay everything human to waste, to remove the cancerous growth that had for too long, far too long, held sway over the Middle World.

But then she heard in her mind the delightful laughter of children and saw little boys and girls playing cheerfully in a playground in a park.

'We start out so perfect and beautiful only to become monsters,' she said to herself in her mind…or perhaps it was aloud, she could not tell.

Tears flowed in streams down Allison's face as she sat there, now hunched over and wracked by the deepest, most mournful sobs. How had we fallen so far, she asked, from these bright little babies to the malevolent creatures who poisoned the lands, seas and skies?

'We must educate them.'

The voice had come unbidden into her mind and its appearance startled Allison. It was not her voice and not anything that she had ever experienced before. Her welling of emotions subsided as her mind scrambled to identify the voice. It seemed to have come from somewhere deep within her, but to be sure she lifted her head and peered around.

She was alone in that little clearing, at least so far as there being any other human beings present.

And yet the voice had been so clear, so precise, so real.

Allison returned after a moment to the darkness beneath her hood. She sought silence and a means to relax once again.

'Those who can be awakened can be saved from the changes which are coming. Those who cannot will earn their rightful fate in death. This is the way of the sacred balance.'

Again, the voice. But this time Allison did not startle. This time she remembered her training and embraced calm.

'How might I be of assistance?' she asked out loud, now quite certain that she had been addressed by someone from the spirit world.

'Learn, grow strong, embrace the First Law and teach what you can to those who are worthy.'

The First Law, the law of the cosmos, the law of natural balance. This was at the very core of Thornish understanding and already Allison knew it well.

'Find your brothers and sisters and teach what you can,' the voice said. *'Be an implement of change and of balance.'*

There was a brief silence in which Allison strained to hear anything more that might be communicated to her…and then, finally:

'Suffer no guilt, you who wear deepest green. Suffer no fear as you tread the dark road.'

And once again Allison felt the many emotions she had felt earlier swirling within her. These lasted only a moment and were gone, replaced by a deep feeling of exhausted peace.

Allison awoke from her rest what seemed like hours later. At first she startled, not knowing where she was and after that she realized that she had actually fallen asleep. How long she had slumbered, exhausted by her experience, was quite evident as she looked up and saw the burnt orange of the sunset sky above the trees.

She got to her feet and picked up her pack. It was slow going at first because her legs and upper body were quite sore from remaining in one position for so long. At last she straightened herself out and after a moment more reverently bowed to the trees, thanking them for allowing her to be there.

Allison did not wish to be caught on the trail after dark but at the same time, as she withdrew from that place, she remembered herself and made appropriate offerings as she went. At last she found herself at the two trees she called the gates, and there, laying a hand on each she thanked them for their help.

Making her way back into the heavier forest cover, Allison walked along rather briskly until she found the main trail. From there it was only about a twenty minute walk to the gravel road where she found her friend Agnes waiting.

'That was a long ritual,' Agnes said as Allison pulled the truck door shut and they rolled away. 'It can get pretty dark out here. Lucky you weren't caught on the trail.'

Allison nodded. 'It was exhausting. I think I fell asleep afterwards.'

'For most people it is exhausting, yes,' Agnes said. 'That probably means you are doing it right.'

Allison began to speak, telling the tale of what had happened to her in the grove, when very uncharacteristically, Agnes raised a finger and interrupted.

'Here is a lesson for you, Allie. I am not sure if I have spoken to you about this but now is as good a time as any. In this tradition there are customs of silence. By that I mean that certain things, experiences, what have you, can be very special and sacred. As you know there is power in secrecy and silence so what I ask of you is that you say nothing more of what happened to you on your Hollowing until you have had time to think about it, to meditate on it first, okay?'

Allison thought about that for a moment and then nodded. 'That's a really good idea now that I think about it.'

'Usually three days is enough,' Agnes replied. 'You can meditate on it, write it in your journal, ponder it however you like and after that you are welcome to share whatever you deem appropriate. Keep the rest for your own sacred journey.'

'Sounds fair.'

'I wanted you to know, however, that I think you did a very brave thing back there,' Agnes added. 'Even from the road there, with the window rolled down, and even after I got out of the truck to stretch my legs while I waited – I could feel the difference in the energy there. Whatever you said or did in there; well done.'

Allison stared straight ahead along the dusty gravel road that would take them to the main road home. As happens in the wilder places, when the sun crests behind the mountains to the west it does not take long at all for complete darkness to envelop the land. Indeed, the road and the surrounding forest on either side had become pitch black in very short order, with the headlights of the pickup truck being the only light at all along that blackened way.

'I am glad that I didn't get stuck on the trail back there,' she said at last. 'Sleeping curled up around a tree with no shelter for the night might be an interesting experience but after what I had going on back in my ritual I think I'd prefer a sound sleep in a bed.'

'How very decadent of you,' Agnes teased.

'But I know I did the right thing back there. Had I been forced to stay the night I know the trees would have been okay with that. Things have changed in there a little.'

Agnes took a hand off the wheel long enough to pat her student on the shoulder before returning it to its place as she drove.

'We do the Hollowing to see our deeper selves and our relations with the worlds,' she said. 'From the energy change back there I can tell that you did what you went there to do. This is a pretty impressive thing for anyone to achieve so early on in their training.'

'I will wait a week or so and then maybe go back to continue my work there,' Allison said. 'For me I think that the woods there need a guardian of sorts, someone who can speak for them and learn from them too.'

'When you go back do you think I could come along?' Agnes asked. 'I would be pleased to meet some of those who I am sure you encountered there.'

Allison smiled. It was a tired, just-before-bedtime kind of smile, yet it had a special energy all its own.

'It would be my pleasure to introduce you,' she said.

3
Heartwood

*'When we seek to master our way we look to understand Önd. Yet in the beginning, few Seekers comprehend that in understanding Önd we discover our deepest selves. This is because we actually **are** Önd; pieces of the will of the cosmos, inhabiting a temporary vehicle of blood and bone.'* - Master Talon

'Un-learning, in this day and age, is easily as important as learning,' Raven said from his place by the fire. 'The sad thing is that today so many kids are being taught outright lies. Do you know what's really sad? That half the time, or maybe more than half, the parents and other adults teaching these lies don't know any better and the untruths perpetuate themselves...it's like a virus, a virus of ignorance and deceit.'

The comment had come unbidden as we sat there in our camp by the river. We had been conversing earlier about a number of different things, not all of which were related to the tradition. Yet as many conversations go there is a time when the words are exhausted and the folk involved become comfortably silent for awhile. As the lull had set in between us I had turned inward, thinking calm thoughts of my own and really just existing for the enjoyment of the hot beverage in my cup. Raven, somewhat across from me, had fallen into a similar state and had been absently arranging embers in the fire-pit with a stick.

It was early autumn and we had come to this place to re-attune ourselves with the world and escape the generally high levels of human activity. I had come out from the city where it was always busy and Raven, even though he hailed from a smaller community, was glad for the chance to get away. We had come to enjoy nature and to enjoy the camaraderie held between those who have sworn sacred oaths together; Hearth-kin at the simple task of living wild – if even for a time.

When Raven spoke it had been sudden and his words seemed laced with either anger or frustration. I could not at first tell which one of these it had been. Yet I looked up and focused my attention on him. Not only was he an elder in my tradition but he was, more directly, my teacher in the old ways. So when he spoke my attention was locked on in anticipation of what he might say next.

After a moment Raven noticed that I was looking at him and with a shrug he told me about something that had been bothering him. A few days earlier he had gone into town to get groceries and gas for his truck when he happened to notice a family walking by. The parents were your typical mundane sorts, not really aware, not really concerned about anything beyond their herd-like desire for material goods, safety, pleasure, food and to continue laboring in what my teacher called the 'slave-cycle.' Raven told me that this was not what attracted his notice, as even in the smallish community where he lived there were plenty of these types of common folk wandering around. What had caught his eye was that their three children, the eldest of whom was probably no older than thirteen or so and the youngest probably around eight, had already been indoctrinated into the mainstream herd-thinking of their parents.

'It was very sad,' Raven related. 'The eldest, a girl of about thirteen or fourteen I'd guess, was already wearing makeup and trying as hard as she could to be like her mother, who looked like she had gotten stuck in the early 70's with her appearance. The two young lads, maybe twelve and eight respectively, were hard at work wearing truck and beer slogan t-shirts and could probably hardly wait to drive trucks, smoke cigarettes and drink beer like their father.'

'I agree. Very sad,' I said.

'When we are that young our former incarnations and memories of these are very close,' my teacher added. 'Our connection with the spirit world is very close. As children we are hooked up properly, the way we should be, to the everything of the universe... to the world. And then adults come along and take it away. It's like clipping the wings of a small, beautiful bird.'

'I suppose that this is the way of things,' I replied after a moment. 'Most of the parents were raised that way and they don't know any different. They pass it on to their kids without even thinking about it.'

Raven looked over at me from his place by the fire.

'But some of us break free,' he said. 'Some of us were guided by our ancestors – our real ancestors, our Pagan relations – and perhaps even by the Elder Kin themselves and given the inspiration to break free. Look at me: I was raised in a very traditional household. Granted, I was lucky and didn't have Christianity crammed down my throat, but in many ways my folks were quite mundane. I was the only one of three kids who turned out like I did.'

'Were all three of you gifted?' I asked.

His comment had spurred my curiosity because Raven himself was very gifted in the area of extrasensory perception. He was a seer of no mean skill and as well had other arcane abilities that he spoke of as a curse...at least when he had been young and unable to control them.

'Yes,' he said at last.

I looked at him questioningly.

'That was a good question you asked,' he replied.

Raven was always the teacher at one level or another.

'In answer to that question, yes. Both of my brothers also have the gift. One ignores it though he suffers to this day from migraines as a result. The other used to think it was a mental illness and sought counseling. Nowadays he moves from fad religion to fad spirituality trying to find himself when all he needed was to accept who he is.'

Raven had told me a few of the stories from his younger days. He had talked about the nightmares and the strange things which had happened to him when he was young. There were times when he could see spirit folk just as plain as day and from time to time dead people had come to talk to him and ask him for help with things. Raven had added a tale or two from the time of his puberty when other things started happening as well. He began to learn how to control the nightmares and from that came a very accurate oracular sense...along with very limited and occasional bouts of uncontrolled telekinesis. Like his brothers, at first Raven had fought the gift and tried to distance himself from it. In later years, however, he realized that fighting it was futile and sought to control it. In the end he had achieved a somewhat turbulent peace with his skills and abilities.

'I'm sorry to hear about your brothers,' I said.

Raven grinned wolfishly, as though he was pondering some cruel joke. The expression would have looked far more at home on the face of my coyote-like grandfather than it did on him.

'Don't be,' he said from behind the grin. 'They are both grown men. They are quite capable of waking up and realizing what's out there. Instead they choose to be slaves.'

In my own experience I had also seen the need, or found the inspiration, to awaken myself. I had been raised in a large household where the reigning philosophy had been a diluted form of Scottish Protestantism. I had been expected to go to school, maybe go to college, get a job and live out my life in the corporate life cycle, slaving away until one day I could actually afford to buy my freedom. A few years later, no longer of use to the machine, I would be discarded and die.

I had no use for that kind of thinking. I was not compliant to that ideal and from a very young age everyone in my family had known I was different. Naturally this did not sit too well with my father, who suspected I was everything from lazy to crazy...and everything in between. Attempts were made to get me to *'grow up'* or be a *'real'* man, but these were to no avail. Indeed, as I grew older, I couldn't help but smile at the thought that my father had at one time blamed possible homosexuality as a cause of my eccentricities. I dared not tell him that I was perfectly comfortable with gay people and had gay friends even though I myself was straight. Surely such a confession would have caused the old man further grief which I did not wish to inflict on his old-school sensibilities.

As it was my childhood and youth were fraught with speed bumps. Though I was not in possession of powerful spiritual gifts like Raven was, I discovered that finding one's way back to the old ways was an uphill battle every single day. So I knew the feeling my teacher was trying to convey with his story about the children in town. I had never been like that; I never wanted to be ordinary or to fit in with the crowd. This created a real strain within me as well because like many little boys I wanted to be like my dad – yet my nature always tore me in the other direction.

So yeah, I understood that...really well.

I wondered though, what had caused Raven to suddenly speak about the subject with such obvious emotion. Surely we had occasionally talked of these things before.

'It just kind of caught me off guard,' Raven said, as though he had gleaned my thoughts (and maybe he had - I was used to this by now.) 'I have said many times the world is changing and those of us who are awake need to be prepared. Well, I guess I was caught emotionally, seeing those little kids and thinking, 'They won't have much of a chance.' I wondered how we can help to awaken more people to the old ways of spirit.'

I remembered the times when he had spoken of the Change-of-Times. He was not the only one to have spoken of such things. I had heard a number of elders talk about the global and spiritual change that was coming, from Mr. Woo, an old Chinese sorcerer I had known as a kid, Mr. Singh, a neighbor of mine from back in the old 'hood, through to various Native elders I had known, including my grandfather. The tale was the same regardless of who spoke about it or what culture they hailed from. There was a time, approaching fast, in which humanity would face a global crisis. This crisis would lead human kind to a crossroads at which a pivotal decision must be made: Either change for the better and live, or continue in the same old destructive ways and perish.

Along with this change of times would come a wide-scale human awakening in which more humans than ever would begin awakening and returning to old ways of thought, returning to their roles as caretakers of the Earth, not the insane despoilers of her. It was as though the Gods were kind and had allowed us to snap out of our industrial stupor, just in time to have the chance at saving out planet.

I recalled something that Raven had said years earlier. Russell had been a constant taker of notes and had written down many of the things our teachers and elders had said. I too was a note-taker, though I don't think my abilities were at par with those of my brother.

Russ had written down Raven's words as he spoke them in 1979: *Before the second decade of the twenty-first century is done the changes will be seen in full force. First it will be weather and other Earth-changes, then humankind will follow with inane political solutions. Finally will come disease and the cull will be in full swing. Those of us still in the cities should reconsider their living arrangements and leave. The cull will not be pretty and we owe it to our ancestors and our descendants to survive in a good way.'*

These words had stuck with me after that. I knew that they were true. There was a storm coming and that many would perish from it. Raven had referred to it as a 'Great Re-Balancing' and I think he was correct in that as well.

'There will be those who will speak about the warming of the world,' Raven had prophesied years earlier, years before I had even known him. *'They will fight about who caused it or whether it was a natural part of the Earth-cycles. Yes, indeed, as I have seen it, the world will get warmer but this is not where it will end. This warming will change the planet and the change will bring the coming of a new ice age.'*

My own tradition, the tradition that Raven and I shared, had been dedicated to helping people re-awaken for decades. The way of the Thornwood had evolved in order to show those who wished it a better way, a way to reclaim our duties as stewards of our sacred world before it was too late.

'Enough grim talk,' Raven said at last. 'While such subjects do need to be addressed we didn't come up here to bring ourselves down in the dumps. We came to talk about hale things and enjoy the world and here we are.'

I agreed. We had spoken of these grim things in the past and indeed our duty to the tradition required us to remain eyes-open about such things. However, there was a time for lighter things as well as for those of a darker nature.

'You know there have never been more of us in the Thornish tradition than there are now?' Raven said after a moment where there had again been a silence. All we could hear was the whispering of the wind, the song of the river and the crackling of the fire-people as they danced in the fire-pit.

'I was not aware of that,' I replied. 'Really?'

'I am talking about the Thornish ways now, not the original lodges,' Raven answered. 'I have no real figure for the Old Lodges, as you can probably guess. They never kept track of such things, but I do know that since the Thornish way came into being we have never had so many members all at once. That is something to be proud of.'

The Thornish tradition, I had been taught from the beginning, had never been a large gathering of people. The emphasis had long been on the quality of the people who were invited in and never the quantity of learners. As the tradition had originally developed out of a secret society, it was easy to see that a number of the elders in the tradition had been more comfortable with keeping numbers small and teachings limited to only a few students at a time.

Yet over time it had been thought that these numbers, these openings for prospective students, needed to grow. With the prophesied coming changes there were a good number of Masters and Elders who knew that in order for our teachings to be of use to people and to the world more had to have access to them.

How to implement this kind of growth was a difficult question. There were thoughts that our ways could end up in the wrong hands and be abused. There were others who feared that some of the teachings could be dangerous if misinterpreted or used by someone who was untrained in their use. Some said that books could be written and that people in general could learn from them. Others suggested that to release too much would not be a good thing. There were arguments for and against such possibilities. In the end it was decided that a new category of membership would be created, that of the Fellows, and that those who seriously sought to know the deeper teachings would seek out actual, in-person relationships with initiated teachers.

Yet as in all such wisely implemented endeavors the going was slow. The usual method of bringing more people to the tradition was through networks of friends and word-of-mouth, just as it had always been.

Of late there had indeed been a number of younger folk coming around. I myself had only been involved for a relatively short time, some five years since I had begun to walk the Thornish path. I suppose in relation to the older folk involved I could be considered one of the *'younger fellas'* as Master Tiva called us.

'How many of us are there, then?' I asked after mulling these things to myself for awhile.

Raven reached over from his seat and took another stick of wood from a pile. He added it on and the fire-folk immediately took to it in a cloud of orange-yellow sparks.

'Right now there are sixteen Masters and students,' he said. 'Not all of them you know, but I bet you can count more than five in your head right now.'

He was right; sixteen was considered to be a high number. Ours had never been a large order to be sure, yet sixteen was more than I imagined.

Raven named them all off and he was right; I recognized about eight of the names he spoke. I noticed he did not mention the names of any of who had passed on. These were actual, living members.

'The reason I am so impressed by this is because we have really not done anything besides what we have always done to find new students,' Raven said. 'It's all about the network of people who know each other and who might occasionally come up with some young person of interest. I'm not sure as to why this has been so effective lately but I am happy it has been.'

'Perhaps it was Russell's work out there, living by example, or maybe Carolyn?' I suggested. 'They are both known for that kind of thing.'

Raven's face took a slightly sad expression as he heard Russell's name. Our friend and brother was no longer with us. He had passed on to the spirit world some years earlier.

'That could be,' Raven said at last.

Again, the comfortable silence returned to the camp and we each sat alone with our thoughts for awhile.

In time, Raven stirred once again from his quiet and got up from the piece of cut log he had been sitting on. When he returned from the lean-to shelter we had built from fallen branches and other forest debris he had an old bottle in his hand. He pulled the top off of it and poured a bit in his now-empty coffee cup. After he had done that he came over to where I was sitting and offered to pour some of the contents into my own cup.

I didn't need to be told what the substance was that he was pouring. I could smell it easily enough and when I did images of sunshine, green woods and flowers came to my mind. It was dandelion wine, one of my very favorite things.

'Emmett's?' I asked.

My uncle was fairly well known for the various concoctions he made from wild roots, berries and flowers, but his most famed creation was his dandelion wine.

'Who else?' Raven grinned, putting the bottle away.

'To the ones who went before,' he toasted, clinking his metal cup on my plastic one.

I toasted back and we drank, offering our thoughts to the ones who had been with us but who had now returned to the land-of-spirit.

'May they watch over us,' I added.

The wine was delicious, as I had expected it would be. Emmett never gave any of it out to anyone unless it was at least a year old. Apparently it aged quite nicely. This cup full was no exception as it went down smooth with a deep, almost rooty, floral taste and scent.

'This is some of the older stuff,' Raven noted after savoring a sip. 'He gave this bottle to me a fair time ago and I was keeping it for a special occasion.'

I was puzzled.

'What special occasion would that be?' I asked.

Raven looked over at me over the rim of his cup.

'You are one of my best students, Qorvas,' he replied, addressing me by my Thornish name. 'You have been like a sponge, learning everything I have had to pass along to you. I am very honored that I had the chance to teach you over the past years. As a matter of fact, you probably know what fellas like Tiva think of you as well.'

'That I might possibly be somewhat acceptable?' I replied meekly.

'More than that,' Raven said, playing along with my attempt at light humor. 'A long time ago we were talking and we all thought that if anyone was going to eventually write a book about our traditions, maybe one day get it out there in the world, it would be either Russell, Carolyn or you. All three of you had the talent gifted to you, the talent to be writers. The rest of us are not so good at writing things down in a way that would maybe make it to a publisher…but you are.'

I wondered what he was getting at. Russell was the guy who I would have voted for in the possibility of writing a book. He was a natural-born writer, took notes on everything, and had a really great style. Sadly, my brother had gone off to the spirit world back in '85 and had left a hole in the hearts of many of us that would never be filled in again. Carolyn was next on that list for me too. She was similar to Russell in many ways as a writer. Yet Carolyn had become ill and mysteriously gone off on a quest somewhere, needing to find something in her life. No one had heard from her in over a year now. All we could do was wish her well and hope she was okay.

I guess, if I looked at it from Raven's point of view, out of three people with an interest in writing I was, at least for the time being, the last man standing. I had never published much more than the occasional article here and there and certainly never a book. It was actually a pretty daunting idea, writing a book about the tradition. The pressure to do it properly and with the deepest respect was quite intense – at least in my own mind. I thought that if I ever did such a thing it would be quite the undertaking, something that would do the elders proud or not be done at all. While I had entertained the idea, in practical terms I had been very hesitant to take up the pen for something like this.

'What we would like to do, wishae,' Raven continued, calling me by the Thornish term that teachers use to address their students, 'is to at least consider the idea of writing and, like Russ and Carolyn, continue to take notes and keep memories so that one day, when the time is right, you may actually have the materials you need to get it done.'

'It's a huge honor, Wataan,' I replied. 'But you know, if I was ever going to do something like that I would have to do it right. I'm not sure I am ready at this point in time.'

'There will come a time when you are ready,' Raven said. 'We are patient. We can wait and when the time is right I know you will do us all a great honor.'

And to that I could say nothing. Instead I nodded my head in the half-formal style Thornish bow, a bow that barely inclines the head, keeping the focus on the object of the bow.

Raven took another sip of his wine.

'Little brother, you know that I always enjoy our times together. This time is no exception and it is always a pleasure to simply relax around a fire with you. To be truthful it is nice that you are also now a Master and I don't have to be quite so formal with you in matters of teaching.'

Yes, I was a Master now. I had completed the tasks of learning set before me and I had been judged worthy to undertake the Master's Deepening. It had taken some time to get to the point where those who were teaching me thought I was ready to move on. I had fashioned my Gar, or sacred spear, and had gone off into the woods for the prerequisite six days of deep introspection and ritual.

A Thornish person undergoes what is called a major Deepening only three times in their life: The Seeker's Deepening, the Master's Deepening and the Elders' Deepening. There is in fact considered to be a fourth Deepening but this is seen by Thornish people as the crossing one makes from the land of the living to the land of spirit. There are minor Deepenings as well and these are considered to be ritual retreats that initiates may embark upon many times during their lives. The Hollowing ritual is an example of a minor Deepening.

The first major Deepening, however, is the Seeker's Deepening. In this process the Learner, one who has been accepted and tutored by an initiated person, is trained in the ways of the tradition and eventually given permission to go off for three days and nights of ritual and meditation. Following the completion of this first Deepening the Learner is given their initiation into the tradition and they are considered to be a Shar, or initiated Thornish person.

The Master's Deepening is much more demanding, both in terms of the skills necessary to be prepared for it and the level of the ordeal itself. It is no simple thing for a man or woman to go out on such a quest and the dangers and challenges are very real. As Thornish Masters, also called Shar Masters, are considered to be the backbone of the tradition, as the primary teachers and collectors of lore, it is expected that only one who has proven themselves worthy through deed, word and a successful Deepening ordeal will be able to serve the Thornwood in a hale way.

The Elder's Deepening, the final major Deepening of a Thornish person's life here in the material world, is undertaken later in life and is seen as an affirmation of years of learning, experience and service, both to the sacred balance and the Great Essence, as well as to the Thornish tradition. This wilderness retreat of meditation and ritual lasts for nine days and when the initiate returns there is no ceremony to recognize the transition as there is for the Seeker or the Master. Other than the fact that a deeper measure of reverence and acknowledgment is now applied to the elder initiate, they still, for all intents and purposes, remain as Shar Masters. After all, when one has accomplished much and served the people well, going on the final Deepening is a true communing of spirit between the initiate and the Elder Kin. It is done for that purpose rather than signaling any other particular accomplishment.

As to my own Deepening, that of the Master, I went out and spent my sojourn in the deep green. When I had returned I was given my initiation. I had not been a Master long and I knew that I had much yet to learn before I could consider myself to be fully proficient in the tradition.

And these thoughts brought me full-circle, around the present and the comments that Raven had made concerning my status and some special event that had occasioned the dandelion wine.

'You know, I don't think I am ready to take on a student if that's what you are getting at,' I said at last. 'I mean, even if there was someone who needed to be taught.'

Raven laughed. It was a full on, honest-to-goodness laugh. There was nothing hidden or cynical in it at all.

Ever since I had begun the preparations for my Master's Deepening I had been concerned about the possibility that one day I would be asked to teach some young Leaner the Thornish ways. I knew then, as I know now, that one of the primary functions of the Masters is to teach and pass along the lore, yet I was one of those people who always felt unprepared, like I would never know quite enough to be trusted to train a new person. I had yet to feel myself worthy of such a responsibility.

I recall quite clearly one day mentioning my reservations in this area to Master Tiva, the old herbalist woodsman who lived up by the river. He heard me out and when I was finished he patted me on the shoulder and said, *'Good. You have a proper dose of Thornish humility.'*

If I haven't mentioned this before I probably should do so. If I have covered it, it will not hurt to speak about it again. Thornish folk have long viewed humility as being one of the most powerful attributes that a real, awakened person can have. It is seen as essential to growth on many, many levels and is an attribute that a Thornish person can never do without.

Thornish humility is not the same kind of thing that most people think of when the word 'humility' is heard. It is not any kind of servile or self-denigrating, groveling or slave-like behavior. To the Thornish person humility is the position of truly comprehending one's place in the greater scheme of the multiverse. It is about being of use, performing one's function as it is known to them through a sacred interface with nature. Thornish humility is about knowing one's place, yes, but this place is not dictated through any petty or corruptible human order. Rather, it is an understanding given through the understanding of balance and the First Law, the law of the cosmos.

Master Tiva once told me something like this: *'Humility is a simple thing, just as all true concepts are simple. Learn about the cosmos, view the First Law in action, and from this glean where you fit in all of this. Are you a sheep*

*who obeys and consumes or are you the wolf who fights...or are you the fox of the
thicket? Are you the serf in the field or are you the hawk that soars overhead?
Your nature and your ancestors help you to find your place; your exploration through
ritual will also help, but once you do know the role you play, you will feel its
rightness of it in your very bones. Knowing your true place is always the key.'*

So for whatever reason I did not see myself as being fully prepared
to teach anyone else yet, even if as a Master I would be expected to do
that eventually.

Raven had long known this and he had not bothered me about
it...not overly anyway.

And now he was chuckling at my discomfiture. I suppose I couldn't
really blame him.

'No, I was not going to ask you to teach anyone,' Raven said at
last. 'Not that there is anyone available who needs teaching at any rate.
However, I was thinking that I might be able to offer you an opportunity
to learn a few things from a new teacher yourself.'

'I am always open to learning,' I replied after a moment of trying to
guess where he was going with his statement. 'If you wouldn't mind
filling me in on who this other person might be.'

Since I had come to the tradition I had had the pleasure of learning
from several people, including Raven, who was my 'official' teacher in
the order so to speak. Yet for some reason I didn't think he was talking
about any of those.

'You have heard of Shale before?' Raven asked quietly.

A sudden chill of anticipation jolted me from my semi-relaxed state
on the rock where I was sitting.

'*Master* Shale?' I asked. '*The* Master Shale?'

'Yes,' Raven replied. He had seen my reaction and living up to his
Vörd-name, I could see that he was much like a great, grey raven perched
on his log, enjoying himself.

There was a Thornish person about whom comparatively little was
known – at least by those of us who constituted the younger generation
of initiates. He was known by his tribal name of Shale and was the
stuff of Thornish legend. It is said that he was the student of Master
Tiva, a Shar who was of the Farers rather than the Spearfolk, and that
he had been particularly gifted. Shale was also known to be a Vardyr
(pronounced Var-deer in the Thornish dialect) which only added a deeper
layer of mystique to the man.

I should explain a bit about Vardyr. In the Thornwood, or Thornish tradition, there are generally considered to be two areas of practice: the Farer way and the way of the Spearfolk, sometimes also called Spear-Carriers. The Farer folk are more inclined to the work of ritual, healing and oracular work while the Spearfolk are more inclined to the more visceral areas such as hunting, heavy ordeal work and the practice of martial arts.

While all initiated Thornish people are considered to be warriors there has been an evolution of special ways – and these have become the Farers and the Spearfolk.

However, over time, a few have emerged who not only display a great aptitude for both areas of work, but who also tend to be far more committed to an ascetic lifestyle, mostly in deep wilderness areas. In the history of the Thornish tradition there have been very few who have taken up this level of dedication to their role as an implement of balance, to give up much of what might be considered a normal human life in order to seek the deeper mysteries and become a more finely-honed blade of the way. These, in the Thornish tradition, are the Vardyr.

So yes, I had heard of the man though I had never up until that point had the pleasure of meeting him.

'It turns out our brother, Shale, has been spending time on the north coast and on the north end of the island for quite awhile. I haven't seen or heard from him in well over five years, but this is the way of things with the Vardyr. They spend much of their lives in solitude, appearing only to emerge when they are needed and often to act as the left-hand-of balance. This time however, Shale found himself in this area and came without pretense other than to visit.'

'That is very cool,' I said, not knowing what else to say.

'Yes it is,' Raven replied. 'So we had a nice visit over at my place the last couple of days. He had heard about a certain student of mine and was wondering if he might have a chance at teaching him a few things. I told him *sure, because my student still thinks he is unworthy to be a Shar Master, at least as far as the teaching role goes, and it might be nice for him to learn a few more things.'*

'You said what?' I asked incredulously.

'That's what I told him,' Raven said from behind an even craftier smile than the one he had been wearing moments before. 'He's intrigued with what he calls your true commitment to Thornish humility and he would like to meet you.'

I thought about this for a moment. Sure, I would certainly like to meet this fellow Thornsman about whom I had heard a fair bit of rumor, yet I wasn't so sure if my teacher had given him the right impression about me.

'Well, you should have brought him out here with us tonight,' I said at last, having decided to roll with my teacher's words and return with an attitude of my own. 'There are certainly questions I'd like to ask him too.'

At this, Raven leaned forwards slightly, so that the flames of the fire cast grim shadows into his face. I have little doubt in retrospect that he had done this precisely to add a theatrical effect to the fun he was already having with me.

'Why don't you ask him yourself?' Raven said. 'He's sitting right behind you.'

At this I fairly leapt off the rock in my urge to spin around to look into the bush behind me. What I had heard regarding the Vardyr was that they were consummate woodsmen, more like fleeting spirits of the green. They were said to be able to move like ghosts and creep up easily on anyone or anything.

But in my own case, as I spun right off the rock and nearly fell on my face, I saw that there was no one there in the gloom behind me at all.

Now Raven was really beside himself with laughter. I returned, with as much of my fragmented dignity as I could, to my rock-perch and waited for his laughter and knee slapping to subside.

At last it did and when he was able to speak coherently again he said, 'But really, he does want to meet you. He'll be coming by the house tomorrow afternoon.'

* * *

'Almost everything in the world of men is a lie,' Master Shale said as he knelt near the cliff's edge with me.

He sported a well-worn Thornish Greencoat while I was dressed in jeans with a flannel shirt. For those who might be interested, the custom of the Greencoat comes from years back in the tradition. No one is exactly sure where it originated. Basically, they are like an overcoat, shin length and usually constructed of a heavy duty material such as duck canvas or wool. Sometimes these coats are a uniform deep green and at other times they are mottled, almost a kind of primitive camouflage, as Shale's was. Traditionally the Greencoat is used as a weatherproof — or rather weather resistant — garment that protects against underbrush and the like, and at the same time provides the wearer with a certain level of insulation and cover.

I had seen several of my Thornish brethren make use of the Greencoat over the years but I had never before seen one so well used and worn as the one that Master Shale was wearing. I had no doubt that it had served him well in his many sojourns in the wild places.

'They avoid the truth of the world and while they do that they await the stroke of balance,' Shale continued, sliding back from the cliff's edge. 'Just look at that filthy mess they are creating down there, harvesting not out of need but destroying for profit. There is no honor in this. There is no excuse a grown man can make for doing such things to the Earth.'

We had remained unseen as we had approached the viewpoint. There was no point in allowing the men below to know that they were being observed. Thornish Warriors appear when they wish to be seen and not before.

Far below us, on the forest floor below, there was a small logging operation at work. They had been removing large fir trees from an area adjacent to the forest service road and already it had left an ugly scar somewhat rectangular in shape. Even though this industrial activity was at least two hundred meters away we could still easily hear the terrible tearing and crunching of bulldozers clearing away debris.

'What do you mean by the stroke of balance?' I asked.

'What do you think I mean by that, nashae Kraa?' he asked quietly. He was not messing around as I had come quite rapidly to know. In retrospect I have come to know that not all Vardyr are quite so serious as Master Shale. He was quite a serious fellow.

His Thornish was quite fluid and he used it as though it was a way of communicating that he used more than he did English. While it was good to hear our dialect spoken by a brother in the tradition I was perhaps a little uneasy about the way he seemed to speak most of the time. His words were delivered in a hard, direct kind of way, with no attempt to soften their reception by anyone or anything

The Thornish dialect, by the way, is a loose collection of words that have found their way into use by the folk since the time of the founding. There is certainly nothing ancient or mysterious about it and indeed, the creation of such a way of speaking was never planned or intended. It is thought to have simply germinated on its own and grown over time. Initially it consisted of either created, borrowed or intuited words that came to various members either from other languages they were familiar with and used, or as gifts from the spirit world. Through contact other members picked up on these words and terms and they came into a kind of unofficial use.

Over time some of the new words that came into use had no traceable source but seemed to have emerged to fit a specific tribal need, to describe things that were uniquely Thornish. Over the years people of the Thornwood had come to accept the existence of this way of communicating and indeed came to enjoy the way that it blended with regular English to get ideas across.

While not a language in itself, it is an interesting lexicon which Thornish people make no excuses or explanation for. The Thornish speech simply is... and like many other Thornish customs it is not something which many outsiders would understand or appreciate. Though naturally, Thornish folk usually could care *less-than-less* (as a Master once commented) about the opinions of outsiders.

Nashae Kraa, as Shale had called me, means student of Raven. Other than the first time we had met, when he had addressed me as Qorvas, my tribal name, he had not deviated from referring to me as the student of my teacher.

'I assume you are talking about the place of Shar in the re-balancing of the world.'

He turned away from the cliff and looked at me. I think he probably would have been quite attractive to women had he not always been wearing the grimness he seemed to prefer. He was of medium build, Caucasian, with dark black hair that he wore very short. He also seemed to have a permanent case of five-o-clock shadow, which I suppose came as the result of his fair skin and the dark hair color. The grey-colored eyes only added to the serious demeanor of this stern and mysterious fellow.

Shale nodded in approval of my words.

'Yes,' he said matter-of-factly. 'Not only us but those of many other tribes and nations who are on the rise. Many don't see it but there are people who have been hidden for generations; secret orders and hidden traditions whose purposes are very similar to our own. We are all rising from the shadows to face the coming storm.'

He paused for a moment and looked alertly around, as if something had caught his attention. Then he turned back to me.

'Many people don't notice these changes that are going on or the rise of various hidden people, but the century has well over a decade left to go. Wait and see and you will notice these things becoming more prominent.'

'I have heard about the coming changes,' I replied. 'Raven has told me, as has Master Tiva and others. My grandfather has as well.'

At the mention of my grandfather, Shale's hard expression softened if only for a moment, and he nodded his head in the slightest Thornish bow.

'Ah, yes,' he said in a respectful tone. 'Your grandfather is well known to me. A great man; powerful, wonderfully dark and very dangerous to cross. You are lucky to be his relative.'

Then he returned to the original conversation.

'The changes are real,' he said. 'I have seen them. People talk about it as if they are on their way but they are already here, little brother. They are increasing in strength. They have come because the natural earth-changes that happen over millennia have coincided with an age of unparalleled human decadence. Sometimes the old powers are slow to rouse but when they do, they unleash forces that have unbelievable power.'

'And most humans carry on with their mundane lives, unknowing or uncaring as to the fate of the world,' I said. I was well aware of the prophecies and from what I had seen, I agreed with their message.

'Yes,' Shale said. 'And humankind in its foolish arrogance believes that it is above the level of any other life on this planet, that somehow the rules of nature do not apply in the case of Homo sapiens. The truth is that no one is above the First Law and when judgment comes down, it is going to come down hard. Many will die. It's our job to make sure that our teachings live on.'

I nodded to that.

We pulled away from the cliff area and silently returned to the bush. We found the trail we had come in on and retraced our path back to the main trail down toward the river.

The most sacred charges of the Thornwood were to comprehend the sacred laws of balance and re-tune with the Middle World, also called Earth. Thornish folk are awakened implements of balance, stewards and protectors of the land and the sacred in the world. The teachings are those of integration and understanding in nature and to pass along this wisdom to those who are able to receive and comprehend such teachings. Yet the tradition is not something which just does its job in the silence of the glades. As sacred implements of the Great Essence, known also as the Great Mystery, and in the service of the Elder Kin and many others, the folk of the Thornwood are the blades of the Warrior as well as the tools of the garden and grove. The Thornish tradition is a tradition of Warriors, not slaves; a way of foxes, hawks and wolves, never sheep or cattle.

It has been said that we will not only play a part in the preservation of the world and the teaching of the worthy, but also in the culling of the world-killers as well. I was never particularly clear on how that last part was to work and what part the 'average' Thornish person (if there was such a thing as an average Thornish person) would play. When I questioned my elders on such things I was told that my own destiny would reveal itself in these matters and through my instincts and training I would play my part when the time came.

But in Shale, I realized I was in the presence of the sharp edge of the Thornish blade. He was hard and dark, probably more so than any other Thornish person I had ever met. I could tell that the First Law, the law that some people referred to as lex talionis, the razor-edged law-of-the-jungle, was his primary creed. He would do his duty efficiently, whatever that duty might be, whether it was tending to trees in a hidden glade, living off the land in peace or wading into chaos with a ruthless intent. Like all Vardyr, Shale was kind of like a Frith-knife laid upon the stones between the Earth and those who would harm her. The phrase *'this far and no farther'* came to mind when I pondered him and the role of his Oath-kin.

Shale was something that the destroyers of the world would have reason to fear.

The grim man in green and gray next to me was an enigma and yet he also gave off what my late brother, Russell, would have called a 'danger vibe.' By this, Russell was referring to the kind of feeling one might get when in the presence of any kind of natural danger, such as a mountain storm, an avalanche or a grizzly bear. When later I was told that Shale's Vörd or spirit-guardian-helper was a wolf, I was not in the least surprised.

We walked along in silence for some time, with Shale in the front, walking the Thornish Warrior's Walk as it seemed he habitually did. The Thornish Warrior's Walk is very similar to what my Native relations might call a Wolf-walk or even a Coyote-walk. The method entails a person re-learning how to move forward in a way that places one foot almost directly in front of the other. The center of balance is slightly lower in this way and the person strives to walk primarily on the balls of the feet rather than landing heavily down on the heel as most so-called *civilized* people do. The purpose of the Thornish Warrior's Walk is to present a smaller, less disruptive profile in the woods, to take less room to move and to leave less distinguishable tracks in one's wake.

We moved ahead silently and relatively quickly using this method. We caused very little disruption to the natural cycles of the forest moving in this way.

Before all that much time had passed we found ourselves back down from the higher ground and were once again moving along the river. I was rather disappointed because I loved the ridge trail and considering that this day was a brilliant sunny one I regretted not getting to enjoy the view from up there for awhile longer.

Yet the deep green of the river as it flowed through the forest floor was also a potent thing to be around. Here there was very little sign of human presence; we were far from any road or main trail. Silence, punctuated only by the occasional rustling of underbrush or bird song, was the music of this sacred place.

At last we came to a small clearing surrounded by pines and firs, with one half descending to the river bank. This place had been used as a camp at one time, long ago, as the small, moss covered stone fire-pit indicated. Nearby, off to one side and partially hidden in the bush was a small, neatly built lean-to of salvaged deadwood and brush. It contained a canvas bag and a generous pile of firewood that looked as though it had been collected from the surrounding forest floor.

'A temporary camp of mine,' Shale explained as I noticed the small shelter. 'Well, not really mine, but it's obvious that Hearth-kin built this fire-pit long ago.'

Hearth-kin is a term used by Thornish people to denote someone who has taken the oaths and been initiated as a Shar. In our way, this indicates that we are through oath, ritual and fire, related to that person as though they were actually blood relations. We take these things very seriously.

I walked over and examined the small fire-pit. Indeed it was very well constructed, with a ring of cantaloupe-sized round stones making up the outer rim and smaller, flatter stones comprising the inner, bowl-shaped surface. The pit was quite deep, probably nearly shin high on a grown man. The stone lining of the pit made an excellent surface which would eventually absorb and reflect back the heat of any fire.

The construction style alone would have suggested that it was of either Thornish or Native traditional design. However, closer examination revealed a glyph carved into one of the ring-stones. It was the Thornish glyph we call Naka, the fire-bowl; the symbol of ritual offering.

'It's Thornish all right,' I said.

It did not take us long to set up a simple camp. I arranged wood in the fire pit and got a small blaze going very easily. Shale, for his part, provided a small metal pot and some camp coffee. I got water from the river and set it to boil in fairly short order.

This was not a camp that we intended to spend the night in but rather it was what could be called a day camp. Such camps were quite common among Thornish people or among many different kinds of traditional people. To sit-the-fire with friends and other kinds of relations was (and is) seen as a very hale way to interact.

It was not long before we had our cups of steaming chicory camp coffee in hand and were sitting across the fire from one another on pieces of log we had rolled over from the wood pile.

I was still getting used to Shale and his mannerisms, yet his counsel had been highly recommended to me by Raven, who as my teacher, kinsman and friend I respected greatly. Even though by tradition Shale and I held the same level of learning-and-responsibility (seen by outsiders perhaps as 'rank' though in the Thornish context this would not be entirely accurate), I did not think of this stern woodsman as my equal. His reputation had preceded him and as well, he had been Thornish far longer than I had. Indeed, there was a considerable difference in age between us as well, though not such a difference as there was between myself and my mentor, Ari. Still to a young man in his twenties, as I was then, someone Shale's age, in his early 40's, who had been Thornish for at least half of his time on Earth, the gulf was seen as considerable.

Finally, after sitting and enjoying the deep forest ambiance for a time, and sipping on that beautifully blended dandelion/chicory coffee, Shale spoke.

'Ya'tela,' he said. 'We begin.'

I was continually impressed at how often he used the Thornish speech rather than English. He had said 'we begin,' which usually prefaces an important process of some kind. In this case I suspected that he referred to the process of learning and teaching. In the Thornish speech there are many such unique words or phrases that mark various activities. In this instance I was reminded that *Ya'tela*, we begin, was also used as a form of greeting between Thornish people. The term *Ya'khola* indicates the ending of something and is also used to say farewell when parting company.

Shale also reached to his belt beneath the Greencoat and withdrew a gleaming blade. I was most impressed with the look of this implement and knew it immediately for what it was: A Thornish Frith-knife. Indeed, this was a fairly large knife, made out of what looked like highly polished and well-oiled carbon steel, it had a blade that was at least 25 or so centimeters (or 10 inches in the old system) long. The blade, as with most Frith-knives, had been forged with a gentle, sweeping curve reminiscent of a bird's talon. The blade was double edged and gleamed wickedly sharp. There was a very minimal guard that looked like it might have been made of brass, and the hilt was a beautifully stained piece of antler.

The Frith-knife is a very respected implement and symbol for Thornish people. Initially, in the early days of the Raven Lodge, it was used as a gift to incoming female students. The idea was that there were few women involved in Thornish life in those days and the blade was handed over as a gift to show that, symbolically at least, the woman should feel safe; that she had a means to defend herself if anyone attempted to accost her. This tradition was based on an old story which had been told around the fires of the Old Lodges, long before the time of the Raven Lodge.

However, this tradition of specifically gifting a Frith-knife to women was not long lived, as a prominent female Thornish Master felt that a Frith-knife gifted to all would promote more feeling of equality and indeed security. Thus in 1962 the tradition of the Frith-knife was altered so that all incoming Learners, male or female, were gifted with a Frith-knife to indicate that they would be treated respectfully and peacefully and the same was expected of them in return.

The word Frith is a Germanic word which refers to the atmosphere of peaceful, respectful interaction which was expected in sacred places, events and among those who were related or who had come together in some way. Among Thornish folk the symbol of the Frith-knife was seen as that of a warder of the peace. Once given, the Frith-knife becomes a powerful symbol of the Thornish way and its practitioners. The knife is used both as a ritual tool and a utilitarian implement and all those who possess one are trained in its use. Tribal law prohibits the baring of a Frith-Knife in sacred enclosures unless the bared steel is a required part of the ritual. Unlike many other pagan traditions which honor the concept of Frith, Thornish traditions allow for the carrying of one's knife within sacred spaces as knives are tools as well as weapons.

After Shale had drawn the Frith-knife he held it before him for a moment so that I could get a good look at it. This is in keeping with the custom and belief that each Frith-knife possesses a spirit and indeed a personality. Showing it in such a fashion to someone peaceful, who has never seen it before, is considered good manners.

'This is Maskwa,' Shale said, introducing me to his blade. Having had a fair bit of exposure to people who spoke the Cree language I was already familiar with the word for Bear. I wondered if Shale, in his travels, had spent time in the eastern provinces or had Cree friends or relations living here.

'The Bear,' I nodded.

Shale pointed with his finger to the curving edge of the Frith-knife.

'The bear's claw, as you can see,' he said. "A good curve which is a very useful thing."

Then Shale laid his knife down, edge out and away from him, on a small, flat stone that happened to be laying on the ground before the fire.

'May there always be steel upon the stones,' he said.

I nodded, semi-bowing towards him.

'May there be peace between us,' I replied. As a matter of fact I had my own Frith-knife with me, but as there was already one blade laid out there was no need for another to join it. I made a mental note, however, to introduce my own blade at a later date. It would be the polite thing to do.

And with that we settled in to talk.

'You remember me saying earlier that the world of men is largely encased in lies,' he said, rubbing his hands over the crackling flames. 'Well, that is a truth I have come to know more and more the older I get. When you get to the point where you can look at the human world from the outside point of view you see that it is in fact a very nasty system of manipulation and deceit.'

'One of the very first things I was taught in the tradition was that so many things in the mainstream world are fabrications made up so that a few can control the many,' I said. 'Since then I have seen it in action more and more.'

'I have been off in the north for a considerable time,' Shale said. 'Weeks and often months on my own, many miles from any sign of human presence, and that is the way I like it. I value true freedom and I am always looking to discover ways that I can fully embrace that. In the deep green places there is much to learn; however, it is also in such places that the spirit-folk, the Shaeda as we call them, speak the loudest.'

The term Shaeda, in the Thornish world-view, is quite complex. It describes spirit-people but perhaps not in the way that many people outside the tradition might see them. To the Thornish person, spirit-people can take many forms and operate on many different levels. They are not necessarily the essences of beings who have died. Indeed, some of them have never lived in the way that human beings understand the term. Some spirit-people are simply different species that exist on different levels of reality than we do and some share the same space in the Middle World as human beings. Some spirit-people are very deep and primal, such as the river folk, the mountain folk or the stone people. Some are represented to us through various elemental powers, such as wind, water, earth and fire. To someone who shares Thornish belief *everything in nature is alive* and, to a greater or lesser degree, holds some form of intelligence. Thornish people also believe that manmade objects and machines can also possess a degree of spirit because they were created from things that were originally from nature and that they often have prolonged contact with human beings.

Everything is alive; everything has spirit. If a person unused to such a concept were to ponder it for a time, with an open mind, the possibilities that open up can be truly staggering.

'I have spoken to Shaeda, though probably not as deeply as you have on your travels far up in the wild places. It is always a powerful and humbling experience.'

'Yes,' he replied. 'If you go with humility and open yourself up to their wisdom there is a lot you can gain from such contact. But you know, little brother, sometimes they tell you things you might not want to hear. As you follow the path of the Black Root you can get drawn into conversations with people who are impossibly old compared to us humans. They know things and sometimes they don't realize that our small minds are only designed to accommodate so much.'

'And they have told you some powerful things?'

'Yes. They have,' Shale said. 'This is part of the reason why I may appear hard to you, that I might have no emotion or sense of humor. There is actually a human man underneath all of my armor and it is quite visible when I am in the wild places. But here, so close to the idiocy of what they call civilization, I tend to close off and armor up, if you get my meaning.'

'I'd say I understand but that might not be accurate,' I replied after a moment. 'Let's just say that I have had a small taste of what you describe and already some of the things I see humans doing makes me sick.'

Shale threw a small stick into the fire.

'It's a start,' he said. 'It's part of waking up and realizing that there are a relatively few human beings, mentally twisted and criminally oriented people, who in their greed have infected many others with their corrupted ways of thinking. This has spread across the world and has brought us to the brink. The world and the Elder Kin have various defense mechanisms against this human disease and our folk, my friend, are one of these defenses. Traditions like our own, not to mention the various Shaeda, have come forward to help in these times.'

'Sometimes it's hard waking up,' I responded. 'I mean, you go through life thinking that the world is a certain way and then, bang! It all changes and you realize that much of what you thought was perfectly cool and normal is anything but. But you know, I woke up years ago and it seems there is always more to learn.'

'The world is still a beautiful place at the core,' my grim friend said. 'But right now she has a sickness and we as friends of the Earth have to help her get better.'

'We need to help more people wake up,' I said quietly.

Shale looked at me very intently and I could see that he was processing not only thoughts but emotion. Perhaps I was fantasizing but for a moment there I thought I detected the slightest sign of a grin attempting to appear on his grim face.

The movement of facial muscles ceased and the man across from me once again became a hard and focused.

'Apologies, little brother,' he said after a moment, and this time I did detect a very slight softening of his demeanor. 'But you know with our age difference I have to keep reminding myself that you are a Shar Master now and no longer a Learner or even Shakai.'

'I know a few things,' I said, attempting to conceal a grin, and nodding. 'I know I have light-years to go, but I try my best.'

'You have a good reputation already,' Shale said. 'And this is why, when Raven asked if I might spend a little time with you, I agreed. I don't have much of a reputation as a teacher, though. I believe I lack the empathy to properly communicate lessons to Learners.'

'I have a similar problem,' I confessed. 'I feel I'm not ready to teach anyone because I still feel like a student myself.'

Now a very slight warmth flashed across that hard countenance and I could tell that he had deliberately permitted the faint lines of a grin to appear on his face. I appreciated the effort.

'We are all students at one level or another,' he said at last. 'I heard the story of your Master's Deepening so I know that you have earned your place.'

I thought about that for a moment. I had shared a goodly amount of what happened in that ritual with others, including the fact that my own ritual lasted nine days rather than the requisite six. This was never intended to impress anyone or serve as evidence of some kind of youthful endurance. I had followed my instincts and come back later, only to discover how impressed people had been. No one had ever done a Master's Deepening of that length before.

'And so, since we are here, I would like you to tell me your answers to a few questions I have,' Shale said. 'It's not a test. Nothing like that. I am simply curious as to where you are coming from in terms of our tradition.'

The Thornish way is not a religious way but rather a pagan spiritual warrior's order. No one tells anyone how to believe but rather students are selected based upon how closely the ways of any potential Learner falls into balance and synchronization with the world-view of the tradition. Certainly there are basic tenets and ideals which all Thornish folk agree upon, but the specifics of such things are left to the individual. As such there are many shades of green among the Thornish people. Shale was asking me to describe my particular shade to him.

So I spoke for awhile. I talked about my beliefs and how I honored the spirits of the land and the Elder Kin of the north. I spoke about growing up in the city and how I had eventually connected with my grandfather and been taught the Indian ways. I spoke about how I had eventually met Ari and the others and my hopes and thoughts for the Thornish tradition.

When I had finished, Shale nodded.

'Interestingly enough, you and I are not so different,' he said. 'I too am from what they call mixed bloodlines. My father was Romanian and my mother was part Cree. Like you I had been taught some of the native ways and later on I made my own way in the world. Eventually I got to visit the old country of my father's family and it was there I met some people who honored the old Gods of northern Europe. It wasn't until later that I ran into Thornish people who were willing to teach and when I found them I realized that I had found a spiritual home at last. I found that the spirit of the Old Gods of the north and the deep Indian spirit of the land is very much at home in the Thornish ways.'

'My road was a long one as well, considering,' I replied. 'I know I am what you might call young, but I have been on the road to awakening for a fair bit of time.'

'No doubt you have,' Shale replied. 'No offense meant to your years. All men gain wisdom at their own rate and I think you have already gathered your fair share.'

'Many of the Pagan people I have met in my life so far really want to play pretend fantasy games as though they are in a novel or a comic book,' I said glumly. 'Many of the others are subconsciously still Christians and they put a coating of Pagan veneer over that. It's like they are afraid to completely let go of that dead end thinking and move forward as a Pagan person.'

'I have seen this too. They are afraid to shatter the chains of the mind that hold them,' Shale said. 'In this act they prove themselves to be unworthy. They are not aware of the sayings we have and even if they were, they would be afraid to heed them.'

'When in doubt delve deeper?' I suggested, thinking of a Thornish saying I felt might fit the bill.

'That is exactly the one I was thinking of,' Shale replied. 'Hale minds think alike.'

When in doubt delve deeper is a saying which addresses the ways in which a Thornish person should deal with the many doubts and insecurities which run rampant in our modern world. It counsels the Thornish person that the truth of matters always lies at the root and in spiritual matters one should always look to nature and to the deeper, more primordial understandings one has of the world for answers. The deeper one looks into the ancient ways the simpler things become and the closer to the surface are the truths.

This is the way of the Black Root; a way of understanding the knowledge and instinctive ideas that will be found both within and without the Thornsman or Thornswoman who seeks.

'It has been hard finding others like me,' I added. 'Until I had the luck of connecting with my grandfather and others like him I was pretty much alone.'

And we sat there for a considerable time sharing stories and comparing ideas about the world. It turned out that indeed we held quite a few things in common.

The common ground that all Thornish people share is based in the primal. Animist belief is at the core, with various additional understandings added. Many hold the specific Elder Kin of the Old North as their guides and inspiration, though not all do. Some are pure animists who prefer only to work with local spirits and others over time have brought stories of different '*gods*' or '*goddesses*' to the circle.

Master Tiva, a Thornish Elder who was held in great respect by everyone, was an example of cultural eccentricity at work in the Thornwood. The child of parents from two very different cultures, Tiva had learned to walk a path that gave respect and honor to the spirits of his mixed Celtic and African bloodlines. Tiva was greatly esteemed and was considered a very powerful Farer and healer.

It should probably be said at this point, for those who may not have considered it, that acceptance into the Thornish community is based upon the way a person walks in the worlds and never by anything like race, culture, sex or their preference of gender in a mate. Women are seen as the equals of men and though there have always been inner societies which revere the mysteries of each, all are seen as respected Hearth-kin.

Among the Thornish folk it is believed that the universe itself is not really a universe at all, but a multiverse composed of uncountable realities and that this entirety of space and time is intelligent. Thornish people refer to this operative intelligence as the Great Essence and view it in some ways similarly to the Native people when they refer to it as the Great Mystery. Thornish people do not ascribe any personality to this Great Essence, nor is it anthropomorphized to appear as any particular form of being. It is seen by us as the intelligent spark that manages the cosmos.

Following this is the belief that life is everywhere and that some forms of life have evolved into different levels of intelligence and form than others. It is held that a very long time ago certain forms of beings came into existence who were the ancestors of the ones we call the Elder Kin, and the Elder Kin themselves are very advanced beings who have achieved much in the ways of intellectual and spiritual technological development. It is believed that certain of these Elder Kin came to the Middle World long ago and that here they took an interest in the primitive beings who would later become human. As such from time to time some of these Elder ones continue to visit this world.

It is thought that human beings were given a great deal of knowledge by the Elder Kin, who helped them along and that much of this old knowledge, called the First Knowledge in Thornish tradition, was somehow encoded into our bodies and our life energies. This is not some radical concept, either. When one observes other creatures in nature they see certain patterns of behavior that seem somehow built in. The general term for this is instinct, of course, but it is thought by Thornish people that the concept and the reality goes much deeper.

Thornish tradition is keenly interested in the process of uncovering clues to this hidden ancestral knowledge because it is believed that humankind was placed here to operate in a stewardship role for the planet. It is believed that this First Knowledge will lead to greater understandings of nature and our role in it. Among the Thornish folk this concept is seen as the root of a great tree (there are individual variations of this image) that is at the foundation of our species. It is referred to as the Black Root, the mysterious way of deepening knowledge.

So fundamentally the role of Thornish people is seen as one of stewardship. As stewards of the land we are awakened warrior-folk who have come to realize the current un-balanced state of the world and have determined to do something to correct the imbalance. This is done through the continual seeking of knowledge (both of the Black Root and otherwise), the gaining of sacred insights, the re-opening of hale relations with the world of spirit and of nature and the educating of those who are willing to awaken.

Yet the Thornish way is not about worshiping the Great Essence, the Elder Kin or anything else. It is about understanding the concepts of nature from a certain point of view, coming to a deep understanding of one's self and gaining power and wisdom from that. Finally it is about utilizing that power, wisdom and deep insight to serve the Earth, to serve one's people and to serve the balance as an implement of balance.

There is a saying which goes:

I hear the Old Ones speak

And in return I am given wisdom and power

With this wisdom and power I serve the Middle World

And my people.

Shale and I discussed these aspects and many more there at that little fire by the river. In the end we were in agreement that we were definitely on the same frequency. However, experience tells and Shale's experience in the world far overshadowed my own. This was to be expected since there was nearly a twenty-year gap between our respective ages.

I was shown some techniques and given some insights which I may not share here. However I will say that the experience was a powerful one and it opened avenues of thought which I had not pondered before. Indeed these avenues of thought, it was fairly obvious to me, could only have come through wisdom gained in the deepest depths of solitude.

'I have seen some things and been shown some things, out there,' Shale said, after a time of silence. 'And those things tell me that these changes the Elderfolk have foreseen and forewarned us about are much closer than we think. I grow frustrated at times because it seems that there are not enough awakened people in the world and I fear that by the time there are it will be too late.'

'I have heard similar things from others,' I said. 'However, Raven, who as you know is quite gifted, has told us about a time of awakening that will come in our lifetime. He has said that a way will come into the world that will allow people unprecedented access to information and that this will really help people to wake up.'

'It will probably lead to some grim times if that happens,' Shale said. 'Because you know that the men and women of the cabals, the ones who act like they are robber barons over a world of field serfs, won't like their chattel waking up and smelling freedom.'

'No,' I agreed. 'But they will at least know that they have freedom as an option where they didn't know that before.'

'Governments have forgotten that it is they who are supposed to obey their people, not the other way around,' Shale added. 'During such upheavals as will come, various corrupt politicians will inevitably be taught the error of their ways.'

'Everything changes over time, my friend,' I said. 'This is the nature of balance.'

'The calm before the storm and of course, the storm before the calm again,' he replied. 'As long as people are willing to wallow in the embrace of the lies, they will remain slaves.'

'The lies?' I asked.

Now Shale actually did grin openly and, it seemed, without having done battle with his sense of self discipline. The grin was something that I would imagine one might find on the face of a boy who had been caught with his hand in the cookie jar.

'I imagine that there is no denying to you that I am Vardyr,' he said.

Vardyr, as I have mentioned before, are a type of Thornish person who has performed certain rituals, made certain declarations and done certain deeds that cause them to stand out from most others in the Thornish tradition. In their most basic form they are Thornish initiates who have become mystics or ascetics, wandering Farers and Spearfolk who find deep meaning in finding a life far from the haunts of humankind. While they are at their core just as Thornish as anyone else who has taken the oaths, they are respected greatly because they have made little compromise between the life of the mainstream and the life of the Shar.

They have sought the concept of True Innocence and True Freedom in a way that many Thornish people can only dream of.

'Yes,' I replied smiling. 'This is something I know.'

'Among us there are certain ideas that to most of the folk might seem rather harsh. Nevertheless, there is deep truth to them. This one we call simply the *Lies*. Most Thornish people think of the solutions to them as the nine hard truths.'

'Ah!' I said knowingly. 'Yes, I know what you are saying then. The Nine Hard Truths are the solution to what you call the Lies. You Vardyr are a hard bunch.'

'The edge of the blade is much closer to the surface with us, my brother,' Shale said quietly. 'In the places where we walk we have no use for sugar-coating anything, nor shielding anyone from hurt feelings.'

For the reader I will briefly explain these things as most Thornish people are taught them. The Nine Hard Truths are a segment of the core teachings of the Thornwood. The Nine Hard Truths are the first segment of the primary teachings that are given to both Fellows and Learners in an effort to assist them with their process of awakening. They basically explain the Thornish worldview in the most basic terms.

♦ **Everything is connected:** Thornish people believe that in the multiverse, everything is connected to everything else at one level or another. Thus what occurs to one creature will, on some plane or another, have an effect on everything else. This is why Thornish folk are so concerned about the sacred balance of nature and that imbalances be corrected as quickly as possible.

♦ **Peace is fiction:** Peace as it is so often imagined in today's age is a fiction. Man-made peace is an imaginary state that most humans believe must be enforced in order to be maintained. True peace exists only as a part of the natural flow and even this is frequently if often only briefly shattered as the balances of life and death are addressed. Thus it is seen that one must look to nature for instruction in reaching a balanced state.

♦ **The Middle World is at war:** Thornish people have no doubt of this. For centuries there have been ruling cabals of human beings who are engrossed with the ideals of entitlement and who feel that they have the right to rule and to despoil the sacred world we live on. Their mentally imbalanced ideas have corrupted the majority of human societies and have caused untold damage to the planet and all of her life-forms. As the Elder Kin and the planet herself take action against this disease they have assisted a great many humans in the awakening process. The awakened ones grow in number each day and work to restore the balance, to heal the world.

♦ **Strength opens doors**; weakness closes them. One need only to look at nature and they will see that strength survives and weakness does not. Human beings who believe in nurturing weakness while shunning strength are walking down the path of misdirection and eventual oblivion.

♦ **Equality is fantasy:** Thornish people believe that all people are unique in special ways and that because of this the idea that everyone is somehow the same is ridiculous. Thornish people celebrate differences and uniqueness and believe that these things are more important than sameness. At the same time Thornish folk see that the idea of reducing all human beings down to a single, monogamous mass is an attempt at disempowering the idea of free potential in people. This is not to say that in general people should not be afforded the same basic respects as any other creature in the Middle World, yet to the Thornish person, greater respect is earned and all persons are not simply afforded this greater respect carte blanche, so to speak. Each human being will gain the respect of others through deeds.

♦ **Freedom is not free:** While those of the Thornwood recognize that in nature all are born with the potential to be free, this is no longer a guarantee on a human-dominated world. It is believed that there are many people who live to steal the freedoms of other creatures and that this behavior is against the natural order. Thus Freedom must be striven for and those who are awakened must be ever vigilant in protecting the freedoms they have.

♦ **Money is a broken tool:** Thornish folk see the interesting and utilitarian tool that the use of currency must once have brought to the world. However, over time, as the resources of the world have been manipulated so that the fruits of human labor end up in the hands of a few, money has lost its meaning. Indeed it has been used as a tool for the enslavement of many living things on this planet. While Thornish people living in the modern times realize that money is at times necessary to live, it is viewed as an (unfortunate) necessary evil. As a part of this understanding it is further seen that the concepts of credit and debt are tools of enslavement. These things are viewed as insidious snares which are specifically designed to steal freedom in the world. Most modern day human beings in the so-called first world, specifically, are mired in the fantasy of debt and credit. In fact Thornish people view the entire credit/debt system as being a fabrication designed to enslave the labor of the people. Thornish folk avoid such things as they are able.

- **Democracy is a failed experiment:** Democracy, along with all other modern concepts of governance, are considered to be failures by Thornish people. The very fact that human beings have been brainwashed into believing that they need to be governed in the first place is at the root of this problem. Democracy, according to Thornish people, has long since been co-opted by corporate and other corrupt influences and today only bears the outer trappings of free society. Thornish people believe that the best modalities of governance are found in the Moot, in which members of each Lodge, under the guidance of Elders and an elected Daar or Kayla (male or female chieftain) make decisions regarding their own actions and fate. Thornish people believe that human structures of governance begin to fail beyond certain population limits and the ideal is a multitude of smaller, tribal nations.

- **Human-made laws are not true laws:** Thornish people see the First Law, the law of nature, as being the only true law. Everything else that might be known as order stems from this First Law. The law referred to as the Fourth Law, known also as the laws of humankind, is not considered to be overly important in comparison to the First Law, as human law is seen as being made to control the lives of other humans. Fourth Law has also largely proven, over many hundreds of years now, to have had a detrimental effect on the planet.

There is a Thornish saying: *When in doubt, ask yourself whether it is good for the planet. If it is good for the world, then it is in keeping with the First Law. If it is not, then it is not in balance.*

Now, in the modern day, Thornish people realize that to blatantly disregard all modern human laws would be to invite trouble with human authorities. Thus, within reasonable limits and to the extent that oaths are not compromised, Thornish folk will operate within the rules of the community they live in. Where human laws are in balance with nature – and there seem to me more of these appearing with regard to the protection of the Earth and her creatures – then walking in accordance with these is acceptable. Thus, not all human laws are seen as bad laws, but Thornish people must keep a keen eye out for those which are potentially harmful and those which are hale.

As such, with regard to people *'wallowing in the embrace of the lies'* Shale was referring to these teachings from the somewhat harsher world view held by the Vardyr.

'There is also hope,' I said in reply to Shale's comments. 'I think that is why we are here in the first place. If there was no hope, why bother trying to heal the world? Why bother helping other people to awaken?'

'I am sure you know the saying, Qorvas,' Shale commented dryly. 'Hope is faith's little sister. It is unwise to trust her overly.'

I nodded at that.

'I have no faith; I have confidence,' I said, quoting yet another Thornish saying.

In Thornish culture the concept of faith is seen as being flawed. It is seen as an expectancy based on unproven ideas or understandings and often used as a controlling concept in organized politics or religious movements. As Thornish people believe strongly in the power of direct experience of the multiverse, they make an effort to go beyond ideas like faith and directly embrace *knowing.*

To the Thornish person, this *knowing* is experienced as a deep, observational, instinctive, 'gut' connection to the reality of something. In Thornish ritual practice, for instance, it is known that the more powerful one's knowing, the more effective the outcome of the work. Thus, one works vigilantly to achieve a state of confidence in their interaction with the world. Faith is considered to be a kind of half-measure, a kind of blind or semi-blind acceptance of either what someone or some doctrine or another tells them to believe.

This is not to say that every Thornish person has absolute confidence in everything they come into contact with, every person they know, or everything they do. What it does say, however, is that people who walk in the Thornish way strive to find the deepest clarity possible in many aspects of life - through direct experience - as often as they can.

As Thornish folk see faith as a kind of half-measure, hope, as faith's little sister, is seen as a wish based on a half-measure.

'Some people see wishes as putting their intention out into the cosmos,' I said in a coyote-like, trickster's way.

'Vas Shælas,' Shale said, nodding. 'The Trickster's ways, yes.'

Shale knew full well that I was teasing him, but he didn't give too much evidence of this other than that almost impossible to detect shadow of a grin.

'Wishes are like the lazy man imagining a fish dinner in front of him, yet going hungry when all he really needed to do was grab his fishing gear and go to the river,' Shale added. 'The common man dreams of food while the Thornsman goes fishing.'

I was starting to enjoy this rather dry but interesting banter.

'I hear what you are saying, brother. But I think you know what I mean about hope in the world.'

'I have confidence, son of Yasgar,' Shale said, using one of the kennings that have been used to describe me. I was somewhat surprised that he was aware of that one and gave him mental *'brownie points'* for his knowledge.

'The reason I have confidence is that I absolutely know that the Elder Kin are with us in this awakening,' Shale said. 'They work closely with the Earth Mother to re-establish the balance. They will not let the Middle World die. In a conference of priorities we humans are of far less value than the entirety of the planet, yet everything is connected and they are well aware of this fact. The death of the Middle World will cause ripples across the 'verse that will affect all of her sister worlds and everything else.'

'I have heard this as well,' I said. 'Raven has spoken about it.'

'I understand you are familiar with Arakos, the hawk-brother?' Shale asked.

'Yes,' I replied.

'Then you know what he says about such things?'

'Yes I do,' I said.

Arakos is a Shaeda – a spirit person - who, some believe, has a particular interest in the Thornish people. He has appeared to a number of Shar over the decades and I myself had experienced his presence more than once while spending time alone in deep green places.

'And what are your thoughts on his opinion?' Shale asked.

'These old ones are unfathomable to us in terms of knowing,' I replied. 'On many levels they try to simplify things so that we can grasp what they are saying. They see so much, know so much that we in these simple human bodies can't really comprehend. But the basic message I think is that the Earth will survive the coming changes. Whether humans will survive them is quite another thing indeed.'

Shale smiled. It was the first time he had done this during our time together and I will admit it caught me off guard. Yet it was not an entirely happy expression which he presented me, but rather it was Cheshire-Cat in its nature; of the primal animal that delights in certain rather visceral and sharp-edged understandings of things.

'Yes, that is the same message as I was given,' he said quietly. 'And it is another reason why I think we humans are being given the opportunity to awaken and fight. We are quite literally, along with everyone else who is worthy of awakening, being given the chance to prove ourselves and save our world. We are also being given the chance to save our species.'

I agreed with him. This was serious food for thought.

'You have your Frith-knife with you then, I imagine?' Shale asked, changing the subject somewhat.

Indeed I did and I showed it to him in much the same manner as he had introduced me to his own. He also invited me to place my blade down on the stone next to his, which was an honor to me. In offering this, Shale was saying that he considered me an equal and a brother – not an everyday occurrence when one meets a Vardyr, or so I had been told.

And after this we sat around the fire speaking about much lighter things, such as hunting, fishing and various camp techniques that Shale had learned over the years. As we talked I discovered that my fellow Thornsman was quite human after all. I could tell that there were various things he was quite passionate and gladdened by. One of these things was the simple joy of fishing alone from the shore of distant, isolated lakes. Another was the watching of baby animals at play in the springtime. He regaled me with a good number of stories concerning baby bears in particular. Though he was a wolf-spirit at heart I could also tell he had a close affinity with the bear people. I supposed that this had played a factor in the name he bestowed upon his Frith-knife.

At long last we noticed that the sky was turning orange with the setting sun. We carefully extinguished the little fire, left appropriate offerings, both to the fire people and to the spirits of the little glade, and when we were done we set out on the trail back toward Raven's house.

We arrived there shortly after night had fully fallen upon the land, and we discovered that both Raven and Tiva were preparing a meal of roast duck and all the fixings. We were welcomed inside with our brothers and spent the rest of the evening feasting and telling stories in good company.

Shale was, naturally, invited to take a room and spend the night which he graciously accepted. It was quite late by the time Raven set out to drive Tiva back to his home and this left Shale and I sitting alone at Raven's large, well-worn kitchen table over cups of tea.

'It has been my honor getting to know you, brother,' Shale told me. 'You know, at first I didn't know what to expect. I am not the most sociable person in the world and don't usually warm up to new people very well. But I have come to know that you are a noble man, worthy of our traditions.'

I thanked him for his words and told him that I too had been honored to make his acquaintance. I had no idea what to expect and indeed I had never met a Vardyr before.

'Actually I think you may have met one other than myself,' he said rather cryptically. 'Not all of us make a big deal about being Vardyr as it is a big responsibility and a kind of…quiet… manner in which we travel the world. So unless someone specifically says, oh, so-and-so is Vardyr, we might not know that they are anything other than a Shar.'

I had not been aware of that fact and naturally, asked who this other person might be.

To that he smiled enigmatically and told me that in this particular case he thought it was wise to respect the privacy of the other.

By this point I was now thoroughly mystified, but I let it go. Showing respect to the identity of the other mysterious person was really the only polite way to go.

'Qorvas, you recall how earlier you spoke about not being…or not feeling…up to the task of teaching, and how you didn't feel that you were ready to possibly teach someone else?'

'Yeah I do remember that,' I said. 'I remember Raven teasing me a bit about it earlier in the day as well.'

'Well, I will let you in on something I have come to know,' he said. 'Few of us are ever ready for it but when the responsibility comes to us it is our duty to accept it, because at the end of the day all Shar are supposed to be teachers in their way. It's part of the reason we are awakened.'

'I realize that,' I said at last. 'Sometimes the doing is harder than the knowing.'

Shale put his hand on my shoulder in a very sincere, brotherly way.

'And now I will tell you something else,' he said in a subdued, serious tone. 'Something you might not want to hear, but I get messages and it's my duty to pass them along, so that's what I am going to do.'

Now he really had me wondering…

'You know that the change-of-times is coming and, as a matter of fact, is already here,' he said. 'The storm is going to grow stronger over time and when that happens we will face challenges, not only as a species on an endangered planet but also as a tradition; as Shar.'

'What do you mean?'

'Right now we are very small as a people. Don't let the record breaking number of Thornish people right now fool you. While this is amazing good news for now it is unwise for us to rest on our laurels. Not enough is being done to bring more Learners into the circle and in time our numbers will shrink again. Hermits like me are not exactly helping in this because we are often faring far from civilization.'

'You do your part,' I said. 'I have learned a lot from you in just one day.'

'Well, what I am saying is that there are those who have foreseen a time when our numbers will grow small again, and that it will be up to a small group of Thornish people to see that our ways don't completely slip back into the shadows. Remember the Old Lodges and how they purposely chose to go back into the wilds lands and fade from the view of men.'

'That's why we refer to it as the Fading. Yeah, I am aware of that.'

'This can't happen to the Thornish way, brother.'

'You are depressing me, Master Shale,' I said at last.

'This is not my intention, brother. However, I am the messenger in this case, and I happen to agree with the message. It's part of why I agreed to meet you. I need you to know that there is a handful of people, our Hearth-kin, who will be needed to carry our message forward and you are one of them.'

'What about everybody else?' I asked, now growing somewhat frustrated.

'Everyone walks their own Wyrd, their own destiny. You know that. You might recall that there were high hopes for Carolyn the writer and her fate has caused her to disappear, at least for now. Our brother Fox has gone to the spirit world and I could go on. There are others who we don't even know yet who will come to help the tradition grow. The idea is to keep an eye out for them. I will certainly do my part when I return to the north, but you need to keep in mind that you are needed to do yours as well.'

'I will remember that,' I said dourly.

'Now let me relay the part of the message I was asked to memorize. This way I can get it done and once I am finished passing it along to everyone I need to pass it to, I can conveniently forget it.'

Again Shale grinned that crafty, cookie-jar-boy grin.

'You will fall asleep for a time, as people sometimes do. People may drift but the tradition will not die. In some it will glow as coals and in others it will blaze.

When you find that you are waist-deep in the mainstream, however, you will awaken again. When you awaken you will find a bear who will help you and you will find a wise man and a Lore-Keeper who will assist you in the rekindling. Then the message will begin to spread like fire. Remember Nauthiz; the need-fire.'

'That's it?' I asked. 'A bear, a wise man and a Lore-keeper?'

Shale nodded.

'I am the messenger, remember?'

'Nauthiz?'

'The rune of the Need-fire,' Shale answered. 'As a Shar Master I hope you know your runes by now.'

'I do.'

I made a mental note concerning this because this rune in particular had been appearing to me quite frequently of late. While not all Thornish people make use of the northern runes there have been a certain number of us who have. My own interaction with them came primarily due to the fact that my own Thornish mentor, Ari, was quite skilled in their use.

'Good,' Shale nodded again. 'Remember the saying; *The weapons of necessity are a bargain with balance.*'

Now it was my turn to nod.

'Would you mind telling me who the message is from?' I asked.

'Can't tell you that, brother. It would upset the balance. I give you my word that it is authentic, however.'

Shale would tell me no more. He seemed adamant on that so I left it alone. Over the years, with the sometimes enigmatic behavior of certain other Hearth-kin, especially those older and more experienced than I was, I had seen many instances of this mysterious message-bringing and at times other cryptic behavior. I had learned not to press no matter how intense my youthful curiosity might have flared, because once the barrier had gone up there was no getting it back down again until the time was right.

'Therein lies the lesson,' Raven had told me once when I had complained. 'The lesson of power-in-silence.'

And so once again I was given meaty things of mystery to ponder.

Shale shifted the conversation and before I knew it we were talking about the rivers that one would find up in Alaska and the Yukon Territory and the deep power that existed there in the northlands.

'It's unbelievably primal and pure,' Shale had explained. 'I think a good deal of growth can be found for our people up there, away from the big cities of the south. One of the things I have been shown is that there will be a lot of disease coming, my friend. Best to not be anywhere near the big concentrations of people when that happens.'

And then Shale went on to describe certain varieties of trees in the north and the various kinds of animals who lived in these boreal forests.

Not long after, Raven returned and joined us in a late night cup of tea. Once we were done we all retired for the night. I found my favorite old place on Raven's extra large couch in the living room, and fell asleep before slumbering embers in the heavy stone heath.

In the early pre-dawn chill a light hand on my shoulder roused me from my sleep beneath the woolen blankets – and I arose, tousle-headed from my slumber, to find Shale standing next to me.

He was dressed for the outdoors, with his greencoat and boots and a substantial backpack already slung over his back.

'Sorry to wake you, brother, but before I go I had one last thing to say to you.'

'Okay, shoot.'

'You will not always be a member of the Raven Lodge.'

'What!?'

Now I was sitting bolt upright. I had made that last in quite a loud, exclamatory tone and caught myself. I had hoped I didn't jolt Raven out of his bed. He could be a rather grumpy one when so roused, as my brother Russell had once discovered.

The Raven Lodge was the lodge of my teacher. It was the descendant of the Old Lodges and as far as I knew, was the only lodge of the Thornish folk in existence. The thought of somehow being cast out or abandoned was unthinkable. Oaths had been sworn and those oaths had been reciprocal.

Once again, Shale was smiling. It was not a sarcastic or teasing smile, but rather a kindly one of understanding.

'I meant that not all things last forever and new things might grow in the shadows of great trees....to become great themselves.'

'Nice wisdom to wake up to,' I said sarcastically.

And for long moments, Shale simply stood there. I knew he had no more to say and would say nothing more to me if I questioned him on the matter.

Finally, he held out his hand. I stood, took it, and we shook.

'Don't worry brother,' he said. 'You will see that it will work out well.'

'It's been an honor meeting you, bro,' I said. And I meant it. It had been rather profound.

'It's been my honor too,' he said. 'I don't travel to the cities or towns too much, my young friend, but in this case I am glad I came and glad I got to spend time with some of the Hearth-kin. I am especially glad I got to meet you and you know what? We will meet again before the storm really gets rough.'

'You have foreseen this?' I asked, half joking and still, only half awake.

Shale's expression became serious, just like in those first few hours I had known him. It was like the weight of the world, a huge responsibility, was weighing down on him, or like he was the gate-keeper of secret things about which he could never speak. His eyes were alight with life and knowing, though, and I could tell that he had been truly glad to have come out here over the past couple of days.

'As a matter of fact, little brother, I have foreseen it,' he said. And with that he tossed me a friendly wave and was gone out the front door with very little sound at all.

I stood there for long moments in the silent living room before the now cold and dark fireplace and wondered about the many things I had experienced over the past years. From the teachings of my grandfather to the tragedy of his death, through to the teachings of Raven and the friendships formed… to now, in the wake of having been briefly tutored by one that I could only describe as a forest mage.

I held my position for a moment more and then, motivated somewhat by the morning chill, I sauntered off into the kitchen to start the stove and get a pot of coffee brewing.

I looked out the kitchen window and saw that a very light coating of early snow had fallen. As I looked I could see that there were still little tiny crystalline snowflakes, few in number, just drifting along through the branches of the nearby pines.

I wondered what would happen if I were to go to the front porch and look out on the path leading to the road, away from the house. I wondered if I would see the tracks left by Shale as he had taken his leave.

There would probably be no sign that he had walked that way, just as, other than the memories I had of his visit, there was no evidence of his ever having been here, in Raven's home.

He would leave no tracks. He was Vardyr.

Life was nothing if not interesting.

And yes, Master Shale had been quite correct in his recent statement to me, about us meeting again. I could feel the certainty of that in my bones though beyond that I had no idea when or where.

Perhaps one day, in the lands of the north, where the night-fires danced in the sky and the potentials were limitless – or somewhere in the myriad of green spaces in between.

Yes, I would see my elder brother again. And we would once again place our steel upon the stones.

4

Hearthfire

'The dark is deeply sacred. So is the wonder of the light, but they are in balance. Anyone who focuses only on the light or only on the dark is out of balance. It's best to learn from both and be embraced by both.' - Master Tiva

Shaara Hawk was Shakai, which is a Thornish term describing one who has been initiated. Among the Thornish people this was the category of learning and responsibility that was also known as the time of the Seeker. As she had completed the Deepening and crossed through initiation she was entitled to be called Shar. And because she was a woman initiate the respectful term of address was Shaara, a feminine version of Shar. Hawk was (and is) the Vörd, the spirit helper/guide of this initiate. It had given her leave to take its name as her tribal name and, honored, she had done so.

Shaara Hawk sat in a dark, quiet place with her Wataan, her teacher in the Thornish ways. They sat in a quiet grove, in the deep shadow of aged maples, in a small, cleared spot near a rushing stream. The sun, which had not long before graced the land with its warm summer heat, was now descending below the mountains, casting the land in the peach-orange glow of late afternoon.

Neither were traditionally dressed. As with most Thornish folk, Shaara Hawk and her teacher most often dressed in casual, everyday clothing when out and about in areas where they might encounter non-Thornish people. The only possible exception to their appearance would have been the two wickedly sharp, semi-curved blades that they had with them. These blades lay on a rounded, flat stone on the ground between them. Known as Frith-knives, these are the primary implement of the people of the Thornwood and are used in a number of applications, including ritual. As it was there were very few people in the area of the woods where they found themselves. It was unlikely that some stranger might happen by and gaze upon their blades.

Earlier in the day they had prepared a small ground-hearth, or fire-pit, in the clearing where they sat. It was a simple hollow in the ground surrounded by nine softball sized round stones that was carefully filled with tinder and small twigs – the beginnings of a small fire.

'Let there be the peace of the blades between us, wishae,' the teacher said. 'May there always be steel upon the stones.'

'And may the ancestors and the Otherfolk watch over us,' Shaara Hawk said.

Following this the two sat in silence for a long moment. Silence is much treasured among Thornish people and they do not seek to constantly fill the natural silences of the world with noise or useless conversation. It is said that a Thornish person masters the skill of basking in silence much like a lizard might bask on a warm stone. This is not far from the truth.

During the silence Shaara Hawk's teacher took a moment to set fire to the fine tinder at the center of the fire-pit. The flames caught and within moments the beginnings of a small campfire were crackling amidst the circle of stones.

After a time Shaara Hawk's teacher broke the silence. As is customary in such things it is considered good manners to wait for the eldest or most senior person to speak first.

The teacher gestured to Shaara Hawk's long hair, which hung in a braid over her shoulder and ended nearly in her lap. Her hair was very long, lustrous, and well cared for. A glossy copper blonde, her hair glowed in the reflected light of both the kindling fire and the setting sun. It had thus caught her teacher's attention.

'You know that you are entitled to the Maka'Sha now, don't you?' he said. 'I think it would look good on you, considering how much hair you have.'

Shaara Hawk smiled.

'Yes, I do know that, Wataan,' she replied. 'I hadn't thought of doing that yet though. I need to find the right feather for the job.'

In the Thornish speech, Maka'Sha means the way of the sacred feather. It has been a part of Thornish culture since it was gifted by the Old Lodges many years ago. In this tradition a person who has chosen to walk in the Thornish way is entitled to wear a feather in their hair or somewhere else on their person. This is a very tribal thing and the kind of feather one might wear as well as the quantity of feathers is determined by the place of the person within Thornish society.

For instance, a person who has not been initiated but who has declared themselves Thornish may, if they choose, wear a single feather on their person. This feather can be from any kind of bird other than a raptor or other protected species. It can also not be black or red in color. The feather used must not be from a bird which has been killed for sport. It must be a 'found' feather; one which has either been dropped naturally from the bird, or taken from a bird which has died in a natural fashion.

For an initiated Thornish person, the wearing of the feather takes on a different custom. The feather must either be a crow or raven feather, which honors one of the Thornish origin stories where Raven brought wisdom to the tribes. Thus a newly initiated Thornish person, a Shar, may wear upon their person a single black feather. A Thornish person who has completed the rites and has been declared a Master has the customary right to wear two black feathers. An Elder in the tradition may wear three such black crow or raven feathers. These are signs of achievement within the Thornish tradition. There are rare occasions when a Thornish person may wear a single red feather in place of one of their black feathers and this indicates that a person is a member of a special society within the Thornwood.

As a Shakai, or Seeker in the tradition, Shaara Hawk was entitled to wear a single black crow or raven feather in her hair. Her teacher was entitled to wear two, though like her he showed no signs that he was wearing feathers at the time.

'You are entitled to two feathers and I don't see any either,' Shaara Hawk teased.

Her teacher reached behind him and brought out a wrapped bundle. From this bundle he produced a short-hafted spear with a large wicked blade. It was a traditional Shar, the ritual implement of the Thornish people. Shaara Hawk looked and saw that just beneath the silver blade, hung on a small bronze ring, were two midnight-black crow feathers.

'I don't have nice, long hair like you do,' he explained with a sly smile. 'So I make do.'

At that the two chuckled softly.

'You are very fussy, wishae,' he said at last. 'You should go and find yourself a nice, glossy feather and tie it in your hair. It would look good.'

'When the right feather comes to me I will do that,' Shaara Hawk replied. 'You know me, where the sky brothers are concerned I tread very carefully.'

'Yes, I do know that,' he replied.

Shaara Hawk had long held a very close affinity to the bird people and thus held them in the deepest respect. It was not difficult to understand, then, that in her mind she needed to receive the right kind of feather in precisely the right kind of way in order for it to be a favorable omen.

'Those are very old feathers,' Shaara Hawk noted, gesturing toward her teacher's Shar.

'Yes,' came the reply. 'They are both from the old days, when Shardai Raven was my mentor.'

There was the briefest moment in which her teacher, Ranek, had a very sorrowful and faraway look in his eyes. Shaara Hawk knew that he sometimes got like that when he reminisced about the earlier years and she felt bad for bringing the feathers to his attention.

Yet, as was also his habit, Ranek quickly shrugged off the old memories and returned to the present. He grinned.

'They are old and worn out like I feel some days,' he said. 'On other days I feel like a kid at heart, full of piss and vinegar.'

'I'm sorry I got you thinking about those days,' Shaara Hawk said sincerely. 'I know you have some amazing memories from those times. I wish I could have been there and gotten to know him.'

By '*him*' she was of course referring to the man called Raven, one of the founders of the tradition who had been one of Ranek's teachers. Indeed Ranek had used the high honorific of *Shardai* in referring to him and the use of that word was reserved for a very few Thornish people of the highest esteem.

Ranek smiled again and shrugged in a very boyish way.

'Did I ever tell you the story of how I got those two feathers?' he asked.

'I am not sure if you ever did, no.'

'I found them sitting on a rock in the woods,' Ranek explained. 'No dead crow, no sign of a struggle and no sign that there had been any other activity anywhere nearby. It was late autumn and so I knew it wasn't an issue of birds fighting or nesting or anything like that. There were just these two feathers, sitting there side by side as though they had been placed there just for me. It was pretty strange.'

'Yeah, sounds like it.'

'So I took the feathers and left a little tobacco there as an offering. It was all I had on me at the time to offer,' Ranek continued. 'I put them in my pocket and hours later when I found myself at Raven's house I showed them to him and told him how I had found them.'

Shaara Hawk nodded her head.

'What did he say?' she asked.

Ranek looked at her squarely.

'He told me it was time for my Deepening,' he replied. 'I was only a Seeker at the time and to tell you the truth I didn't even have a single feather before that. I guess I hadn't taken the tradition seriously though I should have.'

The Deepening is a very special ritual that occurs only a few times in a Thornish person's lifetime. It is a sacred, spiritual sojourn into the wilderness where a person journeys and meditates and seeks out deeper spiritual truths for themselves. There is a Deepening that occurs for one who seeks to be initiated, followed years later by the Seeker who wishes to rise to the level of Shar Master. There is also a Deepening for those Masters who desire to take on the mantle of tribal elder, though not all avail themselves of this. Indeed it is said that there is a fourth Deepening as well; the sacred trip that a person makes when they die and travel to the world of spirit.

Ranek recited the old Thornish memory-poem:

'One for the Seeker

Two for the Master

Three for the Elder

Red for the Vardyr

And white for the dead.'

Shaara Hawk nodded her head at hearing that.

'Maqa'Sha.'

The Thornish term for the feather tradition is Maqa'Sha. *Sacred feather*, quite literally.

'So this was the time when you decided to do that?' Shaara Hawk asked. 'To go and do the Deepening?'

'Yes, about a month later I was ready and I took up the Gar,' Ranek replied.

Taking up the Gar is a reference to a Thornish person crossing the ritual line that lies between the Seeker, which is a form of apprentice Thornsman/Thornswoman, and the role of the Thornish Master. Gar is a term taken from the old Germanic language and means 'spear'. Part of the ritual of the Master's Deepening is the requirement that the applicant for the quest fashion for themselves a functional spear that they take with them into the wild places.

'And you took a spear with you then?'

'Yes,' Ranek replied. 'We all take the Gar with us when we go on the Master's Deepening, even though some of us are Spearfolk and others are Farers.'

Shaara Hawk was well aware of that. She had already experienced a part of the tradition that requests all newly initiated Thornish people to officially declare themselves as Spearfolk or Farers. Spearfolk are Thornish people more dedicated to the arts of hunting and of the deeper Warrior ways while Farers are more specialized in the areas of magic, healing, and crafting. Shaara Hawk, a gifted seer from a young age, had no difficulty in knowing where her path lay and had declared herself a Farer. Farers traditionally carried the stang, a two or three pointed staff, as a symbol of their path while Spearfolk more often carried the spear.

'And did you finally place a crow feather in your hair for that?' Shaara Hawk asked meekly enough. 'When you went out on your Deepening?'

'Yes, I did as a matter of fact,' he replied. 'My hair was much longer then and it was easy enough to do. Once I had completed the ritual, my

Wataan told me that I was now entitled to wear two feathers as the custom allows.'

'It is fascinating how two feathers hanging from the haft of a weapon can hold such a story,' Shaara Hawk said.

'If you want to know something else,' Ranek said. 'I'll tell you about the time when I asked my teacher where the tradition of the feathers came from. I guess I was expecting him to tell me that it had been passed down from some ancient source or something but that wasn't really the case.'

'What did he say?'

'He was blunt about it. He told me that while tribal people had used feathers for many thousands of years, and indeed they had often used feathers to show accomplishments, he had not been given the tradition in any particular way. He told me that in the predecessor lodges to the Thornish ones feathers had been used but mostly only by the Native members of the lodges. Later, when he had received permission to form his own lodge one of the elders had suggested that he might bring the old custom back in whatever way he saw fit.'

'So where did it come from then?'

'Well, other than being suggested to him by elders of the old lodges he told me that he and the other founders had sat council on the idea one night and it kind of came to them.'

'So it was kind of developed into what it is now by them?' Shaara Hawk asked curiously.

Ranek nodded.

'Yeah, but you may recall what has always been said in our tradition; that in the beginning everything was thought up by people. If it works, use it and if it doesn't, leave it alone.'

'We have never made any claims to being any kind of ancient or special tradition,' Shaara Hawk said. 'We are what we are.'

'Yes, we are certainly that,' Ranek replied. 'A tool was needed by the world and in this case it was us. Not like there aren't many others just like us out there. The world is creating many tools for her defense. So yeah, we are what we are.'

'We are what we are,' Shaara Hawk repeated. 'And you know what? I do like the feather tradition. It is very tribal and it is powerful.'

'Yes, it is,' said Ranek. 'It is.'

Again, as though digesting the words they had shared, the two returned to a comfortable silence. All around them the landscape changed as the sun went down. The winds shifted slightly and bird sounds altered as new creatures awoke and joined the sounds of the night. Not long afterward it was suggested that they take advantage of the solitude of the forest to sit Noctua.

The word Noctua came into use in Thornish tradition many years earlier and was borrowed from the reference to an ancient constellation, also known as the Owl. Located at the tail of the constellation Hydra, the term Noctua was also found of interest to Thornish elders due to a secondary reference - one which told that the owl-in-the-stars looked down over the work of mages in ancient times past.

Although the use of Noctua as an astronomical reference has long since fallen out of use in modern times, it was seen as a fitting name for the practice of nighttime sacred conferences between tribal people.

According to Thornish tradition, Noctua is a sacred, though not overly formal, ritual in which one or more people sit quietly after dark and discuss matters which are related to individual members, the state of the world, or the tradition and its function. A single person may sit Noctua, in which case it becomes a form of solitary enrichment, or there might be any number of folk involved.

The topics discussed at Noctua are many and vary from person to person and from gathering to gathering. However, the common denominator is that there is always an atmosphere of trust and respect in place at such rituals. In some cases rituals such as scrying are performed at Noctua. At other times spiritual counseling can occur. Yet other activities include the singing of sacred songs, drumming, the ritual decoration of tools or weapons, and of course the ever-present possibility of deep, meaningful discussion.

Fire is usually present in some form at a Thornish Noctua ritual. This can take the form of anything from a full-out fire-dance circle with a blazing bonfire to a small, solitary candle in a holder. Fire is extremely sacred to Thornish tradition. This is so because Thornish people believe that the Fire-People, the elemental spirits of fire, are excellent guardians, teachers and witnesses to the affairs of human kind. Similar to the Stone-People, the Fire-Folk are regarded as sagely elders who are always welcome in the circle of tribal folk, especially when sacred matters are engaged in.

Additionally, it should be noted that the Noctua ritual is always undertaken at night. Amongst the folk of the Thornwood night is held as especially sacred and many ritual acts are performed after the sun has set. The Great Essence, the intelligence of the multiverse, is seen by Thornish folk as the essence of absolute, fertile blackness; a primordial power so ancient that it preceded light itself. This Great Deepening Dark is viewed as the rich elemental soil from which all life and intelligence originally spring. Thornish tradition holds that dark places, whether inside a structure or outside in nature, are superior places of working. Nighttime, therefore, is seen as the supreme atmosphere in which powerful things might be accomplished. Thornish people do not agree with the commonly held modern mainstream views that connect darkness to evil or other negative forces. Thornish people view nighttime as a sacred friend to be embraced and respected.

There is no custom which dictates the location of the Noctua ritual, although a natural environment is usually preferred over an artificially constructed one. The Thornish custom of the Moot-House, a tribal gathering place usually constructed in the wild, includes accommodation for Noctua rituals.

And so it was that on the night we are describing here the two Thornish tribesfolk, Shaara Hawk and her teacher, Master Ranek, sat Noctua in front of their tiny, flickering campfire. They sat there for several hours, discussing various things which concerned them and these things, sadly cannot be revealed here. It is also a custom of the Noctua ritual that all things spoken of remain protected under a covenant of silence. What is said in the sacred circle may not be revealed to those outside of the tradition.

After a time the two Hearth-Kin concluded their discussions and retired to their handmade brush shelters for the night. As is often the custom when Thornish folk venture into the wild places they take only what they need and very often will refrain from bringing such luxuries as camp stoves or tents with them. Very often Thornish folk will make use of primitive brush shelters or lean-to type shelters for overnight stays.

The morning found Shaara Hawk emerging from her shelter to the enticing smell of camp coffee. Its scent wafted through the air from its place in the tiny battered pot on a warm stone near the fire and brought her senses more fully awake. This was not coffee made from coffee beans in the traditionally accepted sense but rather a mixture of ground chicory and dandelion root that had been brought along in a small bag by Master Ranek.

It was very early. In fact it was so early that darkness still largely blanketed the woods on the mountainside. Only the earliest rays of the sun could be seen high above on the still snowcapped peaks, and the morning cries of small forest birds were only just beginning to be heard.

As Shaara Hawk approached the fire pit to get herself a small cup of the welcoming brew she noticed that her teacher was nowhere to be seen. Ranek's Shar had remained behind and she saw that it was held by two forked sticks that had been pushed into the ground. The two crow feathers on their beaded leather thong tied near the head of the spear blade danced gently on a slight pine-scented breeze. Before the Shar, she noticed, was a small, flat stone upon which were placed a number of small offerings such as berries, tobacco and a small, reddish polished stone. Shaara Hawk nodded in approval when she saw that, thinking that the local spirit folk would probably appreciate the offerings. Possibly some small creature might also appreciate the berries as well.

Shaara Hawk decided to forgo her cup of coffee for awhile and, taking up her Frith-Knife, she walked down the rough trail from the camp to the place where she suspected she would find her Oath-Brother.

It did not take her long to find him. Only a few minutes after she had left the camp and emerged from the woods into open space she found Master Ranek.

Ranek was seated on the ground, on a smooth outcropping of granite that fell away in a sheer drop only a meter or so from where he rested in the Warrior's Wait position. He faced the east with his head slightly bowed with the hood of his coat pulled up over his head. The Warrior's wait position is analogous to the Japanese Seiza position often found in Asian martial arts. It is often used by Thornish people who find the posture to be both elegant and practical.

As Shaara Hawk looked upon her companion and beyond she saw that in the distance, barely over the eastern horizon, was the bright half crescent of the rising sun. The delicate, sweet scent of sage and mugwort reached her nostrils and she realized that Ranek had been making traditional offerings of sacred smoke as a part of his morning ritual.

After a moment more Ranek rose smoothly from his place. He turned and Shaara Hawk saw that he carried a small oyster shell in his hands from which a small tendril of smoke curled. At seeing his kinswoman, Ranek smiled.

'I greet the sun,' he said simply.

Shaara Hawk bowed slightly toward the rising sun on the horizon. She did so in the way of the Thornish Warrior, where while one inclines the head they never take their eyes off of the object of the bow.

'I greet the sun,' she repeated.

The greeting of the sun is a custom that Thornish folk have embraced for years. Not all perform the ritual at sunrise but most make some kind of offering or recite some small form of thankful verse when arising in the morning. Thornish people know also that a spirit of thankfulness and a desire to be positive are important aspects of maintaining good spiritual and physical health.

The Thornish Master Raven, one of the founders of the tradition, once penned a short verse which most Thornish folk take to heart. It is called Raven's Creed.

- **Rise early: Perform morning rites without fail**
- **Tend to your Wolf-Robe: Be sure of your health**
- **Meditate often**
- **See to your Hearth: The Hearth is the home to kin and kin are foundation stone**
- **Relish each day the beauty of the world and the gifts you have been given**
- **Be ever mindful of the luck of your people**
- **Rise each day rejoicing to live, yet prepared also to die**
- **Give thanks and make offerings each day**
- **Sleep with the sun**

Master Ranek squeezed his companion's shoulder in a friendly fashion as he walked past her toward the trail.

'Now that we are awake I think I could use some of that coffee,' he said. 'Have you had any yet?'

'No,' said Shaara Hawk, 'I was waiting for you.'

'I already had some earlier when I got up.'

'I did not know that.'

'Well, I made lots.'

Shaara Hawk smiled as she turned to follow her companion back down the trail. 'You usually do,' she replied.

'Once a boy scout always a boy scout,' Ranek chuckled.

And they passed into the shadows of the pines, rejoined the narrow trail and walked back to their camp. It had been a good couple of days and Shaara Hawk found herself wondering when the next opportunity would present itself to get out into the green.

She hoped it would be soon.

5
Ranek's Tale

'Pain can be a part of ordeal, as can fear. Self control and extreme discipline can also be a part of the Thornish ordeal. One must ask oneself what the purpose of the ordeal is and what they hope to gain from it before they go. Ordeal simply for the sake of ordeal is a waste of time and energy.'- Master Raven

Three days had passed since the young man had stood before the sacred fires of the Thornwood. Three days had passed since he had been initiated and welcomed into the traditions. He had received his tribal name, Ranek, and had been very pleased with this, though at the time he had accepted it with proper humility.

Ranek's world had undergone a profound change over the past year as he had been working diligently toward the moment of tribal acceptance which had occurred only three scant days before. He had been a Learner under the guidance of the Master of the Lodge himself and he had striven to show that he was worthy of being so chosen.

It all seemed to have happened so fast; time felt as though it had flown by. Ranek had come to discover the existence of the tradition less than two years earlier, had made some acquaintances and had eventually found himself in a position to learn more. He felt that he had been searching for so long, despite his young age, and finding kindred spirits such as the folk of the tradition had been a dream come true.

Then he had become a Learner and had made a promise to faithfully learn all that he could under the tutelage of his teacher, Master Raven. He had worked hard and his Wataan, or teacher, had been quite pleased.

Finally, after a period of learning and of challenges, Ranek had set out on his Deepening, which in his case had been three days and nights of meditative solitude on the banks of a deep green river. When he had returned his teacher had informed him that he would be given initiation within the week.

Yet during that space between the Deepening and the ritual crossing, a dear friend of his had died, the victim of an unfortunate automobile accident. The news had staggered Ranek. His friend had only been a few years older than his own twenty-four years and they had been friends for a long time. Ranek felt as though a significant part of himself had been lost with his friend and he grieved deeply.

When Master Raven heard of his student's loss he consoled him and told him that the initiation would be delayed for as long as was required, so that Ranek could do what he needed to do. At first Ranek had resisted this and had wanted to move ahead with the initiation; he wanted to lose himself in the work of the tradition.

Raven denied him this and ordered him to return to the city and be with his family, to attend his friend's funeral in a respectful manner, to allow time for himself to heal.

'You are young and have not fully embraced our ways,' Raven had told him. 'You still need time to go through the grieving process as most people do. Take the time you need and you will find that when you are ready, we will be here waiting for you.'

And so Ranek had done as he was told. He returned to the city and honored the memory of his friend. He was gone for nearly a month before he returned to the valley where his Wataan lived.

Raven greeted his returning student warmly and helped him settle into the spare room he had made ready.

'Take as long as you want, wishae,' Raven told him. 'These things take time.'

Eventually all was made ready and Ranek was given the ritual of initiation, also called a Crossing. He stood in the tribal firelight and became one with the tradition which had adopted him.

Three days had passed since his initiation. Ranek had not only been brought fully into the tradition and given a tribal name, but had also crossed into a greater level of learning and responsibility. He was now a Seeker, one who had crossed over. He now had the right to be referred to as Shar, a sacred implement.

Three days had passed since Ranek had crossed over, become something…more.

On the morning of the fourth day Ranek emerged from his borrowed room to find his teacher waiting for him in the living room and not over steaming cups of coffee in the kitchen as was his usual custom. There was something else different about his Wataan and Ranek quickly noted that it was his clothing. Master Raven was dressed in the formal garb of the Thornish tradition, the Lorn.

The Lorn consists of a traditional pair of soft cloth trousers combined with a high collared tunic which falls below the waist but not below the knees. It is accompanied by a cloth sash and a leather belt at the waist and a sleeved, hooded cloak over it all. Raven's tunic and trousers were black with a grey cloak.

Raven's Shaith, or long-knife, was thrust through the earth-colored sash at his waist and on his left wrist Ranek could see that Raven wore his Maal, the traditional Thornish bracelet of alternating black and red beads. Somewhere nearby Raven would also have his Frith-knife, which was often the companion of the Shaith. The Frith-knife was much shorter than the Shaith and was of a much more utilitarian nature.

Ranek, noting Raven's Maal, reflexively reached over to touch his own as he walked into the room. It had been a gift from Raven when he had accepted him as a student.

Ranek had been surprised to see his Wataan dressed as such although he had seen him dressed this way only three days earlier at the initiation ceremony. He wondered what occasion had prompted his teacher to dress like this again so soon and wondered if there was some ceremony coming that he had not been aware of. As far as Ranek knew the Lorn wasn't something which was worn very often by any initiate he had known. It was worn for some ritual and ceremonial purposes, such as initiations, and he had heard that some of the older Masters wore their own for their daily meditation sessions.

When Raven had explained the Lorn to him, what seemed like ages ago, he had said that the Lorn was a special device which, when worn, triggered the initiate to undergo a kind of alteration of their mind and spirit; to cause the wearer to transition into a special communion with the deeply sacred and to embrace the spirit of ritual and ceremony in a hale way. The wearing of the Lorn was only permitted to those who were fully initiated members of the tradition.

Raven greeted his student and asked him to come and sit down in the chair across from him. Ranek obeyed and sat down in the comfortable chair with his back toward the fireplace. Raven sat back down on the couch.

Between them on the aged wooden coffee table was a ceramic tea pot glazed in darkest earth-brown. Two cups sat there, along with the pot.

Raven reached over and poured tea into each of the cups. The tea was powerfully scented although the smell was rather pleasant to Ranek's senses. He had never experienced anything with quite that fragrance before.

'Yes, the Lorn.' Raven grinned as he looked across at his student. 'I am going to deal with something of a ceremonial nature soon, but I wanted to speak with you before I go.'

Raven did not explain the nature of the rite he would be going off to attend and Ranek did not ask. By now he certainly knew better than that. Ranek knew that his teacher could be very enigmatic if he chose to be. It was very likely a thing for Masters or Elders, Ranek thought. Probably something that Seekers or Learners would not be allowed to attend anyway.

'And so I need to ask you formally, wishae, if you feel you are going to be okay to continue learning from me now.'

Raven had used the term *wishae*, which although used under the tradition of the current formality, calmed Ranek somewhat. Wishae was a familiar term in Thornish culture which most often was used to address a student by a Master who was rather fond of them. The rough meaning of the word is 'younger learner,' denoting someone who is under the care and protection of their teacher.

'Sure, Wataan, I am fine now,' Ranek replied. 'Well, as good as can be expected, considering.'

Raven took an appreciative sip of his tea. Ranek did the same, noting the deep, smoky flavor of the tea. It tasted even better than it smelled, though possibly not quite as pungent.

'Good,' Raven said after a moment. 'After I leave get yourself some breakfast and whatever else you may have to do. After that I would like you to go up to Tiva's house, say, sometime after noon?'

Ranek nodded. 'Anything you want me to bring?'

Raven shook his head. 'Just bring yourself.'

And with that Raven stood up and patted Ranek on the shoulder.

'I'm glad you are doing better,' he said 'See you later.'

And with that he was gone out through the kitchen and then the back door. Ranek noted that Raven did not take his pickup truck which was parked in the front of the house. Wherever he was going was probably not too far away.

Several hours later Ranek found himself on the road to Tiva's house. The road was reached by a trail running through the woods not far from Raven's home. The road was rough gravel, a secondary road that led up into the hills and connected a few residences and properties with the highway to the east.

Tiva was an elderly member of the tradition and a very good friend of his Wataan. Ranek had only met him a few times but from what he had seen Tiva was quite a mysterious fellow. When Ranek had first met him he had not known what to think. The man was of average height and build with brown skin and a head full of wild-looking white and grey dreadlocks. He appeared to be around sixty years of age or so. On closer inspection Ranek had realized that Tiva was not so much a person of African descent as he might have appeared from a distance but was more a Caucasian man with unusually dark pigmentation. It did not stop there, either, as Tiva's odd sounding accent, which sounded like what would happen if an Irish brogue and a Jamaican patois were suddenly but gracefully mixed, only added to the enigma of who this man was or where he actually came from.

Ranek walked along the road pondering this and many other things until at last he found the side trail off the gravel that led towards Tiva's little house in the bush. When he arrived there he found no sign of human life at all. Tiva's place seemed dark and uninhabited. There was only a handwritten note on a bit of paper tacked to the front door.

'Hey brother, go to the back of the house and follow the trail up the hill. When you get to the tin can go left on the trail with the tape – T.'

And so without waiting any longer Ranek followed the instructions and set out to walk the trail behind the house.

Half an hour later Ranek made his way to the top of the rather steep trail. Sure enough, as the note had suggested, there was an old tin can sitting upside down over the end of an old stick set in the Earth. Ranek went left along the much less defined trail – more like a deer or goat trail actually – and pushed his way through the bush.

Ten minutes later the young man emerged into a clearing that half caught him by surprise. Given the thickness of the brush and overhanging trees Ranek had expected that he would be making his way along for a considerably longer time. Suddenly the trail had disappeared, leaving him standing in a wide, well-groomed clearing. Three-quarters of the land sloped up into the bluffs behind a wall of young pines while the rest gave way to a very nice view of the valley to the northeast.

Yet it was not so much the refreshing break from the tiny trail or the very nice view that caught and held Ranek's eye so much as the unusual looking structure in the middle of the clearing did.

Almost directly in the center of the clearing, set in the mossy soil of the area, sat a low dome which looked like it had been constructed of large branches and ultimately covered with a brown canvas tarp. Over the top of the brown tarp a layer of fallen branches and other forest debris had been piled, giving the structure a very camouflaged kind of look. It looked as though it had grown out of the Earth rather than having been placed there by people. Before the small doorway, which faced the northeast and thus the view, was a small stone-circled fire-pit. No fire was currently burning there. Ranek also noted that at various points around the clearing there were stang-poles set in the ground with various talismans like feathers, bones and metal charms tied to them. Each of the poles had two sharpened tines, tips pointing skyward, dyed red at the top and black or brown at the bottom. Ranek had seen these before and knew them to be markers of the sacred directions.

A figure appeared from seemingly out of nowhere, from the trees to the south of the domed structure, and waved to him in greeting.

It was Tiva, who walked toward him smiling a very white, toothy smile.

Tiva was much the same as he had appeared the last time Ranek had seen him; blue jeans and a red and white checkered flannel shirt. Buckskin boots completed the ensemble.

Remembering his place, Ranek bowed slightly as Tiva approached. He used the slight Warrior's bow he had been taught very early on.

'Master Tiva,' Ranek said formally.

Tiva bowed back in the same way. 'Ælan Shar, my young Ranek,' he replied, using the formal greeting.

The formalities completed, Tiva came closer and slapped Ranek on the shoulder in a friendly, fatherly fashion.

'Now a Seeker eh?' he commented 'Congratulations on your Crossing, bro. Oh, and sorry I was not there to see you come over. I had some pretty serious matters come up that I had to be on top of. Otherwise you would have seen me there too.'

It would indeed have been an honor to have Tiva there at the initiation, Ranek thought, for Tiva was definitely the oldest of any of the others he had met. Also, there was a very special kind of energy surrounding the wild and eccentric-looking old man. Ranek liked him and welcomed any opportunity he might have to learn from him. As it was, the initiation had been small and intimate, with Raven presiding, along with Master Corva and Master Ciarán. This had been just fine with Ranek, who disliked crowds anyway.

'Not a problem, Master Tiva,' Ranek replied. 'Perhaps next time.'

Tiva smiled. It was a very warm and genuine expression.

'Next time you will see me for sure,' he said. 'Now come along. There is a bit of teaching for you to attend now that you are Shar.'

The entry way to the domed structure, which Tiva had said was called a Moot-House, was quite low. So low in fact that Ranek had to stoop down to make his way inside. The doorway had been closed with a heavy canvas flap, which Tiva pulled closed behind them as he entered.

'You were taught about the Moot-House I guess,' Tiva said as they entered the doorway. 'This is one type. A Moot-House can take many different shapes.'

Indeed Ranek did know what a Moot-House was. Raven had told him about them but up until this moment he had never actually seen or been in one.

'Mind the slope, bro,' Tiva said just before he entered. 'This is a dug-out structure so the interior is lower down.'

Ranek was thankful for the warning because moments after he

entered into the dim, almost dark, interior he found the lip of the inner wall and stepped down. Had he not been warned about it he might have fallen on his face.

It turned out that the actual floor of the Moot-House was some two feet or more below the grade of the ground outside. Ranek realized that if a person wanted to he could probably manage to stand up under the structure considering the added room the dugout floor afforded.

But Ranek did not stand. He remained somewhat stooped over to avoid the various bundles of herbs which were hanging from the rafters and because there was something about the atmosphere of the place that required one to remain low and in deference. Ranek estimated that maybe, in a pinch, no more than ten people could fit into that modest space – and that would be pushing the limits of the structure.

Entering the Moot-House had been like crossing from one world into another one; a different world from the one he had just left, basking in the early summer afternoon, and into a dim, incense-scented world whose dominant light was the deepest crimson red.

There were small, red glass jars and cylindrical candle chimneys all about the interior of the Moot-House, each one with its own glowing candle. Some hung from the rafters by leather thongs and others were set in small alcoves and on the floor. The only indication Ranek had that the world he had just left was still out there came from the small smoke hole directly above the center of the dome. It let in a little sunlight but not very much. Otherwise the entire experience was something like one might have if they had entered a dim, mystical cave.

The interior was also a place of many different kinds of scent. There was a pervading smell of cedar and sage, along with the unmistakable scent of recently burned mugwort. The structure itself still retained its scent and smelled of old pine and to a lesser degree the smell of cotton-duck canvas. The earth lent her ambiance to the overall scene as well, and it only enhanced the cave-like qualities of the place.

As Ranek's eyes adjusted he saw that he and Tiva were not the only people in the Moot-House.

'Take a seat here, bro,' Tiva said from right next to him, and he saw now by the dim red light that there were folded wool blankets spaced around the middle of the dome for people to sit on.

Ranek nodded and immediately felt ridiculous and self-conscious

116

for doing so, as he realized that no one would be likely to see his nod in the dim red light.

Finding the place indicated to him by Tiva, Ranek sat down. To his surprise the folded blanket was quite soft, thick and comfortable beneath him.

In the very center of the floor was a Harrow, an indoor altar-space or working-table made of stones. The base appeared to be rounded river stones topped with a wide, heavy-looking piece of flat stone. Ranek briefly wondered at the effort it would have taken to carry all of these up here if they had not been found on the site.

At the center of the flat stone there were several items. A bowl that looked as though it had been used for incense as coals still glowed slightly inside of it, two of the flickering red candle holders and a tool that Ranek knew well. This was Shakaika. It was the first actual Shar he had ever seen. The wickedly sharp short-hafted spear was the companion of Raven and was said to have been given to him by the spirits of a very sacred river, which ran not far from where they all sat. Shakaika's name was a variation on certain other words in the Thornish speech, Ranek knew. The name meant roughly *Seeker of Fire*.

The Shar is a very sacred thing to those who walk in the Thornish traditions. There are stories told to those people who seek to learn about the culture of the Thornwood, stories which tell of the ways in which the Shar came to the Middle World. In every case there is the element of the spirit world involved.

The symbology of the tool is well known to all who are familiar with them. The killing edge represents the visceral interface with the material world and the balancing pommel on the other end represents the sacred balance that moves-in-all-things. The haft in between represents the sacred journey and understanding between the two ends of the tool. While the short-hafted spear is always eminently practical and able to be used for anything from crafting or building to combat, it is now largely used as an implement of ceremony and ritual. As an item which could both build and destroy it has long been revered among those of the Thornwood.

The Shar is the namesake of those who have been initiated as well. Male initiates are entitled to be called Shar and female initiates are entitled to be referred to as Shaara. Indeed it is a term in general use among initiates – especially if one is not sure of the position of another in terms of learning and responsibility.

As Raven was the master of the Lodge the honor to place the Shar on the Harrow was his.

'I think you know everyone here?' came Tiva's voice from nearby.

Ranek's eyes had been adjusting the whole time and now that Tiva had spoken he began paying closer attention to the others who were in the Moot House with him. He immediately nodded at his teacher, Raven, who was almost directly across from him. Raven grinned back and nodded. He was now dressed in his usual 'uniform' of jeans and woolen shirt. Ranek thought that he must have finished up whatever it was he had been doing and gone home to change out of his Lorn before coming up the hill.

Ranek recognized Master Corva as well and nodded. She was unmistakable even in the dim light with her nearly milk-white Celtic complexion.

'Master Corva, Ælan Shar,' he said, nodding formally.

'Good to see you again, Shakai Ranek,' she said nodding her head in the traditional bow.

A slight shiver ran down Ranek's back when she addressed him. Even though he had crossed he was not used to being addressed as one. Shakai, in the Thornish dialect is the word for Seeker; the apprentice level initiate rank which he now found himself in. Not for the first time Ranek wondered at the subtle differences between the word that denoted his level and the name of the sacred Shar on the Harrow-stone.

'We have come to talk to you today about something, wishae,' Raven said. 'Since you are now worthy of holding a Shar and being here in this place, but also since you are new to this role, we thought we might have a chat.'

'Of course,' Ranek replied simply. 'What would you like to talk about?'

'Death,' Raven replied. 'It is as good a time as any and seeing as you have just experienced tragedy I thought it would be a good time to cover our beliefs on that subject.'

'I remember everything you taught me when I was a Learner, Wataan,' Ranek replied. His stomach was starting to get a sour feeling in it as he sat there. He did not want to discuss the subject of death at this point. The wound of his friend's loss was still quite fresh.

'I know you don't really want to discuss it,' said Raven, as though gleaning his thoughts. 'But we feel that this is a good time to reinforce our cultural values. Since you went through the Crossing and became an initiate we know you are dedicated to our tribal ways.'

'I am dedicated, Wataan. You can count on that.'

Master Corva leaned over slightly towards him from her place on the floor. Corva was not all that much older than Ranek, perhaps seven or eight years, yet she gave off the energy of someone much older.

'I know you are, brother,' she said softly.

'So, tell us how you are feeling right now, bro?' Tiva asked.

And before long Ranek told his story. He told of the friendship with his late friend and how close they had been. He told of the accident which had taken his friend, of his initial rage when he learned that drunken driving had been involved, and then he told finally of his utter and exhausting sorrow which came with the realization that he would never see his friend again.

Ranek sat in silence for a good while after he had opened himself up. He felt as though somehow his emotions had still been dammed up and that this simple request from his teacher and Hearth-Kin had broken the blockage open.

'Not so,' Tiva said at last. 'You say that you feel you will never see your friend again and to that I say, not so. If you value our ways then you must know it too.'

'The body is a conveyance, a gift of the Great Essence and our ancestors,' Raven added. 'It's a tool for getting around here in the Middle World as you know. It is a perishable vehicle, so once our threads of Wyrd are done here, once we have experienced what we have come to experience, the body will die. As I taught you, we will not live one second more than the time we are allotted. Not one second less either.'

Ranek nodded respectfully to Master Tiva. He was glad that the Moot-House was so dimly lit. He did not want anyone to see his eyes and deduce that tears had been flowing there only moments before.

'I understand, Master,' he said. 'I have not forgotten any of this.'

And to Raven he nodded as well.

'I know what you taught me, Wataan. I believe it, too. It's just that sometimes the mundane programming of the mainstream world reminds me that it's still in there. Sometimes we get caught between the lies of the Abrahamics and the lies of the cabals. Sometimes we get lost and we lose hope.'

'You will see your friend again one day, Ranek,' Corva said. 'Though you won't be as you are now, you will recognize one another. Perhaps you will meet in the spirit world, the place of the Great Essence, perhaps you will meet along the road of the Black Root, or perhaps you will know one another once you have both gone away and then returned in new bodies.'

'There is no fear. There is understanding,' said Raven. His voice was gentle yet firm. 'There is no death, not as mundanes understand it anyway. Death is a gateway, a transition between states. If we hold on to fear and try to hold death at arm's length, or if we treat death like some grim enemy, we are defeating the whole idea of death, which is that it is a gift.'

'It's a gift that stole my friend from me,' Ranek husked back. He caught himself starting to get angry and held himself back from saying more.

'Your friend is gone because it was his time to go,' Raven replied. 'Observe the First Law. It is the very backbone of everything we Shar believe in. The First Law is the law of the cosmos, of nature. In your time how many other animals have you seen dead – besides the ones we eat to stay alive? How many unfortunate little ones have we seen dead at the side of the road, killed by traffic or simply found on the ground, their essence gone? Probably you have seen quite a few. Are they any different than your lost friend? Think about that.'

'I can't just accept that my friend died and should be forgotten like that,' Ranek replied.

'Can you ever forget the animal brothers which you have seen dead at the side of the road?' Corva asked. 'No, I know you haven't, because if you were the type of person to simply dismiss such things from your mind you would not be one of us here.'

'No one is ever asking you to forget any of this,' Raven said quietly. 'But what we are suggesting is that while grief is a natural thing and must be given its time, it must not be allowed to gain power over you. In our way we see grief as leading to various unhealthy states such as anger or hatred…or worse. Our way is a way of balance.'

'Life is deeply sacred,' Tiva said at last. 'All life. When the fire in this world is transferred to the next phase we are not supposed to just shrug our shoulders and move on. That is the way of the world-killers, the ones who are already destroying our world and everything on it. To become callous or indifferent to the value of life is to become like the enemies of the world.'

'Shar are all about life,' Corva said. 'We were created to be the stewards of this planet – all humans were. But not many remember that, which is why some people are awakened. Some people are awakened because the world and the spirits who flow between the worlds see the need for balance. They have created agents of that balance in us and in many others who belong to similar orders and ideals.'

Corva paused for a moment to let what she had said sink in. 'To me being awakened can be the greatest of joys on some days and the deepest of nightmares on others,' she continued. 'As awakened ones **we know**. We are aware of the state of the world and of the twisted, mentally and spiritually ill human beings who continue to kill everything we hold precious. We are acutely aware that the majority of human beings on this planet are woefully unawakened, that for the most part they are interested only in acquiring wealth, eating, sleeping, finding pleasure, and reproducing. All of this bears a deep cost to the world. We who are awakened are aware of all that is broken and of all which must be repaired. We do not hide from the raw wounds our species has ripped in the fabric of the multiverse. Now you are also awake. You have joined us here and we know that you understand your place in the greater scheme of things.'

'Fear serves hatred most of all,' Raven said. 'And hatred serves only itself.'

'Hating is like shooting yourself and expecting your enemy to fall,' Corva added.

'I admit I was becoming hateful at one point,' Ranek said. 'The driver of the vehicle that killed my friend was drinking. But I got past it. I let it go.'

Again there was a deep silence pervading the space between them.

'I could see it in you, wishae,' Raven said. 'I could feel it building up in you when you first came to stay with me recently. You felt frustrated, angry and still more than a little lost knowing your friend was gone beyond the gates. You wanted to do something, be of some use, but you felt impotent to do anything at all...other than hate.'

Raven paused for a moment.

'I know what it feels like,' he continued. 'Imagine a career spent in the military and then think about how many times I have lost people and not been able to do anything about it. So I do understand, my brother. Implicitly.'

'Everything is connected to everything else, little brother,' Tiva said. 'Yes, we are even connected to the ones who are awash with greed and an insane desire to control others. We are connected to the world-killers through life energy and deed whether we like it or not. We are even intertwined with the drunk who caused that accident. These people and their deeds compromise our luck and our Önd, our connection to the Great Essence. This is just one more reason why we as Shar strive for balance...because we are all connected and what happens to one on some level or another affects everything else.'

'I understand that,' Ranek said after a moment. 'Master Raven has taught me that.'

'Then he has taught you well,' Tiva said. 'Everything is a sacred circle and everything is constantly cycling through. If you give anything enough time and don't do anything further to upset the balance, most systems will re-align themselves, heal themselves. Do you understand what I am saying here?'

'That I need to allow myself time to re-align myself. Because everything is connected, my not allowing myself to move beyond my anger has a kind of ripple effect.'

Tiva's response was emphatic yet barely above a whisper in the dark.

'Yes,' he said.

'The thing we call death here in the Middle-World is but a gateway, my friend,' Corva said from her place in the shadows. 'Common folk are taught from a very young age to fear it and yes, it is used by the puppet-masters to manipulate people through fear. Death is not the end. Can you guess why people grieve? They grieve out of selfishness. They miss their friends or their family member and they want to greedily hold on to them even if that friend or relation has come to the end of their wyrdish thread. In our tradition we recognize that it is natural to miss those we care about but we don't obsess about it. Rather, we honor their life as they lived it and in our minds we make them great. We also know without a doubt that we will see them again one day.'

'This is not faith,' Raven said from his place. He had uttered the word faith as though he had something foul in his mouth and was eager to spit it out. 'It is the feeling one gets when they embrace confidence of an outcome.'

'I hear what you are saying, Master,' Ranek said.

'The way of *Doqqa Vor* is the way of death,' Tiva replied. 'We learn about this in our tradition quite early on and I have no doubt that you have been instructed in it. With that in mind you should realize that what may be so frightening to common folk is not so scary to us.'

'Letting go has not been easy,' Ranek said. 'I have done the exercises. I have meditated and exercised and gone through the mantras…but it is not easy. It's like the thoughts keep coming back when I try to focus. Not only that, spending time back in the city…all it did was remind me of the good old days with Rob and now those days are gone.'

'You act as though your friend is gone, erased from existence, yet as a Thornsman you know better,' Tiva said. 'He is with you, even now, not only for the love you bear for him in your heart, not only as a light that shines in your memory, but he really is here with you, watching over you from beyond.'

'If you were as close as you say, it could not be otherwise,' Raven said. 'Once he got his bearings over there I am sure he would have wanted to look in on those he cared about.'

'Once we pass, we blend with our greater selves and with the sacred Essence. The conveyance, the body, the wolf-robe as Raven calls it, returns to the Earth,' Corva said. 'Yet in our beliefs we remain largely who we were before we came to the Middle-World. Death and dying are largely misunderstood by the graylings, the milling herd of humanity who will never awaken. It is a passage to a greater thing, a greater understanding.'

'All part of the sacred cycle, brother,' Raven added. 'The mainstream people fear death because they have been taught to fear it. The powers that be, particularly the Abrahamics, have long used it as a tool of control over people. You have been taught this, and that we do not fear death.'

'There is no fear, there is only understanding,' Ranek quoted.

'And when someone close to us leaves the Middle-World the understanding part becomes difficult; clouded,' Tiva said. 'It leaves us open to the distractions of the easy-ways-out, such as unstable emotions, ignoring the body's needs, potential abuse and other things. Understanding, though, is the key to the healing.'

'I will work on this, my friends,' Ranek said after another comforting silence. There was no hostility in his words. 'I know I have come part of the way, but I need to go further.'

'Honor your friend,' Corva said. 'Never forget him, make offerings for him and occasionally, when you are at peace, speak with him and let him know that you are going to be okay.'

Ranek remembered the Thornish mantra that had already served him well on so many occasions. He recited it aloud now, because he felt it would be the right thing to do.

When I am calm I am at peace.

When I am at peace I am healing

In serenity I find balance

And in clarity I move forward.

'Yes, little brother, we all move forward,' Tiva said.

Again a soft, comfortable silence returned to the room. Ranek allowed himself to be swept up in it, enfolded by its comforting embrace. It reminded him of mediation in a serene place in the woods.

Suddenly a tiny spark of jocularity flared up as memories came to mind. Master Corva had once been called a compulsive meditator by Fox, due to the fact that more often than not she could be found meditating. The comment had been made as a joke and accepted as the good natured jest that it was, yet now, in the silent Moot-House for a mere second or so, Ranek wondered if Corva was meditating again.

'No, I am not meditating, young one,' Corva said suddenly, jolting him out of his thoughts. Either his expression had given her some cue or her powers were developing at a scary rate.

'Sorry,' was all Ranek could think to say, and this triggered off several other muffled chuckles in the room.

Thornish people are nothing if not possessed with a general good sense of humor.

'On to other business,' Raven said at last. 'We have something for you here, since it appears you have earned it.'

Raven took something from a place beside him and passed it over to Tiva, who passed it to Ranek. It was a bundle wrapped in a soft piece of heavy black cloth.

Ranek placed the bundle in his lap and looked at it for a moment before unwrapping it.

The first glimpse he had of the blade was enhanced by the mystical red light of the Moot-House. Its slightly curved, highly polished steel blade glittered along its single, wickedly sharp edge as he held it up in admiration. It had a goodly weight and the hilt was wrapped beautifully with leather cord.

It was a Shaith, the ritual long-blade of the Shar initiate.

Ranek was overcome with emotion at the power of this gift and for a moment could not speak. The gift had been totally unexpected. Indeed everything which had occurred since he had entered the Moot-House had been unexpected. He had not suspected that he would be questioned and counseled by his tribal family and indeed, most certainly, he had not imagined that he would be receiving such an incredible gift as well.

In Thornish tradition there is no custom which prescribes the manner in which an initiate might come into possession of a Shaith, just that eventually it was good to have one. Ranek recalled some of the stories he had been told, in which certain Shar had made their own and others had commissioned them from a reliable craftsman. Others still had received them as gifts from various sources. The Shaith was often worn in combination with the much smaller Frith-knife, something which Ranek already possessed.

Ranek thought about the specialness of the gift and indeed the many other powerful things that he had been given by his teacher, besides the teachings, of course. Ranek remembered how he had struggled with the making of his own Lore-Stone, that holed-stone which represented the desire to learn the Thornish ways and which was the project of everyone who wished to be accepted as a Learner. He had been all thumbs, so to speak; he had never had the gift of crafting things by hand in that way and yet in the end he had surprised himself with the rather good result of his work. That small piece of rounded grey stone still hung around his neck by its leather thong.

Ranek remembered the day he had been accepted as Raven's Learner. Besides the great privilege of being taken as a student by the founder of the Lodge, Ranek remembered how powerful had been the simple gift of the Maal, the simple black and red beaded bracelet which all Thornish people had the right to wear.

'What signs do we have that a person is Thornish?' His teacher had asked.

'First the Lore-Stone, then the Maal, then the Shar and then the Gar.' Ranek had replied.

'And what else might there be?' His teacher inquired. 'Out of the tribal context...perhaps in the street?'

'The Bloodmark?' Ranek had guessed. 'Sometimes the tattoos are visible.'

His teacher had smiled and told him that while all these things were possible the thing he should look for most was the fire in the eyes and the manner of speaking, for these things told the tale of a person's heart more and any other thing.

Ranek could see that everyone in the Moot-House was possessed of this eye-fire. He knew he had it too. It filled him with warmth to know that at last, after so many years of wandering he had come home.

Ranek had been taught many things. It was as though sometimes his memory was overflowing.

And for over a year Ranek had done his utmost to absorb all of the lessons which his Wataan had given him. He had undergone the tests and at last the Seeker's Deepening and become an initiate in the tradition.

Now his teacher had gifted him with a sacred blade. To Ranek it was much more than a simple ritual blade, it was a true symbol of respect between one Warrior and another.

'Make a scabbard for it,' Raven said at last. 'Then go out and spend time with it. Decide if its spirit is male or female and, when you are ready, give it a name.'

'I will,' Ranek said respectfully. 'Thank you for the gift.'

Raven nodded casually. 'Don't forget to thank yourself too. You earned that blade.'

'You have also earned the Bloodmark if you wish to take it,' Tiva said from his place nearby.

Ranek had completely forgotten about that. Most initiates chose to take the mark, which was a tribal tattoo, worn usually on the inner left forearm just below the elbow joint. Raven's was the first he had seen and from the start he had admired its primal form.

'I will think about that too, Master Tiva.'

'And about the blade,' Raven added with a chuckle. 'Don't get too used to such gifts because, as you know, for the Master's trial you'll have to build your own Gar.'

This brought a number of other chuckles from around the small room. The Gar was the sacred spear which was seen as the symbol of the Shar Master, an initiate who had passed into the next level of learning and responsibility in the tradition. Custom required that such an implement be crafted by the individual and could not be commissioned or received as a gift.

'I have plenty of time before I get to that point,' Ranek said light-heartedly. 'I am barely initiated as it is.'

'You do have a road ahead of you before you get to that place on the trail,' Raven said. 'But if you are anything like I was the time will fly and you may have a decision before you more quickly than you anticipated.'

'But for now, welcome, truly, into the tradition…Shakai,' Corva said.

Ranek looked down at the gleaming blade in his lap and felt a deep sense of comfort flowing through him. He thought about the many people who were going through their day to day lives, much like robots who were unaware that there was anything else out in the world, that there was any real depth to the experience of being a human being here, in the Middle World. Ranek reflected on the event in his life which had led him to meeting these amazing people and learning from them. He thought about all of the wonderful things he had been a part of and the feeling of family; of home that it now brought to his heart.

There in the dark, Ranek smiled softly and realized just how lucky he was.

6
Sacred Core

When we speak, in the custom of my own tradition, of darkness, we are speaking of the left hand of balance; of the silent sister to the right handed realm of light. We are speaking of evening as opposed to morning; of shadow in relation to sunshine. We are speaking merely of one aspect of reality in the sacred balance. When we speak of darkness we are not speaking of something bad; we do not deal in such polarities as good versus evil. The world and indeed the multiverse simply is...and balance is the key.'   - *Master Qorvas*

'There are many beings out there which humans might call Gods' Raven said to his student as they walked along the banks of the river. 'There are probably hundreds of thousands of them who may have visited our world throughout the ages; maybe even millions. Some simply visited and then left after a time; others remained and are here still. At least that is our belief.'

'But we call them the Elder Kin,' said the student.

'Yes, that is what we call them, and I have already told you what we mean by Elder Kin and why we call them that,' Raven responded.

The student was quite young, in his nineteenth summer. His name was Allan. He was a Learner, not yet trained to the point of initiation. Raven, who was better known among his people by his tribal name than by his mundane name, had taken Allan on as a student only a few months before.

However, mundane life had not seen the two of them spending as much time together as he would have liked and Allan was not being instructed at the rate which one might hope to teach a newcomer to the tradition. As such, when Allan had informed him of some time he had off from his responsibilities, the older man had arranged for Allan to come and stay at his home for the week. From there they had the opportunity to catch up on many levels.

Allan was the younger cousin of another man that Raven had taught. His name was Russell, though he was known better in the tradition by his tribal name: White Fox. Russell had been an exemplary student and had gone from being a mere Learner with little understanding of the Thornish ways, to a blooded and initiated Shar Master in a relatively short span of years. Of course, Russell's situation had allowed him to stay in the community where Raven lived for sizable periods of time and this had the advantage of more concentrated instruction from several Masters.

Russell had an innate talent that had been evident to his teacher and others from the very beginning. Indeed, there was more than one within the tradition who suspected Russell might one day in the future have taken up the path of the Vardyr, the semi-mythical Warrior-sages of the Thornwood. In the history of the Thornish tradition very few had chosen to walk in that way, for it was a hard path and one which demanded a very special sort of vision and discipline. Yet despite this there were those who believed that Russell might have taken up the spear of the Vardyr and ventured forth boldly into the deeper realms of spirit.

It had come as a great sadness then when the young Thornsman had met an accidental death and had passed from the Middle World. For a tradition as small as the Thornish way, the loss had been magnified considerably beyond the tragedy of a lost loved one.

Following the loss of the White Fox Ari had taken on his spear-brother, a young man who had sworn sacred oaths with White Fox and had become as blood-kin to him. This was Qorvas, another talented Thornsman who had excelled in the training. In fact, by the time Raven had chosen to take Allan under his wing, Qorvas had become Master

Qorvas; he had successfully completed the tasks necessary to become a Shar Master.

Allan had come to Raven in the hopes of being trained several years before, but he had not been ready. Following the passing of Russell he had once again come before the old teacher in the hopes that he could follow in the footsteps of his cousin. Once again he had been asked to wait, to work through his grief before undertaking anything else of a major nature in his life. Allan had agreed and indeed showed great patience for one so young. At last, after a time, the young man appeared on Raven's doorstep inquiring after training in the Thornish way. This time he was judged to be ready and he was given the Maal, the red and black beaded bracelet of the Learner.

'You are now what we call Auga'ri,' Raven had told him upon giving him the bracelet. 'A Learner. Auga'ri is a Thornish term that literally means *sharp-eyes*, so it is expected that you will be just that; sharp and paying attention.'

'Just where does this Thornish speech come from?' young Allan had asked with genuine curiosity.

'It comes from us, where else would it come from?' Raven had replied. 'Some is borrowed from the languages that various founders spoke, some is borrowed from other sources, some is made up because it fits and other bits come from experiences we have had over time in the spirit-world.'

'Some of it came from the spirit-world?'

Raven had eyed his student at that.

'Why shouldn't it? People from the spirit-world have much to teach and every once in awhile they choose to share with us.'

'So the Thornish language, or speech as you say, is pretty much made up?'

'Of course it is,' Raven said, looking at his student somewhat incredulously. 'All ways of communications used by humans is at one point or another made up. Like I say, it is cobbled together from various places. It was never intended to be as big as it is, actually. Back in the day we decided that we wanted a few terms and phrases for ritual purposes and that was all fine and good, but over time it took on a life of its own and continued to grow. Maybe one day it will become an actual language. Who knows?'

Raven remembered well his new student's response to that.

'What do other people think of this made-up talk? I mean, it's gotta be kind of weird.'

At this point Raven had looked his student straight in the eye. 'There are certain areas where I can sense you are very advanced. In other ways I can see a lot of room for learning. We Thornish folk don't really give much of a rat's ass what outsiders think of us or our tradition, I can tell you that.'

Raven had paused a moment to let what he had said sink in. Allan said nothing but had waited respectfully for his teacher to continue.

'A big problem in the world is people going around thinking about what others will think of them,' Raven said. 'What counts is what people you are connected to by blood, deed and oath think of you, people you truly respect. We care what our folk think and what the Elder Kin and our spirit folk allies think. We hold concern to what our ancestors might think as well, but as to what cowans, or outsiders, think? Not usually. If it serves us, perhaps, but that is a part of the charade. I will teach you about that later. No, you need to let go of this concern you have about what outsiders think. Their opinions are, for the most part, less than worthless to us.'

'So, like Russ used to say, we do what pleases us?'

'Within the parameters set for us by the First Law and our traditions, yes.'

Raven smiled to himself as he thought back to that time, not so long ago, when he had begun teaching Allan. Yes, Allan had much yet to understand, but Raven had confidence he would do well.

The two men walked along the narrow trail beneath the overhanging pines until they came to a point where the ambling path reentered the woods.

'You know, there is a very distinct possibility that you will be my very last student,' Raven said to Allan as they passed out of the sunlight and into the cool shadow of the pine forest. 'I am getting on in years, and you know I think I have taught enough people for one lifetime.'

'The tradition will probably not be the same then,' the younger man replied.

'Perhaps not, but you know, that's the way some things go.'

The two men traveled along for a distance in silence. Raven observed his newest Nashae, or student, and noted that, not for the first time, there were distinct differences between this young man and his honored, deceased older cousin. For one thing, Allan showed an astonishing grasp of patience for one so young and for another, he intuitively knew the value of silence. He did not appear to feel the need to fill every single serene moment with questions or idle chatter as his cousin had done at first. Indeed, many of Raven's students had been somewhat overly talkative in the beginning. Young Allan seemed to be quite satisfied with remaining silent most of the time and just observing. He spoke when it was needed, particularly when he had a pressing question, but otherwise he kept to himself.

The White Fox had now been gone nearly four years yet his presence was still strongly felt among many, including the young man walking along at Raven's side. Yet it did not seem to Raven that Allan in any way felt threatened or held back in the shadow of his somewhat legendary cousin. Contrarily, the memory of his cousin seemed to empower him, which was a fine thing to behold.

'About the Elder Kin,' Allan asked after a few more moments of walking along the moss- coated trail. 'I am wondering how those of the Thornish ways view the religious beliefs of others?'

'Ah,' Raven replied. 'Good question. For one thing, the Thornish way is not a religion, as I have told you. We are a culture of Warriors who embrace a deepening animist spirituality. Religion is not the way for people like us. We see religion as having someone interpret the world for you, word for word, like a book. In our way we provide an outline and let you fill in the book with your own experiences. Our way is largely a way of direct experience. The outline we provide is cultural not religious doctrine.'

'Sorry. Yeah, I remember you telling me that earlier.'

'No need to be sorry,' Raven replied. 'Questions are good. They give me the opportunity to clarify things and they give you the opportunity to get our traditions figured out clearly in your head.'

'I'm glad you feel that way. I wouldn't want to be a nuisance.'

'You are certainly no nuisance,' Raven said with a broad grin. 'Not like your cousin was at least...'

Allan looked over at his teacher, saw the wide grin and chuckled.

'I have heard the stories,' he grinned.

'Oh, I have some I bet you haven't heard.' Raven laughed. 'Remind me to tell you a few of those sometime, but about the beliefs of others...'

'Yes, I was curious about that,' Allan said.

'It works like this,' Raven said. 'We offer a kind of generalized respect toward any religious belief that does not do harm to the world. Beyond that, in our worldview, greater respect must be earned. I guess you could say that if you show us consideration and respect, we will show you the same. This applies to our culture, our way of walking in the world, and our interaction with the spirit world.'

'And what do you mean by beliefs that do no harm to the world?' Allan asked, genuinely curious.

Raven grinned again, only this time it was not an expression borne of good humor. This time it carried a warning within it that Allan could read the instant he saw it. It was the look of a wolf warning the unwary from his territory with a not-quite kind of snarl.

'There are a number of religions in this world who are open foes of the Earth,' Raven replied. 'They are not difficult to spot. They are the ones that preach the fantasy that their god created the world for their use and that they can do whatever they want to her without consequence. You see this behavior as it has influenced modern corporations and governments. It is a very dangerous sentiment to have because if you subscribe to such thinking you become an enemy of the Earth, an enemy of nature. If you are an enemy of nature you are not friends to the Thornwood.'

'I can understand that,' Allan said. 'I think I know just the beliefs you are talking about. It's kind of like, *It's okay to chop down the forests or pollute the ocean because our god made it for us and we are going to heaven anyway.*"

'Precisely,' Raven said. 'So where these world-killing philosophies are concerned we always keep a wary eye on their members. Sure there are exceptions and you will find some really fine Earth-friendly people from many walks of life – even the ones that are not generally friends of the world, but in my experience these are quite rare.'

Suddenly, almost without warning, they rounded a corner and came into a small clearing. The clearing was very well kept and had none of the ground-litter of branches, loose stones and pine cones that the trail had. It looked almost as though the place had been maintained by a groundskeeper of some kind.

Allan walked in from the trail and stopped.

'This is very, very cool,' he said.

Around the periphery of the small clearing, beneath the shadowy boughs of the big pines, there were what looked like peeled wooden posts set in the ground. Each post was about the diameter of a man's thigh and a little higher in height than a man's waist, set evenly around the clearing. There were nine posts in all and they looked like they had been there for a considerable time.

As Allan looked more closely he could see that each post had markings of some kind carved into them. Some of them looked as though they might have been inscribed with paint but he could not be entirely sure of that. Time, weather and a liberal coating of soft green moss on most of the posts had done a fine job of obscuring the details one might otherwise have been able to make out.

Raven walked into the center of the clearing and sat down cross-legged near the middle. He invited Allan to do the same.

When his student was seated, Raven smiled. 'You like the way this is set up, do you?'

'Would you mind telling me what this place is?'

'Well there are a number of names for places like this but in the Thornish tradition we call it a moot-place. A moot-place is a meeting place, a kind of quiet, out-of-the-way place where we can meet and discuss things or even teach things. Being out in the woods only adds to its power.'

'And these logs that are set into the ground?'

'These are lore-posts. Lore-posts come up a lot in Thornish traditions but what they are basically is reminders of something from our traditions. These, for instance, have been here a very long time.'

'How long?'

'Let's just say that these were starting to get old before you were born and I can remember them being here for a time before that. One day they will return to the Earth no doubt, but for now they can still do their job.'

'And what job do these lore-posts do?'

Raven stretched his back and looked around the small clearing.

'Well, these old timers are reminders of the elements of the thing we call the Black Stone Code, which, as I think you may have heard me say earlier, is the primary code of conduct in the Thornwood.'

Allan became more alert and focused on his teacher now.

'Yes, I can't tell you how many times Russ mentioned this. I am really interested to know more about that.'

'And so you will,' Raven said. 'This is why I brought you here, and now that you know about this place I ask you to keep its location secret. No sense having young folks coming through here looking for a party spot, if you get my meaning.'

'I totally understand that.'

'This place is considered sacred by us,' Raven said. 'Well, you know pretty much any place is sacred, but this place is one of the spots we have made extra special to our tradition.'

'I hear what you are saying,' Allan said.

Raven gestured around the circle at the posts in the ground.

'The Black Stone Code comes to us over the years from the old lodges of the Black Talon Society as well as some of the other predecessors to the Thornwood as we know it today,' he said. 'The term Black Stone Code was generated from a certain saying.'

'What saying was that?'

'It is said that when constructed with intent, almost any place can be made sacred. However, it is also thought that with nine stones a superior Hörg might be built. In simplicity is greatness often found.'

'A horg?'

'Horg is a word we use to describe an outdoor altar, a place where one might leave offerings and do rituals.'

'Okay,' Allan said, nodding. 'I understand. So the saying says you should be able to build a horg altar using only nine stones?'

'The saying does suggest that, yes. And it emphasizes the importance of simplicity in our way. It's not to say that a person couldn't use more or less, but that they should operate on the principle of keeping things simple.'

'So the Black Stone Code is based on this saying or this idea.'

Raven looked over at his student. 'Yes, you've got it,' he replied. 'To continue along, the Code itself is composed of nine parts, seven of which I will teach you today.'

'Why only seven if there are nine?'

Raven chuckled. 'Now you are beginning to remind me of your cousin,' he said. 'Always so intensely curious, wanting to know everything and to know it yesterday.'

Allan blushed slightly and it was visible despite the shade of the overhanging trees and despite his light but tanned complexion.

'There are nine parts, or staves, as we sometimes call them, yes,'

Raven continued on, 'but for one such as you who are only a Learner at present we feel that the first seven will do the job.'

'For now,' Allan pressed.

'When you are an initiate ask me about the final two staves and I will gladly tell you,' Raven said with a shadow of his former grim remaining. 'But really, the first seven are the ones you need for now, so trust me on that, will you?'

'Sure, no problem.'

'Our Code is not that difficult to commit to memory but to make it even easier it happens to come in a form that is even easier to hang onto. It's an acronym and I imagine you know what an acronym is?'

'Sure, it's a bunch of letters that stand for things and they are put together in a word or code that's easy to remember.'

'Yes, it's a memory aid of sorts,' Raven said. 'In this case the acronym is wardens.'

'Wardens?'

'Yes, WARDENS, kind of like a forest warden, a guardian. That kind of thing.'

'But not like a warden in a jail or anything like that,' Allan said, smiling.

He looked back at Raven who had suddenly lost any of the jocularity he had been expressing earlier. Allan cooled very quickly, afraid he had somehow said something that had offended his teacher.

'You are new to our ways, Allan,' Raven said after a moment, 'and I know there are probably a lot of things you heard from your cousin and probably a lot of things he didn't tell you. However, I imagine that one of the things he never told you was the attitude that Thornish people have about freedom?'

'Not specifically, not that I can remember,' Allan said. 'If I have said something to piss you off I'm sorry. It wasn't intended at all.'

'No, its fine,' Raven replied. 'But in everything, at least for those who are like me, there are opportunities to teach. In this case I will fill you in on the Thornish beliefs concerning freedom. Freedom is the greatest gift in existence along with the sacred gift of life. We believe that to take the freedom of other beings—and as animists we have a much longer list of what constitutes a being than many other traditions— is one of the highest crimes. There is even a word for it in our dialect.

What do you know about the Thornish speech? Besides what I have already told you, that is.'

'Russ told me a little about it but not much, and of course I remember what you had to say about it awhile ago.'

'Okay, I will repeat a bit here. The Thornish speech is a collection of words we have developed or borrowed from various places and we use these words or phrases mostly in ritual work. It's not really anything as complex as a language but it works for our needs. In this case, because of its importance and because it is largely a warning we have a special word. That word is Raan'Skonda. This basically means 'freedom-stealer' and it is one of the most powerful derogatory words we have. Thornish people do not believe that human beings have any right to imprison or enslave any other being, anywhere, at any time, for any reason. Anyone who does so or who through their acts or profession supports this kind of thing is not considered to be a person in tune with the sacred balance. There is zero honor in a person who makes a living from the imprisonment of other beings.'

Allan looked as though he had swallowed a frog.

'You mean like a prison warden, right?'

'I know that you were making a play on words there, my young friend, but I thought I might as well take the time to educate you on that point. As adults we can choose our path in life and in the modern world that means we can choose our profession. People who choose to go into professions that abuse, enslave or imprison other beings are out of balance with the sacred First Law of nature. These folk are not the kinds of people who we consider to be friends of the Earth.'

'I'll remember that one. Sorry.'

'No need to be sorry,' Raven said. 'Like I said before, questions and invitations to be given knowledge are always good.'

'Sorry for all the side-tracking though,' Allan said rather contritely. 'I really do want to hear about WARDENS.'

'Then I will tell you,' Raven said. 'We have arranged the first seven staves, or parts of the Code into the acronym of WARDENS. And to start I will tell you what the letters stand for.'

And Raven went on to do just that.

W   –   Ward the Sacred

A   –   Acknowledge the Law

R — Revere the Elders

D — Defend the Tradition

E — Embrace the Self

N — Nourish Loyalty

S — Seek the Black Root

'Now, there is a lot more to this than just these simple points,' Raven said. 'When we say *ward the sacred*, what do we mean? We mean that those things that we know to be sacred, such as the land, our families and oath-sworn kin, true innocents, sacred places...all of these are sacred and must be protected.'

'Could you tell me what a true innocent is?' Allan asked.

Raven nodded.

'Good question,' he said. 'A true innocent is any being which has retained its pure essence with regard to the laws of nature. That is, they are true to their role in nature and have not deviated from their place in nature and caused imbalance.. With the exceptions of small children, certain Shaeda and a very rare few human beings, almost all other beings you will encounter in the worlds are true innocents.'

'Shaeda?'

'Spirit people.'

'Okay, I got it.'

'Acknowledge the Law,' Raven continued. 'What we mean by this is the First Law, or the law of nature. Thornish folk will always hold the First Law as the highest law. All other laws, especially those created to control or enslave men, are considered to be lesser considerations.'

'So you say there are more of these laws?' Allan asked.

Raven smiled.

'I am glad you are asking questions. Better to figure these things out now than be up at four AM scratching your head about them. Yes, in answer to the question, we see there being four main categories of law. The first of them is the First Law, the law of the cosmos; the law of nature as we experience it. It is the primal law and the one Thornish people look to the most for guidance. The Second Law is what some might call the Law of the Gods, or the Elder Kin. These are sets of rules and ways of doing things which are held by the Elder Kin and may or may not affect us. Many of these are beyond the comprehension of humans.'

'And the other laws?'

'The Third Law,' Raven continued, 'is the Law of the Tribes. This is the cultural and traditional body of law which exists in most primal cultures. The rules of behavior in the Thornish tradition, for instance, are considered to be Third Law. The last law is what we call the Fourth Law. This is the law invented by humans to control other humans, basically, and to a Thornish person it is the least important of all the laws. In fact, over the years there have been Thornish folk who have debated whether the Fourth Law could be considered more of a program of indoctrination than a real law, but that is conjecture.'

'Yeah, I can see how some of that would be up for debate,' Allan said.

'So let's move on,' Raven said. 'You will be hearing about the Code quite a bit at this stage in your training so don't worry if you miss anything this first time around.'

'Okay, I'm all ears.'

'Next we have Revere the Elders,' Raven continued. 'This is a really straightforward one, but it does demand a bit of clarification. You might recall my saying that respect is earned. Well, in our culture we are willing to give out some respect based on certain things. One of these things is age. As a result we will show deference to other humans who have achieved a good number of years of life here in the Middle-World. Therefore its is always good manners to treat elders kindly no matter if they are from our tradition or not. Now this doesn't mean that we bow down to someone or that we put up with someone being an asshole, mind you. There are plenty of old people who are wastes of skin just as there are many young people who are the same. It's up to you to be able to judge who's who in the zoo, if you get my meaning?'

'I might not have been around for nearly as long as you have, but I sure do get what you are saying,' Allan replied. 'I give everyone a chance to prove that they are an okay person. If not I move on. Good manners are never a bad thing to have.'

'You have good instincts,' Raven said. 'And you are right about manners. In general we pride ourselves on being polite whenever this is possible. Most people have the mistaken impression that folks who walk in a tribal way are somehow uncouth savages but they would be wrong in this. Primal folk are most often the very essence of good manners…but of course this depends upon what one's idea of good manners are.'

'Act with consideration and general respect unless given a reason to act otherwise?'

'Very good!' Raven said, clapping his hands together in a friendly way. 'You have it figured out. Let me add that in the case of Thornish people we treat our elders with extra special respect and consideration because by the time you are an elder in our tradition you can bet that reverence is truly earned. Now, I should point out as well that not all elders are human, of course, but the same rules apply. We have beings all around us who are quite ancient. Take the stone-people for instance, or some of the tree-folk. There are also spirit-people around who are older than this planet is, so always move with caution and if in doubt side on the side of good manners.'

Allan looked at Raven with what appeared to be a new sense of realization at his last words. 'I never really considered that part,' he said. 'Good to know.'

'Yes, it never hurts to have good manners. There are some things out there that could do you in in a fraction of an instant. Others can stain your luck for generations and we don't want to get on the bad side of anyone, especially beings like that.'

'Understood.'

'Okay we are at the letter 'D' in our lesson,' Raven said.

'I feel like I am learning the alphabet all over again,' Allan joked.

Raven smiled. 'In a way you kind of are,' he replied. 'Now here we have Defend the Tradition. This one also really doesn't need much in the way of elaboration. As a distinct culture of pagan people we know that there will always be those who might be a threat to our ways. We always protect our traditions and we protect our own first, yet we strive to be good allies to those who support and befriend us.'

'In other words we don't put up with any crap,' Allan added.

'You may remember when I said that people who want to talk down our ways or our way of speaking are considered to be less than worthless? Well, the same applies here yet we also have the wisdom to keep a wary eye on those who may prove to be a threat. We defend our ways literally, but for the most part also feel no need to debate or defend our existence in word wars with fools.'

'Well said,' Allan agreed. 'Wasting breath debating with idiots is the worst waste of time.'

'Next we have 'E', which stands for Embrace the Self,' Raven said. 'You would not believe how many people seem to think this is not every bit as important as the other ones at first. Can you build a sturdy house on shifting sand? No, you need a solid foundation. I will tell you that there is a Thornish saying which goes: *The first circle is the self.*' What is meant by this? Well, what I mean is that in order to be fully functional in the world, in order to be fully effective as a steward of the land, we must come from a strong foundation. A strong foundation comes from knowing and understanding yourself fully and completely without compromise. Following this we befriend and come to love ourselves. This is very important. I can't emphasize this enough. For most people it is a work in progress and that's fine, but the process is what is important too.'

'So we work to strengthen ourselves through self-understanding and building genuine good relations with ourselves?'

'Yes, wishae,' Raven said. 'Wishae is a kind of friendly term we teachers use to refer to our students, by the way. I knew you were going to ask so I beat you to it. And also, a mirror is among the excellent tools we have available for this process. Talk to yourself in the mirror from time to time. Don't be shy. Look at the person you see in the reflection as a brother, an ally and best of all, as a friend. In the end you will not be disappointed.'

'Something I'll have to think about for sure.'

'Next we have 'N', which stands for Nourish Loyalty and Love,' Raven said. 'Here is one which is very potent as well. In the Thornwood loyalty is amazingly important and it binds the tribe together. Knowing, absolutely, that someone is there for you, that they have your back unconditionally, no matter what, is an astonishingly powerful thing. Indeed, it's one of the main reasons the Thornish tradition exists, to create these tribal bonds for people who might not otherwise have any. Tribal loyalty is the antithesis of the modern day dog-eat-dog world. It defies the slave-programming of the modern governments and the domestication efforts of the theologists and the social scientists. And really, when you think about it, tribal loyalty interacts with and supports all of the facets of tribal life. There is a saying: *Loyalty is the root of the thorn-tree*' and we strongly believe this is true. In the Thornwood, when you think of the term *you bet your life,* 'if you have a Thornish brother or sister at your back you truly can, without the slightest hesitation.'

'I can remember having that kind of feeling of loyalty one or two times in my life, but this was with individual people like my late cousin,' Allan said. 'But never with a large group of people.'

'Something to think about then,' Raven said. 'Now we move on to the last stave, which is the letter 'S.' This one may bear a bit more explanation and it's a thing I will need to teach you in detail over time. S stands for Seek the Black Root.'

'The Black Root?'

'Ah yes, I should tell you about that as well,' Raven said. 'In the tradition we walk we have certain core beliefs. I have already told you in the past about the Elder Kin and how we believe that human kind as we are today came to the world as a result of the Elder Kin's involvement.'

'Yes, I remember that.'

'Well, another of these core beliefs that we share is that of the Black Root,' Raven said. 'To us the Black Root is a symbol of what other tribal people might call the First Knowledge or the Primal Wisdom or even the First Teachings. What we mean by this is that we believe that our species is gifted with original knowledge that is encoded into our bodies and our spirits. We believe that this First Knowledge is built into all living beings and it accounts for what many might refer to as instinct. However, in beings like humans we believe that this First Knowledge is more complex than that and that in working with it we can learn more about ourselves, our world, and our purpose in being here in the first place.'

'Kinda like an operating manual of sorts?'

'Kind of like that, yes, but a lot more. We believe that the First Knowledge holds the keys to our evolution not only as a species but as a spiritual life-form as well. We hold that the original knowledge was at one time somewhat more available to us for our use, but as we became civilized, and I use that term very loosely, we began to lose touch with nature, the sacred balance, and many other things that are our birthright. These days we strive to understand what we have lost and to seek it out and learn from it. We believe it will make us much more powerful and as such we will be greater Warriors and stewards of the land.'

'So, why the term Black Root?' Allan asked.

'Back in the old days one of the men who helped us found the Raven Lodge came to us from a tradition that used that term. They used it for the exact same purpose as we do, only that tradition was more internally focused and arcane in nature. Nowadays we see the Black Root as a symbol of something deep and primal, growing into the dark Earth like the roots of a great and mighty tree, a Tree of knowledge if you want to look at it that way. Some of us see the Black Root differently, as a great crystal vein winding through the Earth, or as a great dark underground river. What matter is that it is mysterious, very primal, and it holds the key to some very ancient forms of understanding.'

'You say the men who originally coined the term Black Root were arcane?' Allan wondered aloud.

Raven looked over at his student and then away into the shadows beyond the trees.

'Yes. They described themselves as forest mages. They had all but faded from the world when one of their folk came to us and befriended us,' Raven said with a dreamy, unfocused look on his face that lasted only a moment. 'But this was a long time ago by your youthful measure. We learned a lot from each other and we adopted the word he used to describe what we had been calling by other names…yet it was pretty much the same thing all along.'

'So, *Seek the Black Root* really means that we should make a point of trying to find bits of this First Knowledge wherever we can?'

'Yes, that's right.'

'So how do we do that?'

'There are a good number of ways of doing this,' Raven said. 'We meditate, we sit out, we perform ritual and we study the oral and written work that might give us clues to follow. I have found that one of the best sources is to go out into nature and commune with the Otherfolk. They are often quite helpful since most of them are far older than us and have been here longer.'

'Otherfolk? I have heard that one before, from Russell.'

'Otherfolk is another term we use to describe spirit-people or people who are not normally visible in this world. There are many, many different kinds of people in the multifold realities of the world, wishae. Not all of them are visible to the average human being. At this very moment we are surrounded by many of them and only the ignorant man would say that just because he can't see, hear or touch something that it's not there. So we use the term Otherfolk to describe these people in general. There are of course quite a few more specific terms we use as well. Shæda, for instance, is another word we use to describe some of these people.'

'So over time a Thornish person will get to know these spirit people and others like them, and through that they can learn more about the Black Root?'

'Seeking the Black Root is a lifelong process, my friend,' Raven replied. 'It is a big part of being Thornish because knowledge is power. With power we can interact more efficiently with the Middle-World and other places, we can re-connect with our spirit teachers and allies more efficiently, we can defend ourselves against trouble from outsiders, and, most importantly, we become better at our job which is to steward the land. Think of it like sharpening a good knife. A dull blade does no one any good and, as a matter of fact, a dull knife can be dangerous. Better to have a sharp edge at all times. It is better to have a well-tuned instrument when you sit in the orchestra of life, eh?'

'I think I understand,' Allan said with a furrowed brow. 'It's a lot to get my head around.'

'It's a start,' Raven said with a grin. 'After a time you will see that it's not nearly as confusing as you might think.'

Allan and his teacher sat in silence for awhile. The little grove was very silent, save only for the slightest murmur of the river in the distance, and the occasional sound of some small animal scurrying in the trees or in the underbrush. Allan took time to absorb all that he had been told and he wondered how much of it he would be able to retain over time. He was glad that Raven had said he would repeat things to him when he needed it. He though that this would certainly help.

'One day I think these old teaching poles will rot off and sink into the ground,' he said suddenly, and just as suddenly wondered why he had said that.

Raven did not object. In fact he chuckled.

'Just like us, my young friend,' he said. 'We are like these poles in that at one time we were bright and shiny and new to the word, standing proud in the light of the world. Yet eventually pretty much everything gives in to time and returns to the stuff it was made of. When that happens, at least with these poles, someone might come along and put new ones up. Or maybe that won't be done at all. Maybe a new place will be found and this little space will be left alone. It all depends on what the land wants and what our tradition needs.'

'I know from the stories I was told on the Native side of my family that everything is a sacred hoop, a sacred circle,' Allan said.

'That is very true,' Raven replied. 'Everything is a circle, a cycle in nature and we are part of that cycle. All we can do is try to play our part in the best and most hale way we can.'

Once again they were quiet again, this time for a long while. Finally Raven spoke again.

'Do you remember I told you about the man who came to us from that older tradition and who shared some of his knowledge with us?' he asked.

'The guy who used the term Black Root? Yes.' Allan grinned.' Despite everything I have been cramming into my brain over the last few days I'm pretty good at remembering things from only a few minutes ago.'

Raven grinned back.

'Well, there was another fellow from the old traditions who was somewhat of a student of the older guy. He was a good friend as well and a very wise fellow. He once said something very powerful and we have preserved his words so that others can learn from them. He said this:

'The key to living this life well lies in the realization of the inevitability of physical death. Enjoy what you are given, for each incarnation is finite.'

'This is one of the reasons we strive to do what we do,' Raven added. 'We as Thornish folk know that our time here in these physical bodies is limited. We are here to learn and to experience and, most importantly I think, to evolve as beings, so while we are here, in this cycle of life, it's important to do our best to serve the balance; to be good people and when we leave here, we go knowing we made a difference in a good way.'

Raven suddenly stood up and brushed pine needles from his pants. He stretched his arms and invited Allan to stand up as well.

'I think we have been here for long enough for this short lesson,' he said. 'I find that it's best to keep lessons short and to allow the student to experience them in a natural environment if possible. Fresh air is good for the mind and short lessons are easier to digest, if you get my meaning.'

Raven then reached into his pocket and pulled out a small leather pouch. From this pouch he poured a small pile of what looked like dried herbs into his hand. He showed the little mound on his palm to Allan.

'Much like they do it in your grandfather's Native way,' he said. 'Here we have a mixture of tobacco, mugwort, sage and other special things. Most of our folk keep a little bag of these kinds of offerings at hand to give to the Otherfolk and to the land as thanks. It's always important to be polite, you know.'

'Could you tell me what a Farer is?'

'A Farer in our tradition s a person who applies themselves to healing and various forms of crafting, usually with a fairly heavy addition of what you might call magic.'

'That's cool,' Allan said. 'Kind of like Medicine people in the Indian traditions.'

'Somewhat like that, yes,' Raven replied. 'There are two primary callings in the Thornwood, the way of the Farer and the way of the Spear-folk. I told you what the Farers are so I guess you can guess what the Spear-folk are.'

'Warriors?'

Raven smiled and patted Allan on the shoulder with his other hand.

'All Thornish people are Warriors to one degree or another. We all have what we call the Blood-fire, the bright spirit of one who goes forth to do what needs to be done. However, there are some of us who are more drawn to the way of the hunt and the way of the defender and guardian, so yes, you could say that Spear-folk are somewhat like more specialized Warriors.'

'And which are you?' Allan asked.

'At first you were kind of shy, now you are just pouring out the questions,' Raven joked. 'Well, you have known me for a while and you have been to my house. Which do you think I am?'

Allan did not hesitate.

'A Warrior,' he said simply.

Raven nodded.

'Do you remember my friend Agnes, from the coffee shop the other day? She is a Farer.'

'She's Thornish!' Allan widened his eyes in surprise. 'I had no idea.'

'There have never been many of us but we do have a tendency to stick together,' Raven laughed. 'Yes, she's Thornish. Does a Thornish person need to have a particular look? We don't often wear any particular garment or hairstyle if that's what you are looking for. Part of our way is to blend in among the people of the outer world. We don't make a big deal about advertising who we are.'

Allan grinned sheepishly. 'Kinda caught me off guard is all.'

'Well, next time you see her you will know, but keep that as private matter, will you? You can let her know that you know and you can do that by calling her Wataan, a Thornish word that means teacher, and she is that. But the whole rest of the community doesn't have to know.'

'Do you mean that we have to hide who we are then?'

'What I mean is that we are selective in allowing our presence to be known,' Raven said. 'There are two reasons for this. The first is that we operate in a continual sense of balance and deepening humility. This means that we don't expect to be celebrated and we do what we do because it is our way. The second reason is that there is still a lot of intolerance in the world. Many great crimes have been committed because of intolerance and we think that the days of such grimness are not gone from the world. So for security for our folk we are, for the most part, quiet about our existence as a people.'

'I understand that, for sure,' Allan said. 'I can see the hate that people have for others. I'm Native and I have had it right up in my face.'

'So yes, you do understand,' Raven said. 'It's terrible that you have experienced hatred like that but good that you understand through firsthand experience.'

And with that Raven walked over to the base of a nearby tree, knelt on one knee and poured the mixture at the base of it. Allan could tell that Raven was saying a few words, probably words of thanks, but he couldn't make out what exactly it was that he was saying.

When he was done he nodded slightly toward the tree and indeed inclined his head at a respectful angle as he looked around the little grove. It was obvious that he was offering his thanks. Allan also nodded his head in a slight semi-bow and silently offered his thanks for the space and the beauty of this little place.

After a moment more they turned to go.

'Where are we going now?' Allan asked, curiously.

'I am going to walk back to my place and make a telephone call. I think there are one or two people that you should meet today.'

Allan wondered who else he would meet who was walking in the same way that Raven was and he wondered even more about what kinds of things they might be able to teach him. In getting to know Raven he realized that he had opened up a whole new world that in years before his older cousin had only hinted at. Now he was on the verge of becoming a part of those very same things. For some reason he felt that this was creating an even closer bond between himself and his now lost cousin and this gladdened him beyond words.

'I will do my best to learn whatever any of you have to teach me,' he said.

Raven looked at him for a moment and Allan wondered if the older man was searching his face for signs of honesty or perhaps even signs of his relationship with Russell, who Allan could tell Raven missed as well.

Finally Raven smiled once again and turned to walk down the little trail.

'It's a good start,' he said.

7

Flow

The more common person of spirit, when approaching the great unknown asks: 'What can you do for me?' The Thornish person asks: 'How may I serve?' - Master Shale

Qorvas sat alone by the gently swirling waters of the river. The river here was not overly wide nor exceptionally deep. In some places it was barely more than a creek and in others, such as the place where the young man was sitting, it widened out somewhat to allow its graceful green waters a slightly slower passage. Further along the river would come into rapids and a faster flow.

Qorvas was not fooled by the apparent mellowness of the river. He had come to know its deep power soon after he had come to this valley and though he was relatively new to the ways of the Thornwood he had already been given many potent lessons through those waters.

The weather was fine on that clear autumn day, which was welcome to the young man since the preceding two days had been fraught with winds and rain. The shadow of the nearby bluffs at whose base he sat had only enhanced the effects of the cold and damp, as any hope of warmth was lost as the sun passed behind the peaks. Thus, having already been hit with rain twice, on the third day the Thornsman was pleased to wake up beneath clear skies.

Qorvas had chosen his place in the forest deliberately. There was a considerable concentration of power in this place – much more than the surrounding woods – and he had chosen to go and do a sitting-out there.

In Thornish tradition this kind of sitting-out is also known as a minor Deepening. A Deepening is a form of ritual meditative retreat in which one seeks to open themselves to greater understandings. Such a ritual always takes place in a natural environment where the student may perform certain rites or just sit peacefully and become one with the surroundings. In Thornish tradition there are two kinds of Deepenings; the minor Deepening, which is explained above, and the major Deepening, a special transitional rite which may occur only three times in a Thornish person's life. To be sure, the minor Deepening was often also referred to as a Séta, as most Thornish folk preferred to avoid referring to it as something minor – which it was anything but.

In the case of Qorvas, he had been inspired to come to this place two weeks earlier, when he had experienced a trio of dreams concerning the river and the powerful place along the widening flow. For him, messages of importance often came in threes.

He had dreamed that he had gone to the special place by the river and that he had received powerful teachings from the spirits of the land. The dreams had been extremely vivid, something which Qorvas had long seen as a sign that he was receiving communications from the Otherworlds.

Normally, when he was not visiting or training with his teacher, Qorvas lived in the city. He had been a city dweller for most of his life and while a portion of his loyalties and roots did indeed lie in Vancouver he had long since opened himself to the call of the wilder places. As such he left the city and sought adventure in the green places as often as he could. In this instance, upon heeding his dreams and also desiring a break from the mainstream he called his Teacher, who immediately agreed that he should come up for a visit.

Qorvas had stayed with his teacher for two days before setting out. After that he had gone off to find the special place beneath the mountain where the sacred river flowed widest and then narrowed again in a series of rocky cascades. His plan was simple. He would live quietly and minimally there in that place near the riverbank, make the appropriate offerings and hope to receive a teaching or two.

The first afternoon, even though the weather had turned grey, was a delight to Qorvas as returning to these woods and to the river was exactly the same as if he were visiting an old friend. More so, in fact, because in such cases the Thornish person viewed the sacred places as more than friends; more as family.

He delighted in the sights and sounds of the river valley and in all of the subtle nuances that were to be found along the trail. At last, when he had come to the special place, he took from his pack a simple cotton duck canvas tarp and arranged a very rudimentary shelter using several sticks and fallen branches found nearby. In front of the small shelter he arranged some local stones in a very small circle so that his modest fire needs could be accommodated. During his stay he would be taking only water and occasionally a cup of special herbal tea, so not much wood, which was collected from nearby dead wood, was needed.

Qorvas settled in and made himself comfortable. He sat and waited. Many things might occur when a person situates themselves alone in the wild places, the very least of which will be a deepening sense of peace and serenity. To those unused to such things the experience might eventually degrade into anxiety or frustration when the stay became too uneventful or even perceived as boring. To the person who was experienced in such things however, the perception of the thing was much different. It was an opportunity to experience deep calm and a oneness with the Earth.

Other than taking the opportunity to seek deep peace and meditate on the bank of the river, Qorvas did very little for those first two days. He simply existed, and this was good enough for him. He knew that in the ways of the spirit world things seldom went as humans imagined them to go and patience was a valuable key.

The third day was a delight for reasons mentioned earlier. In fact the nice weather was the first one that Qorvas (or anyone else around there, for that matter) had seen in a week. It had been rainy over much of the coast and this had extended inland to the valley where he found himself camped. He took advantage of it by setting a few of his things to dry on branches around his shelter. His brown pullover hoodie, which he often wore when he was meditating, had gotten quite damp over the previous days and he had experienced difficulty getting it to dry over his meager fire. He hoped it would have a chance to completely dry out in the much warmer breeze that was flowing through the pines.

The day went idly by and Qorvas simply enjoyed the experience of the day sitting by the water. Finally, as the sun edged her way past the peaks and brought shadows across the land, Qorvas returned to his little camp, put away his things, and set to kindling a small fire. He had consumed only water for the first two days and now he hoped he would be able to enjoy a cup of tea in front of his shelter. He was glad to discover that his pullover jacket was now completely dry. He shrugged it on against the beginnings of the night-chill.

At one point Qorvas reached into his bag and pulled forth a soft deerskin bag. He set it on the ground before him and loosened the ties. Reaching inside, he first brought out a piece of black linen about thirty centimeters square and set this on the ground. He flattened it out on the dirt and then reached his hand into the bag once more. The piece of cloth was a casting cloth, a place where one might cast tines, stones, bones, or any other oracle which had found use within his tradition. In the Thornish way a black cloth is used because black is representative of the Great Essence of the manifold universe. To a Thornish person black represents numinous power and the source of all life. As such it is seen as a perfect shade for the casting of the implements of Wyrd. This is different from the kind of cloth upon which most users of the old oracles cast, when indeed they cast upon cloth. In other traditions a white cloth is more often used as it represents purity, light or perhaps a clean slate.

From the deerskin bag Qorvas produced a single stone tablet about a centimeter square. It was black pipestone upon which he had carved each of his personal runes. As Thornish people who cast the runes prefer a particular rune-set, the rune he had drawn was but one of the thirty-three which normally resided in the bag.

All of Qorvas' runes were so carved upon black stone tablets. They had been individually inscribed and ritually colored with a mixture of ochre, blood and other pigments. Each of the runes had been empowered through individual meditations and in rituals mostly taking place in the forest at night.

The runes had served him well and even though he had been interested in them and had worked with them over the years in one form or another, he knew that even should he live to a ripe old age he would be permitted to fathom only the most superficial of runic understandings.

The runes are mystical doorways into the world of spirit,' his teacher had told him. *They are not only gateways, each of a very specific nature, but also each one is a living, conscious being capable of very powerful teachings...if one approaches with reverence, respect and the appropriate offerings.'*

Qorvas was well aware of this and in keeping with the tradition he made a small scrape on his finger with the edge of his knife and touched the tiny bead of blood to the rune as it came out of the bag.

We do not do things as perhaps some of the other traditions might,' another of his teachers had told him one night, not all that long ago. *We know for a fact that the power of such oracles as the runes are not for the use of common people. They are very potent; very dangerous if used incorrectly. Imagine finding a small trickle of water flowing through a hole in a wall and sticking your finger in there. Imagine doing that, not realizing that just beyond that wall was the unstoppable power of a vast lake, just waiting to break through. Imagine that unstoppable force there, just on the other side of that wall and what it could do if it decided to push through that small hole, all at once!'*

In his studies Qorvas had come to see that what his mentors had told him was very true. He had learned but the tiniest fraction of what he imagined there was to know about the runes, but already he could sense their distinct and primal personalities. In particular he knew from experience the potency of Kenaz, the fire-rune and Laguz, the rune of primal waters. He also knew well primordial Uruz, the sacred bull of ancient and fathomless life-energy. Ior, the deep-Earth serpent and changer of faces and Eár, the rune of the Mound and the worlds beyond this one.

Now Qorvas reached into his worn rune bag once more. He hoped for guidance; direction for his workings this night. He had decided to pick one rune only and see what it might have to say to him on this quiet, darkening day.

The young Thornsman tossed the rune on his waiting black cloth to see which rune had come to guide him and he saw that it was Nauthiz, the need-fire.

'In the darkness and cold is the need-fire desired,' Qorvas said to himself.

The need-fire is the potency of the primordial laws at work, the essence of action and reaction in the multiverse. That, and the effect which such things might have on the ebb and flow of the individual luck...as well as the Ord; the collective luck of gatherings of people. Qorvas knew that Nauthiz, especially as the rune before him lay in the upright and facing position, was indicative of the principle of right action...and that when one encountered resistance to things in the world and pushed past them, a gain in understanding and strength could be achieved.

Qorvas looked at the rune for a while longer in the deepening dusk and at last he took the rune up in his left hand.

'Thank you, my friend, for sharing your wisdom with me tonight.'

Then he touched the rune to his forehead, allowing it to sit there for a moment to absorb a small amount of his essence. Finally he returned the rune to the bag to be with its mates, followed by the now folded casting cloth.

Qorvas put the bag back in his larger bag and set it aside. He turned inward for a time, so as to contemplate the deeper meanings which the need-fire-rune had conveyed to him.

'All runes are tricksters of a sort,' his teacher had told him. *'They coyote-teach. They will almost never give you a direct answer to anything but rather they will talk around what you have asked. They will give you peripheral clues and expect that if you want deeper truths you will hunt them down on your own.'*

Night fell completely around Qorvas and his tiny campfire, and as is the way in the forest, it did not take long for the surrounding woods to become completely black. Qorvas sat and watched the blackness deepen all around him, and not for the first time, marveled at how his tiny camp became an island of light in a vast sea of sable night.

Qorvas wasn't sure what caused him to awaken in the deep hours of the night. It might have been the sudden flare of the tiny fire which he had been sure was extinguished. It may have been out-of-the-ordinary sounds that penetrated his consciousness or it might have been something rooted further down in his subconscious that triggered him to instinctively wake up. In any case he woke up from his peaceful sleep very quickly and within seconds found himself sitting bolt upright with his hand on the hilt of his nearby hunting knife.

Little more than a meter away he saw that indeed his little fire-pit was lit with the merry dancing of the Fire-people. Wood had been added and the flames licked somewhat higher than they had when he had tended it. He knew without a doubt that he had completely extinguished the blaze before retiring for the night and it was a mystery why it was once again in operation.

For a second he considered that it might have been his teacher, come out to speak with him or take advantage of an opportunity to pass on a lesson or two. His teacher, Raven, had done this in the past and the ability to pass quietly in the woods – day or night – was something which Raven had long since mastered.

But something did not fit with that theory. It did not feel like Raven, although there was a definite feeling of presence in or around his camp, something that had not been there before.

There was also a scent, reminiscent of wild flowers that hung in the air amidst the smells of Earth, water and evergreen trees. Considering that it was autumn such a scent was unusual in that place to say the least.

Qorvas sat in silence for long moments, there in the even darker shadows of his small shelter. He waited and although his awakening had been abrupt he did not move himself any further. His senses probed the blackness beyond the fire-pit and around the perimeter he had set for his sojourn in the green. He brought forth abilities which he had been honing for some time now, senses that went beyond the normal faculties of sight, sound, smell and the tactile senses. He attempted to feel the area around his camp with his spirit-senses, to try and discover the nature of whatever or whomever had come to his camp and then not properly announced themselves.

Finally he had it. His sensory sweep stopped suddenly in a place just off to one side of the opening of his shelter. The feeling of presence was very strong there though at this point he was still not overly sure of exactly what he had detected.

At first Qorvas was somewhat unhappy at having been jolted awake in the middle of a restful slumber. Indeed he had never been the easiest person to live with in such cases and had been known by a good number of friends and family as a morning grump, not a morning person at all. Yet he also realized that while it was certainly in the AM, it was still black as pitch in the woods outside his little haven.

Qorvas restrained himself from making any untoward comment to whomever was out there. He felt no fear and further enhanced his calm using methods from his training. Finally, he swung his feet around and emerged from his shelter.

He saw her right away and for a brief instant fought to retain his composure. He succeeded with maintaining what he hoped were zero visible outward signs of his wonderment; that he was surprised to see a hooded woman standing in his camp.

Finally, he stood up and looked at her. She stood there silently not all that far away. Apparently she was not armed or at least not seeming aggressive in any way.

She was of average height and build from what he could see beyond the cloak. The garment covering her enclosed her head so all he could make out was a glimpse of a female face in the flickering light – that and wisps of long, black hair flowing out of the hood. It seemed to him that her complexion might have been that of perhaps a Native person or someone whose ancestors had come from a more southerly clime. Of course he could be sure of nothing in the dim light. Otherwise she was covered from head to ankle by the cloak, which appeared to be of some earthy color. He had difficulty making it out in the firelight.

She said nothing and stood there, just outside the brighter light of the fire, looking at him.

There was something slightly unnerving about her and Qorvas deduced that it was not her sudden appearance in the middle of the blackened woods. There was an unusual energy present and he suspected that this mysterious woman was the origin of that energy.

'Welcome to my camp,' Qorvas said finally. His training served him well and he knew, as all Thornish folk do, that hospitality, even if meager, is a very sacred thing.

Now a voice emerged from beneath that hood. It was soft, feminine and most definitely touched with an accent. It was not so much the sound of the voice which caught him off-guard but the content of her words.

'You are Qorvas, student of Raven and son of Yasgar.' She spoke these things as fact, not supposition or in the form of a question. Her words were meticulously spoken as though she was a person of significant rank and class. Her voice had the slightest tinge of an accent that Qorvas guessed might have come from an original, non-English tongue.

She knew who he was, who his teacher was and indeed she had used the kenning he held for his own father. Not many people would have known these things outside of the traditions, but Qorvas was certain he had never met this person before.

156

Yet if indeed she was somehow of his tradition then Thornish rules of courtesy demanded a polite response. Qorvas offered the traditional Thornish bow.

'I am Qorvas,' he replied. 'Ælan Shar.'

His suspicions that his enigmatic visitor was from his own tradition were confirmed when she returned the bow in like fashion.

'Indeed,' she said. 'Ælan Shar.'

Ælan Shar is a formal greeting of respect in the Thornish tradition. Its meaning is roughly *'to bring firelight and balance'* and had been one of the first things he had been taught as a Learner. That she had returned the greeting in the way that she had done so told Qorvas much. The odds that she was an initiate and possibly even a Master in the tradition were very good as far as Qorvas was concerned and so for the sake of decorum he was glad that he had greeted her respectfully.

'May I know your name?' Qorvas asked, curious as to the identity of the stranger.

After a pause the woman finally spoke. 'I am not…permitted to say at this time.'

'May I ask then, why you are here?' Qorvas then remembered his traditions and added, 'May I offer you some tea perhaps?'

The hood shook in the negative although he sensed that she was pleased by the offer.

'Come with me,' she said, and with that turned and walked smoothly away from the firelight.

Qorvas followed somewhat hesitantly, though he was glad he had been wearing his pull-over hooded coat to sleep in. It now provided a welcome barrier against the chill night air.

Looking up, Qorvas noted that the weather was once again on the change. Where he had gone to sleep beneath a clear, star-filled sky he saw now that a patchwork of mottled clouds was coming in overhead from the west. Beyond the cloud layer he could detect the diffuse light of the moon cresting overhead. He found himself hoping that the moonlight would be able to break through the clouds – if even for a while – just to keep him from tripping in the deep dark.

The cloaked woman walked down toward the edge of the river and then turned left, following the bank along until it crossed the boundary of the sitting-out area which Qorvas had set for himself. In Thornish tradition there are no hard and fast rules on such things; Qorvas had simply set himself that perimeter in order to keep distractions to a minimum.

He continued to follow her until he heard, in the darkness ahead, an increase in the sound of the water which told him the river had reached a cascade point in its course. He continued along for a distance further until he saw the woman standing at a small gravel covered flat space right at the river's edge.

Qorvas looked down to see that his footing was all right in the darkness. Beneath the trees at that time of night everything was still as black as pitch – even though the banks of the river were somewhat more open to the sky and afforded a bit more light. He had nearly tripped several times in following the woman, who seemed to move effortlessly through the gloom, and he had no wish to fall on his face.

Looking up again he noticed that the woman had once again disappeared from his sight. He wondered how she could navigate so efficiently in the darkness and marveled at this because not even his teacher was so adept.

Finally reaching the flat spot where he had last seen her, Qorvas stopped.

'Where are you now?' he asked of the surrounding dark.

'Here,' came the reply.

Qorvas looked around somewhat confused for a moment – and then he spotted her; a lighter shade against the opposite banks of the river. As she moved from an erect standing position to a crouch near the water, Qorvas wondered how on Earth she had managed to cross the water, which at this point was running quite deep, possibly chest deep or deeper, and was cascading quite turbulently over rounded ancient stones.

Upon further examination, at least what further examination he could make given the lack of light, Qorvas was amazed to see that the strange woman did not even seem wet for her efforts. He knew the river course well in this area and was certain that there were no footbridges or other means by which she might have gotten across in a dry fashion.

'Come closer to the river,' the mysterious one said. He found it odd that he was able to hear her voice so clearly despite the sound of the rushing water. Yet another question to be pondered.

Qorvas walked down closer to the river's edge and eyed the woman suspiciously. He was starting to get the idea that she might not be an ordinary person – if even a member of his tradition that she appeared to be. He wondered if perhaps she was not human at all but possibly a spirit person of some kind, possibly even an Elder Kin. He had heard of spirit people taking semi-corporeal form before and had heard some strange stories from elders concerning such things, but he himself had never experienced anything that was as real seeming and interactive as this. Yet Qorvas' logical mind intruded on these thoughts and convinced him that there must be a more mundane explanation for what was happening. Possibly even this might be a test of some kind sent by Raven to see what his reaction would be – or possibly he had just come across a member of the tradition he had never met before.

'There is no such thing as coincidence,' Master Tiva, an elder of the tradition, had taught him quite early on. 'Everything happens for a reason even if we cannot glean those particular reasons ourselves.'

And so Qorvas set his thoughts aside and walked to the river's edge as had been requested.

The woman pointed out a place about halfway between where she was crouched and the shoreline where Qorvas was standing. There, wedged between several large rocks, was a broken branch that had been caught upright by the current and was sticking nearly vertically out of the cascading water.

'This is like you,' the lady said. 'You are like a stick which has been caught between stones and resists movement even though all around you a current flows.'

'I don't understand,' Qorvas said. 'A metaphor?'

'Reality,' came the reply. It now had a somewhat stern edge to it. 'Think, young student; think about your place and where you are in the world. You are Shakai and you should know. Think about the frustration you are feeling with your life in the city and the anger than builds up inside when you feel torn between worlds.'

Shakai; the Thornish term for a person of Qorvas' level of learning. The rank was that of the Seeker, or the initiated apprentice whose role was to learn and grow in the traditions. She was aware of Qorvas' position in the tradition. She also knew things which he was sure he had not shared with anyone else connected with the Thornwood. How did she know these things and yet he had never met her?

Suddenly the general illumination increased and Qorvas looked up to see that he had been granted his earlier wish for bright moonlight. All around him that which had been either black or shades of dark grey now added silver and blue shades to the tapestry of the woods. It was truly magical. Now he could see, in brief glimpses of her hands and shadowed face, that she did indeed have a mysterious, darker complexion. Qorvas could not recall having met another Thornish person who looked like this Lady did, which as far as he was concerned, only deepened the mystery.

'What are the rocks then, in this analogy you are making?'

'The stones that hold you from beneath the rolling waters represent your will,' came the reply. 'Will is constrained by the mind and the minds of the young are often undisciplined, impetuous, slaves to emotion. You are such, young Qorvas.'

'I am here though, unlike many,' Qorvas replied. He had taken a breath and calmed himself, for, hearing her words he had begun to react in exactly the way she had just described. 'I am trying to learn control and I am working on my inner balance,' he added.

There was a long pause in which only the voice of the river and the night-song of the surrounding trees could be heard. The trees whispered in the gentle autumn breeze and it seemed to him that they were encouraging him to remain at ease; in balance and unperturbed by this unusual experience.

'Yes you are, which is part of the reason I have come. The other reason is that your brother has asked it of me and he is not yet strong enough to come to you directly.'

Qorvas dropped his gaze to the ground before him. He felt a current of cold energy tingle its way up his spine and into the base of his head. *His brother.*

He knew without asking for clarification exactly who she was talking about. His spear-brother, his best friend and one who he had loved dearly had died only about a year and a half before. Qorvas suddenly felt a rush of emotion and felt the blood rushing to his cheeks as he thought about his lost kinsman. He fought the emotional outpouring that surged upward and as well he held his discipline and stuck to the topic at hand. To babble questions like a young Learner at this stage would, he felt, do no good at this moment.

Qorvas did not know exactly who or what he was speaking to at this time, but one thing was eminently clear to him. She knew things, things that very few could know, and for that he continued to listen.

'You are stuck and I have come to help you with that,' the woman said after a time, as if in answer to some of his unspoken questions.

'Watch the stick,' she said. 'It sits there, wanting to re-join the flow but it can't do it as long as the rocks are holding it. It stands at an awkward angle, opposed to the flow.'

'Yes, the flow,' Qorvas said without really meaning to verbalize his thought. Raven had taught him about this many times and illustrated it to him with examples and lessons.

'Flow you know about,' she said. 'It is far more than the current of the river here. It is sacred Önd or Qaa as we call it; it is life energy that moves between all living things. It is everywhere and it connects everything. It is the deepest expression of the Great Essence, the song of the life-mother and the spark in the fabric of being. As well, it is the mesh from which sacred destiny is woven.'

'This I understand,' Qorvas said. 'What can one do to return to the flow?'

'When you resist the flow you are not doing anything but stagnating your own destiny, young one,' she said. 'Knowing when one is out of synch with the flow is the first step.' And for a moment she simply remained where she was, silent as if in deep contemplation.

'There are ways,' she said after a time. 'One can either find a way to wiggle free, one can get assistance or one can stay there stagnant until the power of the current eventually rots one off at the base. Then it will be too late. Then one will not have learned the lesson and continued the journey in a hale manner.'

The woman made a slight gesture and the stick leaned over somewhat in its place, more now, toward the surging water.

Qorvas was not overly surprised with this act. He had witnessed minor examples of telekinesis before in his life. Most of the time these were unexplained and other times, at least twice, he had seen such thing deliberately initiated by certain gifted individuals. Now he wondered if he was witnessing a third such example.

'That small gesture is an example of help. But you see, it does not fully accomplish the purpose of freeing one back into the flow. Also the lesson is only partially learned, which could lead to folly.'

Qorvas though about something that he had been taught by Corva, a Master in the tradition who had taught him the rudiments of meditation.

'*Sometimes a partially understood lesson is worse than no lesson at all,*' she had said.

He believed it. He had seen the misapplication of lessons in the past. None overly disastrous, yet still, they had been unfortunate.

'How then does a person return to the flow on their own?' he asked. 'Is it a strengthening of the will, as you suggest?'

'The will can be greatly increased through understanding,' she answered. 'But the true art of it is in the *knowing*. Will is forged in many fires but one of the most important ones is the fire of knowing. Knowing is understanding; knowing is belief; belief strengthens the threads that connect everything. Once we learn how to strengthen our grasp of the connecting threads, anything is possible.'

There was a momentary silence and then: 'One learns to let go,' she said. 'Holding on is indicative of attachment. Attachment to too many things becomes a deep weakness. It is the fodder of the herd animal, not of the free thinker. Unlearn the lie which tells people that they have to have things and hold on to emotions and materials as though they are somehow essential to life. Let go of these things and the flow will return you to balance.'

'Holding on to these things can make one a slave under their own designs,' she added. 'And such is not the Thornish way.'

'What steps can a person take to let go?'

'Practice the rites, live the Code, meditate, embrace joy and don't allow emotions to rule you but rather treat each event as something which requires attention yet not a knee-jerk reaction. Step outside the situation and see it objectively. Never allow yourself to be hung like a puppet on strings. Avoid becoming angry. Learn how to step beyond simple belief...**know** instead.'

'I see,' Qorvas said somewhat quietly, though he was certain she could hear him quite as clearly as he could hear her.

'Embrace life, young Shakai,' she said. 'You hold much anger in your heart. You believe that being a Warrior is to be angry and reactive and fierce all of the time. This is not so because in our tradition we see the Warrior as being wise and understanding in all things. The wise and understanding person has become wise through years of learning and he has become understanding by taking a step back and observing the larger picture. The larger picture shows us that everything in the worlds is intimately connected to all else. Nothing is truly separate. When you learn – truly learn, that you are not in any way separate from the multiverse then you will understand why it is important to embrace flow.'

And she moved her wrist again and the stick broke free. It fell with a splash into the churning current and was quickly carried off into the dark.

'It goes to the sea eventually,' she said. 'As we all go to the sea in the end, the great sea of energy that everything comes from and that everything returns to.'

'Learn to let go of the lies and the attachment and the hate,' she said at last. 'It is not easy as my student will tell you herself. It is a challenge to open oneself up to that which is greater and then…to truly understand where one lives in the world.'

Qorvas realized once again that he now had far more questions than he had answers. He felt them welling up inside him and while he tried to decide which question he should ask first he realized that the mysterious woman was simply no longer there.

She had disappeared in some way or another. There was now no sign that she had ever been there at all.

On the morning of the fourth day Qorvas packed away his few belongings and, leaving offerings for the spirit-folk of the land, he set out on the trail back to his teacher's house. When he arrived there he recognized the battered old pickup truck parked next to that of his teacher. It was the vehicle of Corva, who he had come to know somewhat.

His teacher, Raven, welcomed him inside and before long he was seated comfortably at the worn old kitchen table with a steaming cup of coffee in front of him. His tribal relations were interested in hearing about his adventure, if he was willing to share, and so Qorvas told them the tale.

As he did he realized that the expression on Corva's face had gone through a number of changes as she listened. Raven's face had remained passive throughout.

Finally, when Qorvas had finished speaking, Corva said, 'I think I know who that was.'

'I do too,' said Raven, 'though her appearance is somewhat surprising. Brother, you must have really needed that kick in the pants.

Consider yourself lucky to have received it from someone as respected as Jhaar.'

'Jhaar?' Qorvas asked, repeating the name with its odd soft 'g' start. 'You know her?'

'Yes, she is Corva's teacher's teacher, one of them anyway, from back in the old days.' Raven said.

'In other words she was Ciaran's teacher and then, later, she also taught me.' Corva added.

'I have never met her before,' Qorvas said.

'Not surprising, since she has been gone from the world for years,' Corva said quietly.

Qorvas sat there, dumbfounded. He wondered if any of what he thought had happened, had actually occurred, yet the details were still there, quite clear, in his mind. In Thornish thought when one dies this means simply the expiration of the physical body, or conveyance as Raven sometimes said. When the body expires the essence of what one is, who they were, and everything they are returns to the spirit world where it usually rests while waiting to go on another corporeal adventure.

The spirit of the person, it is taught, shows but the smallest hint of itself in the physical body here in the Middle-World. There is a much greater vastness lying behind every individual, like a great spiritual iceberg beneath the energy sea. Sometimes these essences, these spirits, returned to the Middle-World to watch over those who they care about and sometimes to impart lessons. And it had obviously appeared to Raven and Corva that Qorvas himself had just experienced such a communication.

Neither of them were overly surprised. Thornish people do not hold themselves aloof from the ways of the spirit world. Quite the opposite, actually.

'She was right what she said about flow,' Corva said after a moment. 'Flow is everything and yeah, I did have my battles while I was learning to fully let go.'

'Maybe you can advise me on that then?' Qorvas asked hopefully.

Corva looked at him with a rather intense gaze for a moment or so more and then she said, 'I'd be happy to. I wouldn't want to get my ass kicked by her *that* way...again.'

And to that Raven chuckled. It was a deep, good natured sound.

Corva joined in and looked at the older man as if the two of them were sharing a particularly delightful little secret.

'Care to share?' Qorvas asked, somewhat put out at not having been included in the joke.

Raven looked over at him with a friendly grin.

'In time, my friend,' he said. ' In time.'

8
Black Trail

'The darkness is where everything and I mean everything has its beginning. It is the primal place, the place of the Great Essence, the Dark Mother, and everything else we hold sacred. Do yourself a kindness and spend time in the dark. Just listen and feel and before long you will be amazed at the things the dark can teach.'

- Master Ciarán

'Qorvas is the name of a sacred trickster,' the grey haired Warrior said as he crouched behind the massive, moss covered fir tree. 'Qor is the name of one of our sacred teachers; an Elder Kin, but it also means to struggle, to fight, to strive. Vas refers to one who teaches through tricks and sideways behavior. Together these two words have created an interesting combination.'

There were two men crouched behind the remains of the tree, one older and grey haired yet still of strong frame, and one much younger, sporting long reddish-brown hair. Both were dressed in dark-colored flannel shirts and denim trousers. Both wore thigh-high animal skin boots that made their movement on the trails whisper-soft.

The downed tree was truly massive; lightning killed long years before it had eventually fallen to its side in the deep brush and had gradually become a home for animals, small seedling trees and moss – lots and lots of moss.

After the older man had finished speaking, his voice barely above a whisper, the younger man turned to him with an odd look on his face.

'I know the meaning of my tribal name,' he whispered back, rather perplexed at why his teacher should choose the current moment to remind him of the origins of his name. 'At my naming ceremony you were the one who gave it to me.'

The older man grinned through a stubby forest of grayish-black beard stubble. They had been in the woods now for some time and neither of them had made the time for anything beyond eating, sleeping, the bare necessities of cleanliness, and, of course, the primary reason that they were out in the forest to begin with: The sacred tradition of the hunt.

'I might have named you but in truth I have to give Tiva the credit for coming up with it,' the older man replied. 'Tiva is very imaginative, you know.'

The younger man's expression of bewilderment had not changed. Their trail had brought them into an area where it seemed that something truly violent had very recently happened. They had not determined the cause of the disturbance and yet his friend was reminiscing and talking about plays on words.

'I still don't get why you are bringing it up now,' he said. 'It's been...how long?'

The older man's brows furrowed and he began to roll his eyes somewhat. It seemed that now it was his turn to express bewilderment.

'You know that there is usually a point to some of the odd things that might come out of my mouth from time to time,' he said wearily. 'My tribal name is Raven. Ravens tend to fly overhead and see the bigger picture. Your tribal name speaks about a trickster but doesn't specifically name the trickster...'

The young man seemed to be at a stumbling block as to his teacher's train of thought. Though his expression had softened somewhat he was still unable to glean his friend's deeper meaning.

'Sorry, you have lost me,' he said at last.

'What is your Vörd, your sacred guardian-teacher animal?' Raven asked after a long silence.

'Is this a trick question?'

'No. Just answer my question, will you?'

'My spirit-teacher in that way has always been Coyote. You know that.'

'Ah, yes, but I wonder if you know it? Maybe since the trees are too thick for Raven to get the bigger picture from above, imaginatively speaking, maybe Coyote, who is paws-on-the-ground, might have a better way out of our current dilemma.'

'I don't know,' said the younger man, somewhat petulantly. 'I seem to remember being teased about how people like eagles, hawks, owls, ravens and the like fly overhead and get the bigger picture while people like bears, wolves and coyotes stumble about in the brush, bumping into trees.'

Now the older man nodded.

'We meant no insult.'

'Yeah, I guess so.'

'So, do you see what I am saying then?'

The younger man, Qorvas, nodded his head after a moment.

'You want a Coyote solution to the situation we have in front of us.'

Raven nodded, a grim look of satisfaction on his face.

'Yes,' he said. 'That would be good because in a moment we are going to go past this tree and down into the clearing on the other side. I sense that what we are about to see will probably be one of the most powerful opportunities for teaching that I have ever had, not only with you but with anyone I have ever taught.'

A cold sense of anticipation rose once again in Qorvas' chest and throat. During the low crouching stalk that they had recently used to get to this point he had been feeling it as well but when Raven had begun talking about name-origins he had, for a brief time, let go of the tension and began to re-embrace a sense of calm. Now, once again, the grimness was entering his bones. He saw that there was a look of serene determination now residing upon his teacher's face and he couldn't decide whether it was the kind of look a man might wear when entering a holy temple or whether he was contemplating ritual suicide.

'Well, my Coyote-self suggests going at whatever we decide in a roundabout manner. I have found that plunging in directly can sometimes cause more trouble than its worth. Better to be crafty and get as much information as possible before doing anything and when you do go, come from the blind side.'

'That's what I expected a Coyote might say.' Raven chuckled. 'And you know it might be just the ticket to get us through this with our skins intact. Sometimes wisdom comes with a terrible price you know.'

Now, in Qorvas' heart, the chill deepened. All around them there were the multitudinous signs of autumn, yet to the young man it suddenly felt like he was in the bleak depths of winter.

The two men had been in the deep woods for four days now. On the first day, when they had decided to undertake the sacred hunt they had prepared themselves by sitting overnight in the Moot house and speaking about their plans. Following this they had washed themselves in the waters of a nearby rushing river, a river whose leaping green waters had been snow on mountain peaks not all that long before. After this they had returned to the Moot house, which was basically a simple structure, sanctified for meditation and ritual, and partaken in the last meal they would have before going on the hunt.

To Thornish people something such as the sacred hunt is especially sacred. Indeed, the taking of any life so that one might eat is considered to be a powerful act, never, ever taken lightly even if that act is as simple as harvesting from a garden or picking fruit. All life is sacred and is treated with the utmost respect. Raven had taught Qorvas early on that in the ways of the tradition, which he sometimes described as *being at the tribal root which all northern peoples shared*, it was always important to show deep reverence to the land and the spirits who dwelled on it or in it.

The sacred hunt, in which a wild animal is stalked and slain for food goes even beyond the normal levels of reverence shown for one's food. There is a tradition within the tradition that is followed and this includes a simple ceremony, ritual preparation and a last meal before the hunt. It is held that when a person kills for food they should not be full of food and satisfied but rather they should be hungry and showing their need of the food. As such, following the ceremonial meal in the Moot house there would be nothing substantial to eat for the participants save for very minimal fuel, usually in the form of dried jerky pieces, dried fruit or pemmican. Following the sacred meal, the two hunters slept in the Moot house to await the dawn of the next day.

Day two started very early and they rose before the sun. They set out into the forest and walked for a goodly distance before they came upon the signs that the elder of the two, Raven, had been looking for.

Their prey had been an older white-tail deer, a buck considerably past his prime. Raven had spotted him several times during the summer months and had noted that the deer had a pronounced limp. He had deduced that the problem had come from a back leg that appeared to have been damaged in some way and had not healed properly.

'This is the kind of four-legged that men should hunt,' he had taught his student. 'We've learned much from our brothers of the First Nations about this kind of thing over the years. The good hunter culls the weak and the crippled from the herd. He doesn't take the best or healthiest because those should be left to strengthen the herd. No, a truly honorable hunter, if he has a choice and his people are not desperate for food, will choose to help the herd by taking the weak and encouraging the strong.'

Qorvas was not new to this way of thinking. He had been fortunate in having been taught to hunt originally by his uncle Emmett, a trapper wise in the ways of the woods.

Once the two hunters had found the sign they were looking for they began to make their way along various game trails, ways that Raven knew the old buck and other deer frequented. For an entire day they went along in this way, seeing many other animals but not catching up to the particular four-legged that they were looking for. That evening they slept in the forest, in a small clearing with no campfire. They wrapped themselves in their blankets and nodded off as best they could.

The next day greeted them soon enough with the faint light of the rising sun peeking over the nearby peaks and down through the branches of the surrounding trees. The men rose from their places, rolled their blankets and set out on the trail once again. At last they caught up with their quarry about midday as he drank from a small lake in the highlands. Qorvas, thought it would be the perfect time for them to take him, but Raven demurred.

'No,' he had whispered from their place at the forest edge. 'All of the places of water are deeply sacred. Many come to drink here and we shouldn't disrupt the peace in this area. We'll wait and try to take him on the trail.'

And so they waited. Raven was the eldest and indeed the teacher. Qorvas accepted his wisdom and did as he was asked. At last the buck finished taking his drink and wandered back into the forest uncertainly on his injured leg.

The sight of this caused Qorvas to feel a rush of emotion that he quickly brought under control. Wild creatures, he had learned long ago, were highly empathic and many had abilities that bordered on what humans might call telepathy. They could feel thoughts and other such things and a sudden outburst of these feelings might just be enough to trigger a panic in them.

As he watched the buck drink Qorvas thought that it could be the buck's very last time at the peaceful lakeside. At this thought Qorvas felt a deep sadness for his four-legged brother and the urge to weep welled up in his chest. He thought of the discomfort his deer-brother must be in with his damaged leg and yet he also thought about the brilliance of life force which still burned ever so brightly in his furry chest. Qorvas felt ashamed of even thinking to take the life of this magnificent animal - even if it was done in reverence and done for food. He felt the connection with the buck as one might feel toward a much-loved sibling or friend.

His memory flashed back to the thought of another injured deer he had seen, years ago, while learning to hunt with his uncle Emmett. The deer in that case was much more crippled and in the end, taking him had been a mercy. Still, Qorvas had felt a powerful sense of guilt and sadness as the act of killing had been carried out. He had learned firsthand the incredible power of taking another life and the deep inherent responsibility that came with such acts.

'Taking life should never, ever be something that a person takes pleasure in,' his uncle had told him. *'It should never be satisfying or anything like that. It's an act of violence and of taking. You should always feel sadness and pain in your spirit when you kill.'*

The hand on his shoulder brought Qorvas back to the present and he saw that his friend, Raven, was looking at him with concern.

'You are pondering the kill, aren't you?' he said quietly. 'I can sense it in you and see it on your face.'

'Yes, I am,' Qorvas admitted. 'I feel shame in it.'

Raven's lips formed into a straight, grim line across his face. His eyes were hard.

'It is good that you feel emotion regarding this,' he said. 'Shame might be going overboard a bit so you might want to be a bit easier on yourself. You hunt to offer sacrifice, not only of your prey but also of yourself. The Elder Kin watch us as we do these things and they wait to see what kind of men we are. In order to live, every single being on this planet must in some way rely on the death of something else for food. This is the way of things.'

'I understand,' Qorvas replied. 'But as you know, understanding does not always make it any easier emotionally.'

Raven's expression softened.

'I understand what you mean,' he said. 'I am glad that I took you as a student. You have a clean spirit and a good heart. You take no pleasure in the kill.'

'No, I don't. I understand the need for the hunt, but I take no pleasure in killing my brothers.'

Raven nodded in understanding.

'We need to go,' he said, gesturing across the clearing, past the lake and toward the spot where the buck had entered the brush. 'Or we will lose our brother.'

'Maybe I'd be okay with that,' Qorvas said.

'Maybe I would too,' Raven replied. 'But the ritual has begun and we should see it through. If it is our destiny to complete the hunt, then that's what we will do. If not, then we will have learned valuable things from these days in the woods.'

The two men had again taken up the game trail and had followed their quarry throughout the day. The buck, despite his handicap, was still given to bursts of speed along the trail and had put considerable distance between them. Qorvas admired his spirit and understood that even if they did catch up with him today it was unlikely they would take the prey. The sun was rapidly falling in the west and he knew that Raven would never make a kill after dark.

Qorvas' prediction proved true and it wasn't long until Raven declared the hunt over for the night. Once again they found a small clearing off of the beaten path, pulled out their blankets and settled in for the night.

This time, however, the men did not immediately turn in and go straight to sleep. There seemed to be a restlessness in the air that kept them awake for some time despite the fact that they were both tired. At last, as the curtain of night enveloped the woods in black autumn softness, it found the two companions leaning up against the trunks of trees, quietly talking.

'I understand how you were feeling back there, wishae,' Raven's disembodied voice said out of the pitch of night. 'I was in that same headspace once and held onto it for a long, long time.'

'Did it ever go away?' Qorvas asked.

'It changed as my perspective changed,' Raven said. 'I began more and more to see the threads of wyrd that bind all of us together, and as I saw that I realized that like my quarry I too would one day be brought low by something or other. Maybe that something would be illness, maybe it would be an accident, maybe it would be a bullet or other violent thing, or maybe even it might be old age. What counts is that there are very few creatures in the worlds that are ageless. Human men die. All creatures that I know of here on the Middle-world die.'

'It is difficult,' Qorvas said from his place in the dark. 'I mean, logically I totally see what you are saying, but in my heart I always feel this deep sadness when I hunt or when I fish, when I take a life. Even when I buy meat at the store or when I harvest fruit or vegetables I realize that these fellow beings are giving their lives for me, so I can continue on.'

'Like I said, I am glad I took you as a student,' Raven said. 'You have a good heart. There is nothing wrong with feeling sad but you should also take that sadness and transform it into the deepest respect for those you take in order to live. When you honor them so deeply they know you for the true Warrior that you are.'

After a long moment of silence Qorvas spoke.

'I guess it's a work in progress.'

'Yes it is,' Raven said. 'Life is a very precious gift. Life and freedom. You honor both in the way that a good person should. You behave as a Thornsman should, or any true tribesman for that matter. I'm proud of you.'

'Thank you, Wataan,' Qorvas replied somewhat more formally. 'I do my best.'

'All true hunts are a sacred ritual,' Raven said. 'Those who don't see it as such are ignorant and foolish. There is deep imbalance in the heart of people who go out into the woods to hunt but see it as a sport or something to be done and gotten over with. When we hunt, we prepare ourselves, then we ask for permission. Following this we go out on the trail and apply our skills. We go hungry to show our need and we deeply revere the animals we take for our food. When we kill it is an act of deepest reverence and we thank the fallen for their sacrifice.'

'And this is not just a way we learned from Native people either.' Qorvas added. 'From what I've been taught this was probably also the way of our northern European ancestors from long ago, back when those tribal ancestors roamed the old country.'

'Yes.' Raven replied. 'Our tradition owes the First Nations people a lot though, because the Thornish tradition wasn't born in Europe. It was born here in North America and we had already lost a lot. Our friends helped us to get it back and we can never forget this.'

Qorvas said nothing from his place in the clearing. He had heard his teacher's words and knew that what was being said was very true.

'There is deep power and deeper magic in this primal act,' Raven said in a quiet, respectful, almost awe-filled voice. 'We are privileged to walk the Black Trail.'

The Black Trail is a concept within Thornish thought that describes the path of one who walks in a sacred way. It teaches that as primordial darkness is the source of all life, the path that the life energy takes is like a dark subterranean river. When lives interact and some are taken in the process this is seen as a sacred exchange; an exchange necessary for the continuation of life. Thornish thought takes this idea one step further when it discusses the ways of those who walk in the manner of Warriors.

Warriors and hunters are similar in that from time to time, in the execution of their duties, they may come into situations (more often than the people of other paths) where the taking of life is necessary. In the traditions of the Thornwood, when a person fully embraces the sacredness of the old ways, particularly when they are engaging in battle or the hunt, it is said that they walk the Black Trail.

In the case of Raven, who had, as the Thornish saying goes, *brought his own meat to the table,* he had brought his personal beliefs, that of the Old Gods and Goddesses of northern Europe, into his Warrior practice. A reverence for the Old Ones of Northern Europe had been very common amongst Thornish people from the beginning. Among the Thornish folk, while there is a core of agreed upon beliefs and understandings, there have been instances where initiates have 'flavored' their own Thornish path with their long held understandings of the cosmos.

Raven held a closeness with the old Germanic deities. He had been raised with them and had a deep connection with the ways of his northern European ancestors. When he had adopted the ways of the Black Talon Society as a younger man he discovered that the old ones of his youth easily found a home around the campfires of his new understandings. Raven already believed that the old Gods of the north were Elder Kin, ancient and powerful relations of vast intelligence and technological advancement, and so the matter of acclimating his beliefs took almost no effort at all.

The Thornish ways are, at their core, deeply primal and deeply animistic, yet there has been considerable color added into the traditions through the examples of a number of Masters who have adapted the way Raven did. Just as Raven had brought a powerful Germanic flavor to his own interpretation of the tradition, others such as Master Ciarán and Master Tiva had brought a taste of their own Celtic and Caribbean heritages into the mix.

As the venerable and eclectic Master Tiva had once said: *'You can put all the flavors you want in vanilla ice cream but at the end of the day it's still ice cream.'*

And so it was that those Masters who had adapted to the Thornish ways thusly often passed their particular cultural ambiance on to their students. Of course the students could personally adapt as they wished within reason, but a number carried on in the ways of their teachers. As long as the core of the Thornish beliefs were kept, no difficulties were experienced.

In the case of Qorvas, his own path through the Thornwood was somewhat similar to that of his teacher, although he tended to delve into the more primal mysteries and relied more on networking with local Otherfolk than working with the Elder Kin directly. As well, since Qorvas was the product of both European and Native American blood and culture his interface with the tribal was representative of this.

'You know well what I have to say about Ullr and the Black Trail, wishae,' Raven continued. 'When I am out here in the silence and the darkness of the forest, and especially when I am on the hunt, I can sense his presence, watching and guiding me.'

'I know,' said Qorvas. 'You have told me this and I certainly believe that you have an ally in him.'

Ullr is a particularly ancient northern God who was revered by people living in the northern and possibly central areas of Europe from prehistoric times. A guardian of the deep Earth and of the season of winter, Ullr is also an Elder Kinsman associated with the sacred hunt, of warding over sacred oaths and of single combat.

Raven had held a close association with Ullr ever since he was very young and had been introduced to the old ways by his paternal uncle. Indeed, Raven had a special harrow, or indoor altar, set up in his house to honor Ullr and a sacred space made of piled stones for the same purpose in the woods on his property. To Raven, Ullr was a very potent ally and a wise teacher. The Old One had assisted Raven on a good number of occasions and in return Raven had offered him deep reverence and long lasting loyalty.

'The Black Trail, the way of the Warrior and the sacred hunt, is the purview of the Master of Yew-Dale,' Raven said, using a kenning for Ullr. 'He watches over those who are loyal to him and he is never an easy teacher. He is uncompromising, stern and hard. Some think that he is without emotion or empathy but this is not true. He is one who has little time to waste on the weak or the foolish.'

'I hope he watches over you well, Wataan,' Qorvas said. 'It is good to have alliances with powerful Elder Kin.'

'Indeed, since you are my nashae, my student even now, I know he is watching over the both of us,' Raven replied. 'I have little doubt that old Yellow–eyes Coyote is out there too keeping an eye on you...keeping you out of trouble as they say.'

At that, Qorvas grinned in the darkness. It was true enough that he was a strong friend to the one people call Coyote. The Native trickster and teacher did not seem to fit with the Germanic flavor that Raven had brought to his teachings, but Qorvas was the product of the mingling of worlds. Since he had been a small boy, tutored by his maternal uncle to some degree, Qorvas had known his affinity for wolves, foxes and coyotes. Yet as he matured and came into his late teens the young man had come to know that the one who had long been watching over him was Coyote.

The Coyote that Qorvas knew was not the bumbling trickster that some groups of Native Americans told stories about. Nor was he the semi-suicidal, violent character often portrayed in children's cartoons. Rather, he was a shadowy teacher who gave up his lessons sparingly and even then always with work on the part of his pupils. Coyote was demanding but not in the way that Elders like Raven or Ullr were demanding. His teachings held a certain element of chaos blended with an almost childish playfulness that many adult human beings had great difficulty understanding.

From a very young age, Qorvas had experienced no such difficulty in comprehending either his ally or his teachings. Coyote and Qorvas were, from the beginning, much alike and so the mutual understanding between them came with relatively little strain.

Master Tiva, who was a somewhat playful character himself, had been very intrigued by the relationship held between Qorvas and the one he called 'Way-Way' or *'Old Uncle Coyote.'* While Tiva's Vörd (The Thornish term for one's primary guardian-teacher-ally) was Fox, he was close enough in personality to comprehend the relationship the sacred-trickster and Qorvas held. He had once jokingly referred to Coyote as a *candy-coated straight razor.* By this he was referring to Coyote's dangerous and quite often lethal primal side. Qorvas had understood the reference immediately and found it darkly amusing.

'I think we will get him tomorrow,' Raven said after a time sitting in silence. 'I know this country pretty well and I think we might have a shot if he ends up where I think he might.'

By having a shot, Qorvas knew that his teacher was referring to the immaculately kept rifle he kept in the moose-hide scabbard next to him. Other than their belt knives the aged Lee-Enfield rifle was their only hunting tool. A relic from the Second World War, this wood and steel long-gun was the only implement-of-the-hunt that they had brought along with them. Raven affectionately called the rifle *'Ol' Betsy'* and despite her weight was the only firearm he hunted with. Qorvas suspected that the inconvenience of having to carry around a gun that was at least twice the weight of a modern rifle was a part of the ordeal that Raven subjected himself to every time he hunted. He probably considered it to be part of the price he had to pay in sacrifice, to give of himself in the process of seeking to kill for food.

There was again a short silence during which Qorvas found himself wishing for a nice little campfire, and perhaps a tiny cup of coffee or herbal tea. Raven interrupted the fantasy with a question.

'Did you notice the sign I was examining earlier as we came back down into this valley?' he asked.

'Which one?' Qorvas answered. He had seen Raven stop on several occasions looking at sign and for the most part had taken the time to explain his discoveries to his student.

'The one higher up on that big cedar, where the tangle of roots crosses the trail.'

Qorvas remembered that one. The trail had suddenly dropped off somewhat between the boles of two very ancient red cedar trees and the younger man remembered thinking that the tangle of mixed roots just at the edge of the drop were one of the many reasons why it was unwise to travel the trails after dark. There could certainly have been a good chance at tripping there in that weave of tree-fingers.

Qorvas also recalled Raven stopping and examining a patch on the tree on the left hand side of the passage. He remembered that Raven had said little but told him he would have been glad for some wet weather; weather that might have made for the leaving of clear tracks.

'Yes I remember that,' Qorvas said. 'There was this big bear-rub there on the tree. Looked like it was maybe left there by a bear scratching himself.'

'I don't think it was a bear,' Raven said somewhat enigmatically. 'I think someone rubbed up against that tree, either deliberately or by accident, but I don't think it was a bear that did it.'

Now Qorvas was genuinely curious.

'What was it then?' he asked anxiously. 'Looked like fur to me.'

'I could be wrong about this, so let's wait and see what we find in the morning.'

Naturally Qorvas probed for more information but his teacher would say no more about it. Qorvas had learned that once Raven had decided to withhold something there was no way of getting it out of him until he was ready, if ever, to reveal it.

Shortly afterwards the two men became quiet and settled into their blankets for the night. Qorvas noted that this night was considerably colder than the last two had been. He wondered if the autumn was drifting into winter much sooner than expected this year.

The fourth day found the two men awakened early by a light misty rain that had come in from the east. Raven had grumbled something about being glad Ol' Betsy had been wrapped up for the night as it was *'really a bitch to get rust spots out of her old barrel.'*

Decamping did not take long, and after a very small bite of beef jerky and a swallow of berries and water, they were back on the faint game trail and heading north.

Qorvas was beginning to feel the days without a proper meal taking their toll. He found himself hoping that indeed they would bag their quarry on this day so that they could begin the process of taking the meat home.

The two had been walking and carefully following the signs before them for the better part of half a day when suddenly both of them froze in place. The sounds of a tremendous crashing had come echoing through the trees, sending hundreds of bird flying and the creatures of the underbrush to become instantly still and silent. It sounded to Qorvas almost as though there was a great battle of some kind going on in the forest ahead of them; a battle that was not taking place with steel weapons or firearms but rather a physical combat between large bodies crashing in the brush.

At last, seemingly as suddenly as it had begun, there was a sudden, high pitched cry in the air. It did not come from any human throat that Qorvas had ever heard before. The sudden cry ended abruptly and the crashing seemed to cease, leaving the forest in a deep, almost unnatural state of silence.

He looked to where Raven was still frozen in a half crouch near a large Douglas fir tree and saw that his teacher had not grabbed for either his rifle or his belt knife. Finally, Raven took Ol' Betsy from the scabbard across his back – ever so slowly – and then motioned for Qorvas to follow quietly.

At first Qorvas had imagined, from the volume of the commotion they had heard, that the conflict would be close by, possibly even right around the bend in the trail they were approaching. Yet as they traveled with extra stealth along the path he realized that the battle must be a considerable distance away. Raven did not hesitate and moved forward with a grace that belied his nearly seventy years in the Middle World. He seemed to be perceiving signs along the way that Qorvas, even though well trained, could not detect and the younger man began thinking that quite possibly his teacher was using senses beyond the norm to guide him.

179

At last, without any prior indication, Raven veered off into the brush at the side of the trail and radically slowed to a slow-moving crouch. He was stalking now with his knees bent low and his torso slightly bent forward at the waist.

Qorvas stepped off the trail as well and slowed his pace, following his teacher as best he could without disturbing the silent modality that his teacher had entered.

Curiously enough it was at this time that Qorvas dissociated somewhat from what was going on and began pondering in his mind why he still thought of and referred to Raven as his teacher. According to tradition once a Thornish person had undertaken the Deepening to become initiated, the one who had taken on the task of teaching them until that point was no longer strictly a teacher but rather termed a Mentor. Once a person was given their tribal name and considered an initiate it was up to them if they wished to continue having a teacher-student relationship, though most elected to continue. The teaching relationship at this point changed and the relationship became less formal and more collegial in nature.

Qorvas shook his head and dismissed the semantics of the thing from his mind. He realized that his body had been silently stalking along behind Raven despite his inward dalliance, and that amused him somewhat.

Raven signaled him to come in behind him as he rounded a massive, rotting stump. Qorvas did as instructed and followed his teacher around and down-slope somewhat as the incline brought them to the side of a great, downed Douglas fir tree covered in moss.

Qorvas noted that even though the sounds of the great commotion had ended some time earlier, the natural sounds of the forest had not yet returned. This was odd because in most cases the natural rhythms of the small creatures did not often wait for long periods before going back to their natural flow.

There was something else too: Qorvas had detected an odd scent in the air yet it was very faint and he could not quite put his finger on what it might be.

'As I said, this will be a powerful moment, wishae,' Raven said. 'When we go past this log I want you to be very alert and pay strict attention. Focus. Don't drift. Be open to all you might see. Let your Coyote teachings guide you.'

All Qorvas could do was nod in agreement. He had no idea why his teacher had shifted gears in the way he had, but he knew from numerous experiences that his older friend and oath-sworn Hearth-brother was gifted with senses and abilities that few other men possessed. As well, there was a strong sense of trust between the two men. In the Thornish tradition this is known as Kin-Trust, and it is something that must truly be experienced to be understood properly.

'Okay, off we go,' Raven said. And, taking up his rifle in one hand he swept to his feet and swung around the end of the fallen tree.

Qorvas got up and followed.

The space beyond the tree continued down-slope and Qorvas could see that the landscape all around for a good distance formed a kind of shallow bowl-shaped depression in the ground. Here there were considerably more fallen needles and leaves littering the ground and as they moved it was considerably more difficult to do so without making any noise. Still Qorvas tried his best and kept up with his friend as they descended the gentle slope.

Finally, after using tree after tree as both a stop and a barrier the two hunters made it down to the very bottom of the slope. The last of the brush was gone from the area and the central part of the great woodland bowl was clear to see.

Qorvas stopped short as he rested against the trunk of the final tree before the space cleared out. He blinked in amazement several times before doing anything else and found himself wishing dearly that that he had brought along a rifle for himself.

The clearing at the bottom of the slope was somewhat flat and largely devoid of any debris. With the exception of a portion of moss-covered boulder that emerged from near the center of the clearing the area was devoid of underbrush or any other kind of growth that one might expect. Dried autumn leaves and the fallen needles of coniferous trees littered the floor of the space but not much else...and it looked as though an elephant had charged straight across it and off again into the woods on the other side.

There were huge scrapes in the ground that bit through the leaf cover and into the dark ground beneath as well as broken bits of branches probably dragged in from the perimeter. The very feeling of the place made Qorvas certain that this had indeed been the location where the commotion they had heard had happened.

There was blood spattered all over the place; on the leaf cover, on the surrounding soil and on the brown, black and green surface of the ancient protruding boulder. Bits of what appeared to be hair or fur were scattered all over the place and as he got closer Qorvas could see that this hair and blood seemed to be most concentrated near the waist-high rock in the center area. He noticed as well that there was more blood as well as hair smeared along the path that had been scraped through the clearing and up the far slope to disappear into the brush and trees beyond. The rich, metallic scent of blood combined with the dank musk of wet fur and soil, made the atmosphere nearly overpowering. There was another scent too; it was something that Qorvas couldn't remember ever having experienced before. It was exotic, primal, heavy and the scent of it stood his neck hair up on end for reasons he couldn't fathom.

And there in the midst of the aftermath of this chaos, the thing that had immediately caught the young hunter's attention, froze his blood and locked in his imagination, was the object that lay upon the rounded mossy top of the boulder. It was the entire rear leg, from hoof to rump, of what had once been a rather large deer.

Qorvas also realized now what the unusual smell was that he had detected earlier was fading. Earlier it had been very strong but now it was disappearing fast.

'Stay where you are for a minute, wishae,' Raven said, and deftly walked around the perimeter of the clearing.

Qorvas had absolutely no problem with that. He remained stock still and took in the scene before him. It was as though two (or more) very large creatures had fought for supremacy here in this ordinarily quiet little place…and one had emerged victorious. The other, well most of him anyway, had been carried off with the victor.

It was obvious that the deer had lost the conflict and it seemed certain to Qorvas that this had been the very same deer they had been stalking over these last days. What was eerily uncertain to him though, was the nature of whatever it was that had taken the buck and then had left, almost as an offering, this large portion of meat sitting there on the top of the boulder. Surely it was not a bear that had done this. Qorvas had seen bear kills before and they had been nothing like this.

Finally, Raven completed his inspection of the perimeter and left up-slope toward where the rest of the deer (he assumed) had been dragged. He paused for a moment up there, looking down the trail, still within sight of his student, and then returned to join his companion.

Raven's expression was very serious now as he looked at the boulder that stood, half buried in the dirt, in the center of the clearing. He examined the large haunch of deer leg as it sat perched on the top of the stone but did not touch it.

'So, Coyote, what do you think happened here?' he asked at last, deadly serious.

Qorvas hesitated only a moment before speaking.

'It's pretty obvious this is the source of the commotion we heard earlier,' he replied. 'It looks to me like something quite big jumped our buck here, killed it and then went off into the bush on the other side there with most of the meat.'

Raven was still circling the boulder with its dripping prize, examining it in detail as he did so. 'Anything else?' he asked his young companion.

'I can't for the life of me explain why whoever it was would leave this big haunch of the deer here on this rock, but what I will say is that whoever made this kill must have done it with a bow or something like that. Otherwise we would have heard a gunshot.'

Now Raven was crouching down near the end portion of the deer leg, observing it closely.

'You are close, little brother, but I will tell you straight up now that it was no bow that did this. This four-legged brother was killed by someone who took it down by hand. Only after he was passed off to the spirit-world did they cut him up. I imagine they did the cutting with a stone tool of some kind.'

Qorvas was incredulous.

'Stone tools? What, are we dealing with Fred Flintstone here?'

Raven gestured for his companion to come closer.

'Look at where this bone is cut,' he instructed. 'See how it was chopped? How the bone and the meat gave way to the tool? See the fineness of the grooves? No knife did that.'

'Maybe an axe?'

Raven straightened up.

'Maybe it was an axe, yes,' he replied, 'but I am fairly certain that it was not a metal axe that was used to cut this meat.'

Qorvas was confused. He had a very quizzical look on his face to which his teacher asked: 'What would Coyote think?'

Qorvas reached down within himself, to his primal core and opened up to the urgings of pure instinct. In his experience this was the place from which his Vörd most often chose to communicate with him, besides in Visions and dreams.

'Whoever it was, was hungry and they made the kill quick with whatever tools they had. Whoever did this must have been a good tracker, silent and really, really fast because even crippled this buck would have been way faster than any man would have been. When they had killed the deer they took what they needed. And left.'

Raven nodded. He walked over a bit from the boulder, found a space on the leaves and needles which was clear of blood, and set down his small pack. He then took Ol' Betsy, un-chambered the round that had been in her breech, and returned the rifle to her scabbard.

'But what does your Coyote friend think? Dig deep for the pure communication, not the logical thoughts.'

Qorvas' head snapped up and he looked at his friend carefully.

'What happened to the guts?' he said suddenly.

Raven nodded again, this time with a grim smile on his face.

'Yes,' he said, holding the 's' sound of the word slightly longer than usual so that it produced a satisfied hiss. 'Why do you think that was?'

'Because they wanted to use everything, Native style?' Qorvas answered.

'Again you are correct,' he said. 'And why is it, do you think, that out of the entire carcass we have been cheated out of, there is only this last rather choice cut of meat sitting here on this rock?'

To this Qorvas had no answer. He shrugged and held his arms out in frustration.

'I have no idea,' he said.

'Perhaps I can help you out in that regard my friend,' Raven said. 'Go around the other side of the boulder, to the spot where the leg bone was cut, and tell me what you see there.'

Qorvas did as he was told and walked over to the spot that had been indicated. What he saw there sent a sudden chill up his spine.

'Did you put that there?' he asked, hoping that the answer would be in the affirmative but yet dreading that it would not. He had seen the symbol that had been scrawled there on the side of the boulder before, though in the past it had not been so crudely scrawled, nor painted in deer blood.

The drawing he saw there before him in the rapidly drying fluid was in essence a bind-rune. It consisted of a simple arrow shape pointing vertically upwards and the shaft of the thing running downwards in a straight line to end in another rune, a three-pronged rune, tines downward, that was known as the Yr rune. Interestingly though Qorvas saw that above the point of the arrow tip, otherwise known by some as Tiwaz, was a crudely scrawled circle, also inscribed in the lifeblood of the prey. Qorvas had indeed seen this symbol before.

'Where have you seen that symbol before?' Raven asked without answering Qorvas' question.

'On the stone altar behind your house,' Qorvas replied. 'Painted in red on that big flat piece of granite behind your offering space, but the one painted behind your house is a lot neater looking than this one.'

Raven nodded his head.

'No, I did not put that there in front of you, to answer your question, but I find it very interesting that someone did,' Raven said. 'It confirms something that I have suspected for some time; that certain kinds of folk have been visiting my property and satisfying their curiosity as to what I do around home.'

'Who would that be?'

'Whoever took this buck from under our noses, that's who. Same people.'

Qorvas' brows furrowed and his face took on an angry expression. He had begun to imagine that perhaps someone they knew had followed them into the bush and was now playing some kind of sick joke on them. To Qorvas the hunt was very sacred and as much as he himself enjoyed a good joke or trick he also knew that the hunt was no time or place for such antics.

'Are you suggesting that someone we know is being an asshole?' he said, loud enough for anyone in nearby earshot to hear. 'Because if that's the case I'm going to kick someone in the head.'

'Do you honestly think that this was done by anyone *you* know?' Raven asked, seemingly gleaning his student's thoughts. 'That somehow they managed to follow us without my knowing about it, or doing this without using a gun or a bow?'

Qorvas shook his head.

'No, I guess not,' he admitted. 'Probably the only people I know who could sneak around you in the bush and not be detected would be my grandfather or my uncle.'

'Precisely,' Raven replied. 'No, this is not a joke, my friend. What this is, for you, is a supreme moment of understanding. It is a moment where doorways you might not have known were there, are suddenly opened for you – if you dare to look inside.'

Qorvas stood silently, looking at Raven with an intense curiosity but said nothing.

Raven let him wait on silence for a few moments before speaking and when he did the words that came out of his mouth cause Qorvas' jaw to drop slightly.

'Okay, I would like you to get that cloth game bag out of your pack and wrap up this piece of meat. Wrap it twice and put it in the larger canvas bag. We can take turns carrying it or maybe I'll just let you handle it for the trip back since I am already carrying Betsy.'

'We are…we are going to take it?' Qorvas finally blurted out. 'We are going to just take it?'

Raven looked up from where he was adjusting the strap of his rifle sling.

'Of course we are going to take it,' he replied. 'To refuse an offering would be…well, it would be rude.'

'What!?' Qorvas' frustration had by now caused him to lose his usual respectful manner and he was now looking at his teacher in absolute bewilderment. 'Sorry, bro, but you have me really confused here now.'

Raven finished what he was doing and walked over to Qorvas. He put his hand on his student's shoulder in a fatherly way and looked into his eyes.

'This was an offering,' he said quietly enough. 'A gift. It was left here because the ones who took this buck knew we were already hunting him. They must have needed the meat more but they remembered their manners and left us a choice portion for our own uses. These ones are tribal people and they are pretty good at making sure that we don't see them very often. I'd bet that they can even out-sneak the best human woodsmen. They are very, very good. I admire them.'

The side of Qorvas' mouth turned upward in the slightest smirk at hearing this.

'My Coyote side says that it is good that people out here have manners,' he said semi-sarcastically. 'I'd rather not be on the bad side of something or someone who can rip a full grown deer in half with their bare hands.'

'Yes, they do have manners of a sort,' Raven replied. 'And after all since they took the trouble to leave that mark, they were quite literally addressing the gift to me.'

'I am pretty blown away by this,' Qorvas said.

'I have been suspicious for quite a while now that there are times when I have been making offerings that I was being watched but I could never confirm that. I think maybe they are curious about my spiritual rites and that is where whomever left this gift for us saw the bind rune. I use it to represent Ullr on my offering place both in my yard and elsewhere. Now it all makes sense.'

'Maybe to you it does,' Qorvas said. 'I wonder why I have not met these mysterious Indians or why my grandpa never mentioned them to me.'

'In all my years here I have never met one either. This is the very closest I have ever come to it and I am pleased that they like me enough to show respect in this way. Perhaps something will come out of this little adventure and we might see them around one day. Oh, and they are not Indians. Not in the way you are thinking anyway.'

'Who are they then?' Qorvas asked earnestly enough. 'If you don't mind telling me, since they have pretty much blown our whole hunting trip.'

'I bet Coyote sees this as a gift rather than a failure,' Raven said coolly. 'You need to open yourself up to his teachings more than you have been. A powerful thing has happened here and we have not only been permitted to experience it but we have been gifted as well. Think about what I have taught you about the Black Trail. This is what it's all about, wishae; it's all about making contact with the primal, the visceral, and the deeply magical.'

Qorvas nodded his head. When he lifted his eyes to regard his teacher again he had a crafty grin on his face.

'So I guess at the end of all this we can finally get something solid to eat when we get back, eh?'

Raven smiled back.

'Good. That's Coyote talking.'

'Seriously though, I really want to know. Who are these people?'

'I'm sorry that your grandfather never told you about them and I guess I mistakenly thought he had. He used to call them the Moon Brothers. That little red circle you saw on the boulder, the one above the bind rune? That, as far as I know now, is their sign. I don't think they have reading or writing so whoever left us the note there was working from memory.'

'The Moon Brothers?' Qorvas said with a wave of realization suddenly washing over him. Indeed, his grandfather had told him stories of these people though he had never imagined he would ever have contact with them. The tales his grandfather had told were stories of hunters and trappers getting rare glimpses of them while out deep in the woods or even sometimes in the mountains. They were massive people, covered mostly in dark, thick hair, who had lived in the wild places since times immemorial. Grandpa had told him that they were relations to humankind but whose ancestors had taken a different path from man, choosing the wild and primal ways over the modern ones. Sometimes, he was told, people had helped these distant cousins, but for the most part it had been these other ones who had, from time to time, helped people in their times of need. It was said that they were generally kind and gentle, although there were stories where men had gotten too close to their homes or had done disrespectful things and had paid the price.

Qorvas' grandfather had called these people the Moon Brothers because it was said that they preferred to come out during the times when the full moon glowed brightly over the trees of the deep forests. Some had even suggested that the Moon Brothers had certain spiritual practices which they preferred to hold during the light of the moon.

It all came together in Qorvas' head right there and then and he shook his head at the thought of it all. He wondered if his grandfather had ever had any direct experiences with these mysterious people even though he could not remember him specifically saying that he had. Perhaps if he had, the experience might have been so powerful that Grandpa might have kept it to himself. Now that Qorvas' grandfather had returned to the spirit-world the younger man suspected that he might never know for sure.

Qorvas walked over and set his pack down, heedless of the drying fluid that was splashed on the needles and leaves. From the inner bag he pulled out the cloth bags that Raven had mentioned and began to wrap the large haunch of meat. When he was done he tied a cord to it much like a sling and set it next to his backpack.

When he was done he turned to see what his teacher was doing and saw that Raven was standing near the boulder. The older man had one hand on the stone and was gazing off toward the space that the deer had been dragged into. Qorvas wondered upon seeing this, if perhaps the other hunter or hunters who had taken the deer were lurking out there, watching them, or if perhaps they had simply gone their way to get the meat home...wherever home was for them.

At last Raven took from his pocket a small plastic bag and dumped the contents on top of the boulder where the haunch of meat had once been. He then waved toward the direction he had been gazing and Qorvas imagined that he was waving farewell just in case someone had indeed been watching.

He walked to where Qorvas was standing and hoisted his pack and rifle.

'We should get going,' he said. 'There are no doubt a good many of our four-legged relations around here who can smell this place and will be wanting to check it out. We'll take a straighter route back and should be a good distance from here by the time the sun sets.'

'Fine by me,' Qorvas said, still somewhat numb from the whole experience. 'By the way, if you don't mind my asking, what kind of offering did you leave there?'

Raven smiled as kind of guilty smile. It reminded Qorvas of the kind of expression a little boy might have had when he had been caught with his hand in the cookie jar.

'Hard candy,' he said. 'I always carry some just in case of emergency you know. Every once in a while I leave some in various places as an offering because I think there are those who like such things.'

Now it was Qorvas' turn to play the role of the strict adult.

'Not good for the teeth,' he said, but his stern visage quickly softened into a grin.

'No, not very good for the body, but good for the mood I think,' Raven said. 'When we get back I will be offering some of this meat up to Ullr as I am sure you can appreciate.'

'I have no doubt that you will,' Qorvas replied.

'It's important to reciprocate a gift with a gift,' Raven continued. 'Ullr has guided me many times over many a year and has taken the time to teach me when I needed to be taught. Part of my skill in the woods comes directly from his mentoring.'

'Balance as always, is very important,' Qorvas replied. 'That I understand completely. I wonder if you will ever have mysterious people watching again you as you do your rituals out back there.'

Raven started up the slope along the way they had come into the clearing and as he did so he turned to look at his student. There was a wistful smile on his face.

'Hey, you know, any time they want to they are welcome to come and visit,' he replied. 'In fact they are always welcome to join me.'

Qorvas watched his teacher hike up the incline and a moment later he followed him. He thought about what Raven had just said and, knowing his older friend as he did, he had absolutely no doubt the invitation he had just made was authentic.

Qorvas chanced one last turn of his head toward the boulder in the clearing as he rose to the top of the slope, and as he did so he could see the glitter of the hard sugar candies sitting there on the top. He wondered if indeed one of the Moon Brothers would come back into that clearing later on and take the gift that had been left there for them. He wondered if they would actually like the candy or if they would marvel at how things that looked like small colored rocks could taste so good.

He turned his attention back to the trail and took to following the path through the brush that Raven had made in front of him. He knew that it would be a long, hard push if they were to get a reasonable distance from this place by nightfall, and like Raven, Qorvas had no interest in spending the night discouraging foxes, bears or coyotes and maybe even wolves from coming by to investigate the deer meat they had.

Once again the image of a big, hair-covered Moon Brother sitting and enjoying the taste of the rock candy flashed into his mind as he walked. He smiled at the thought and realized that when he had arisen that morning he would never have been able to predict what would happen that day.

'Candy is bad for the teeth,' he said to himself as he smiled and walked.

'What was that?' came Raven's query from up ahead.

That guy has the ears of a fox,' Qorvas thought to himself.

'Nothing,' he said out loud. 'I didn't say anything.'

'Well, get a move on, wishae,' the older man said. 'We are racing the sun.'

9

The Bladed Key

'The Way of the Warrior is that of the Bladed Key: An instrument of fate thrust intentionally into the locked doors of destiny. Turned with will and discipline, the Bladed key opens chambers of power and wisdom.' - Master Qorvas

At the base of high glacier topped mountains, at the foot of primally deep green forests, along the shores of an ancient river, two men sat in a camp around a small yet cheery fire. All around them the land was awash with the heavy rain of an autumn storm and the two were comforted by the fact that a day earlier they had constructed a shelter for themselves that was built up against the mouth of the shallow cave they were now camping in. A natural ledge, which protruded out of the rock wall above the cave opening, combined with a structure of carefully arranged sticks and brush, had further protected the men and their little fire from the assault of the hammering rain.

The two men, dressed for the woods in water resistant jackets, woolen trousers and sturdy boots, were very much at home in such places as this – especially the older of the two, who had spent more time in the wild than many. The younger man, one barely past his mid-twenties, was a relatively new student in the tradition the older man practiced, and he listened with keen ears to the story the older man was telling him.

'And to this day no one really knows what became of that old Master,' Qorvas continued as he took the now-boiling steel pot off of the fire with a forked branch. 'One day two younger fellows went looking for him at his house and the place was completely empty. Not only that but the place looked as though it had not been occupied for years. There were vines growing in through the windows and there was even a barn owl living in the rafters of the roof.'

The younger man nodded and sat there for a moment, pondering what Qorvas had said. Qorvas looked at him for a moment and realized that once, long ago he too had looked somewhat like the young fellow seated by the fire. Qorvas too had sported his hair long, though his companion's hair was yellow blonde and Qorvas' hair in its prime had been a dark cedar-brown. Like Qorvas in his youth, his young companion was also working valiantly on a mustache, though it was still rather wispy and fine, no doubt to the endless consternation of its grower. The two men, younger and older, were of similar average build and Qorvas saw that it was there that the physical similarities were the greatest.

The Thornsman sighed inwardly and thought for a second about the magic of youth, yet he also understood that considerable power and understandings were available only to those, like himself, who had been around the proverbial block a few times.

'Maybe he had left much earlier and no one had noticed?' the younger man suggested. 'You did say that his house was off of a relatively isolated road into the mountains.'

Qorvas took the small, steaming pot and set it down carefully on a nearby flat stone. He then took a tin cup and dipped some of the hot water out, using it to fill two of the three metal cups that sat there. Herbs bubbled to the top and filled the small space with the aroma of mint and spices.

Qorvas gestured to the cups, indicating that the younger man take a cup.

'Careful, these metal cups can get pretty hot.'

The younger man took the cup and held it up so that he could smell the brew. He sniffed appreciatively.

'We were discussing Master Tiva,' the younger man prompted, as though for some reason Qorvas had forgotten.

Qorvas had certainly not forgotten and his curiously raised eyebrow caught the student's attention.

'Sometimes we can take a second or so for a detour and not lose track of what we were saying,' Qorvas said. 'And besides, I am not exactly ancient, you know.'

'Sorry.'

'No need to be sorry, just be more observant. A person's eyes and body language can teach you much if you pay attention.'

For a moment there was no more talk. The two men sat in silence before the brightly dancing fire, savoring the cups of tea in their hands and simply appreciating the storm.

'What you suggest—that he could have moved out earlier and not had anyone notice—is a good supposition, but unfortunately for your theory it was not the case,' Qorvas said. 'One of Tiva's students, Wolf, went up there about a week after he was last seen. Wolf often did that, just to see if Tiva needed anything. The fact is that when they arrived there, there was no sign that anyone had lived there in maybe years. A good number of people were quite blown away by that I can tell you. Of course there were also those of us who weren't in the least bit surprised.'

The young man, whose tribal name was Wulfgar, raised an eyebrow and peered at Qorvas across the fire for a moment, saying nothing.

'I have heard that,' he said finally. 'Björn told me a bit of the story. He told me that Master Tiva had warned certain people that he would be leaving.'

'This is quite true,' Qorvas said. 'After the passing of Master Raven, Tiva, who was quite close to Raven and considerably older, told a number of us that he was planning to go to the mountains. He told us that he was getting weary of the Middle World.'

'So he went to the mountains as in went on a trip or Doqqa 'Vor?' Wulfgar asked.

Qorvas smiled grimly. 'He did not specifically say Doqqa 'Vor. However, I know that he was getting tired of the world and tired of people. He was eighty or so, don't forget. He had been around the block a few times.'

In Thornish culture, the term Doqqa 'Vor refers to the ceremonies surrounding the end of physical life here in the Middle-World. It is considered to be greatly honorable that a Thornish person has some say in the manner of his or her passing. As we know that at least physically we have no control over the circumstances of our birth and some early periods of our human lives, it is desired that we will exercise some control over our adult lives and certainly the manner of our passing.

In the ways of the Doqqa 'Vor it is not considered honorable to die the death of a coward or the thing known as a straw-death. The straw-death or bed-death is where one dies of a disease in a bed. Slow, wasting deaths in hospitals are considered to be almost worse than anything else. It is considered weak and is most undesirable among Thornish people. Thornish people do not think in the same way as most modern folk do concerning these things. They adhere to the understandings of the First Law, the law of nature and the cosmos. As such there are a number of ways in which a Thornsman or Thornswoman might find an honorable death. The first is the *Long Walk*. In such a case a person who is preparing to die, whether this is from disease, old age or some other reason, just walks away into the wilderness, there to meditate and commune with nature until their physical end comes.

The second way of the Doqqa 'Vor is known as the *Way-of-Striving*. It is also known as the way of battle. To end one's life in the act of doing something worthy or even in combat, is considered a great honor, especially if one's death is taken while striving for something worthwhile. To die in a glorious fashion, in a way that may be spoken or sung about, is a passing of great honor indeed.

The third way is known as the Way of the Knife. In this way a Thornish person terminates his or her own physical existence through the use of a bladed implement of some kind. Such a passing as this, it should be noted, has never occurred in the living memory of the tradition, nor is it recommended to anyone. ***Only a fool scorns the gift of life***, as it is said, and the taking of any life, including one's own, is a very serious matter indeed. The way of the Long Walk is seen to hold much greater honor and even then it is done only in very special circumstances by fully initiated people who are of stable mind and who are well versed in the Thornish traditional ways. Life is considered to be an exceptionally sacred gift and for someone to take it lightly and simply use a sacred ritual to 'escape,' as it were, rather than to fight, is not considered honorable.

As has been mentioned, the ways of Thornish people are primal and close to the land. They are not the ways of most modern folk and it has never been the mission of the people of the Thornwood to convince anyone outside the traditions of the validity of Thornish ways. They are the traditions and they have served for many years.

In the case of Master Tiva, he had never specifically said he was going to perform the Doqqa 'Vor or any other such ceremony, nor did he ever say that he was going on the Long Walk. All he said was that he was tired of the modern world and that he was probably going to go to the mountains.

'So he may have simply moved away and not made much of a fuss about it,' Wulfgar added as a suggestion.

Qorvas grinned somewhat cryptically.

'Well he certainly did move away, that's for certain.'

'But the condition of the house?' Wulfgar said. 'He used to have it so neat and clean. I mean it was full of stuff. Plants, jars of mysterious stuff, decorations, masks and weapons, but it was always well kept. It was a very cool place.'

'How do you know this?' Qorvas asked.

'Björn told me.'

'Ah,' Qorvas said. 'You know all this happened some time ago. It is not something new.'

'I am just really...mystified about how one lone old man can disappear like that and then the house kind of comes apart as if no one has been there for years.'

Qorvas took a long moment before saying anything else. He tentatively sipped his tea and found that it was still far too hot to drink. He felt the sting of the metal cup edge as it lightly burned his tongue and inwardly chuckled. He should have heeded the same warning he had given only moments earlier to Wulfgar about hot cups.

'You are Shakai now, Wulfgar,' Qorvas said at last. 'You are now a Seeker. You are an initiate and you are expected to know a thing or two at this stage in the game.'

'I'd like to think I do know a few things,' Wulfgar said, slightly smiling but still unsure of the meaning behind Qorvas' words.

For a second or so more, Qorvas sat there by the fire, looking at Wulfgar with his piercing green eyes and somewhat stern visage partly hidden under his reddish-brown goatee.

'You are well aware of the fact that Tiva was of the Farers, right?'

Qorvas asked after he had allowed the student to sit uncomfortably for a moment more.

'Yes, I know he was of the Farers.'

'And I am sure your Wataan has told you that among the Farers there are individuals who possess very special skills and abilities? Some who could perhaps be called sorcerers or Medicine-people or something like that?'

Wulfgar hesitated only for a moment before nodding in the affirmative. He didn't say anything but Qorvas could tell the younger man was busy processing information in his head. Finally, he spoke.

'You mean sorcerer, like old Augustus from the stories, or Agnarr or Black Coyote, right?'

Qorvas smiled.

'And I know your relation with Black Coyote,' Wulfgar said. 'He was also your grandfather. Raven was your Wataan, your teacher.'

'Yes,' Qorvas said, continuing to smile. The smile remained but the eyes behind it were a little frosty for Wulfgar's taste.

'Did you actually know Augustus or Agnarr?'

'No, they were before my time, just as there are some who were before your time,' Qorvas replied. 'Though our tradition is not really that old, we have been around long enough to establish a timeline of sorts.'

Now it was Qorvas' turn to ask questions. 'Tell me, Shakai, what, in your understanding, is a Farer?'

Wulfgar realized he might be being tested. He straightened himself up and looked over at Qorvas who was patiently awaiting an answer.

'A Farer is a person with a particular focus, here in the tradition,' he said. 'We have the Warriors, and we have others among whom are the Farers. Farers are people who have talents and interests in things like herbalism, healing, oracular work, crafting and things of a kind of magical nature.'

Qorvas nodded.

'Good,' he said. 'And you know that Tiva was probably one of the greatest Farers of all.'

'He was a man of Var too,' Wulfgar added, to impress Qorvas perhaps a little more.

Var the Far-Farer was the name given to a primordially ancient Elder Kinsman known for his many travels, his hunger for knowledge and his expertise in the ways that many might call magical practice. Though the term 'Var' was of mysterious origin it was thought to mean 'far' or 'distant', in reference to the travelling nature of that old spirit-person. Even though there was a Norse Goddess who was also named Var, this was seen as a separate thing and unrelated to the Thornish use of the word. Over the years, some Thornish people had come to equate the Far-Farer with the Norse God, Odin. Others considered him to be something other than that; perhaps a different form of spirit-person or ancient ally. All Thornish people agreed, however, that the Far-Farer was a powerful role model.

'And do you think that perhaps Master Tiva, with his advanced knowledge of the many worlds, with his understanding of the use of power and his relationship with the Far-Farer, might have had a few tricks up his sleeve when it comes to moving a household?'

Qorvas was silent a moment and watched what he had said sink in with the student.

'Wow,' Wulfgar said after a moment or so. 'I guess that's why some of the old guys weren't so surprised by what happened.

'One of the things that will eventually sink in with you, Wulfgar, is that the way of the Thornwood is about a lot more than a gathering of people who have forged a unique culture and who strive to re-connect with the old ways. We are what the great Qor called a *Rekindling*; a rebuilding of something greater from a few primal sparks. We and others like us represent what humanity is supposed to be, not the pathetic wrecks that so-called modern western civilization has produced.

'Modern civilization, and I use that term very loosely, has produced some really amazing things but for the most part much has been lost during the two-thousand-year-long experiment of monotheism. Much has been lost forever but much is also recoverable. One of the things we are recovering here is the wide-eyed wonder of comprehending the real magic in the world; the real energy that exists right in front of us. Most are blind to this but we are not...and we are reawakening every day.'

'So what Tiva did was no big deal then?' Wulfgar asked.

'Not so much, no,' Qorvas replied. 'Because to those of us who know, the world is a much more complex place than others might think. It is far deeper, far more mysterious and far more imbued with power than even we can fathom. Master Tiva simply stepped sideways and was gone. Where he went no one here in the Middle World knows, but we do know that he went there with intent. We do not mourn his loss but instead we teach his lessons, tell his stories and do what we can to honor his name.'

'So, we are a Rekindling then?'

'Yes my young friend, we are a Rekindling,' Qorvas replied, tossing another small stick in the fire. 'We are but one stick of firewood in a much bigger blaze. There are more and more gatherings such as ours appearing every day. Some have been hidden and silent for hundreds of years, if not more. Others have always been visible. Regardless of this, what is happening is that the Elder Kin, the spirit folk, and the very world herself have begun allowing us to re-awaken. The world-killers and spirit-crushers for many generations worked very hard to extinguish our spark but they failed. Now we are slowly coming back, building a great bonfire with many other people, many of them Pagan like us. Eventually the blaze of that great bonfire will burn away the filth and lies of the last many years.'

Qorvas noticed that although the rain had certainly not let up, it had slowed down somewhat. He attempted another tentative sip of his tea and found at last that he could drink it without char-broiling his tongue. The cool autumn weather had certainly been of assistance in that regard.

'Björn has spent a lot of time telling me much the same kinds of things,' Wulfgar said.

'Good,' Qorvas said. 'It's his job as your teacher; your Wataan.'

Suddenly a dark shape appeared from the bushes directly across from where Wulfgar and Qorvas were seated. The shape came closer until both of them could easily see the man who had emerged, stripped to the waist, barefoot and swaggering towards them in the rain.

'Who has been speaking my name?' he roared good naturedly.

And indeed, the voice of Björn Hammarson, gravelly and hoarse, certainly matched his barbaric appearance. A man of average height, Björn made up for it with his well-muscled upper body. The multitude of tribal tattoos and his plentiful gray hair and beard did not take away from the somewhat savage appearance.

Qorvas grinned as he saw his friend and Hearth-Brother walking across the clearing toward them. Naturally, he was soaking wet from a dip in the river.

'Did you have a nice swim?' Qorvas asked.

Björn smiled brightly.

'Of course!' he declared 'It's a perfect day for a man to go swimming.'

He looked at his student sitting by the fire. 'It's a good day for a man to go swimming, not sitting about sipping tea like an old grandmother,' he said. But the bright smile remained and Wulfgar knew his teacher was only playing around.

Björn walked over toward the shelter and when he had passed underneath it he almost immediately began removing his clothes.

'Hey, don't get any of that water on me, trickster!' Qorvas said, leaning so as to avoid the drips of water streaming from his soaking-wet friend.

'Who is the joker here? Not me! I am not the one who tied his brother's boot laces together last week,' Björn laughed.

Qorvas tried to retain a straight face but could not. After a moment he snickered.

'Worked pretty good too. You fell flat on your face.'

'Lucky it was in the bushes and not on rocks or something.' Björn disappeared into the back of the shelter and began rummaging around in his pack for dry clothes.

'Did you really tie his laces together?' Wulfgar asked.

'What can I say?' Qorvas smiled, shrugging his shoulders. 'I am the grandson of a dark trickster. Sometimes I can't help myself. Goes with the territory.'

A few minutes later Björn re-emerged in dry pants and a red and black flannel shirt. He dropped down by the fire on the other side of Wulfgar.

'I mean; how can a guy not notice that his boot laces have been tied together like that?' Qorvas asked in mock amazement. 'It's like, you go to get your boots and you notice that they are tied together. You swear and grumble and untie them. You don't exactly put them on anyway and try to walk.'

'It was dark,' Björn said in a somewhat subdued tone.

'Didn't you feel that the boots were still connected when you put them on?' Qorvas asked, grinning.

'It was dark and...well I had indulged a little in the mead. You know that.'

Qorvas' face now took on a sober, matter-of-fact tone as he turned to Wulfgar.

'Well…yes, there was that,' he said. 'And it was dandelion mead. How often do you see that? Not often, which is why my brother here was so eager to sample it well.'

Now Björn's smile had returned fully. 'And sample it well I did!' he exclaimed.

Björn shifted his weight a little and settled in to his seating position. 'You need to watch out for this guy, Wishae,' Björn said, 'He is a consummate SOB when it comes to the trickster's game. He has got me many a time, let me tell you.'

'I'll keep that in mind,' Wulfgar said, grinning.

'What's this? Herbal tea?' Wulfgar said, leaning over and sniffing Wulfgar's cup. 'Argh!'

And with that Björn once again got up and shuffled back into the shallow cave. A moment later he returned, this time bearing a brown glass bottle with a metal screw-on top.

Björn grabbed a cup and poured a dash of the contents of the bottle into it. A thick herbal scent quickly infused the air and was quickly swept away by the prevailing breeze. The great gray-bearded Northman then took the metal cup and raised it to his lips, taking an appreciative drink.

'Ah!' he said. 'Now that's a Warrior's drink!'

Wulfgar looked at his teacher for a moment and then looked back at Qorvas. 'I don't know how he can drink that stuff,' he said.

'What? Absinthe?' Björn inquired. 'Maybe a bit too strong for ya, laddie? I tell you it's a man's drink and once you grow a little bit more of a liver then maybe you will like it too.'

'I think its maybe for the sake of not killing my liver that I stay away from that stuff.' Wulfgar said with a wrinkled nose. 'And besides, the taste doesn't exactly do anything for me.'

'You have to admit that drinking high-end absinthe out of a battered camp cup probably takes away from the experience a little though,' Qorvas commented.

Björn eyed his cup for a moment and then tipped it back, draining it. He then placed the little bottle behind him and sat back.

'Yeah, maybe a little bit,' he admitted.

'So the dip in the river was good?' Qorvas asked.

'Yes, it was good,' Björn replied with a shake of his long grey hair. Droplets from the still-wet mane splashed in the fire and sizzled upon the ring of stones. 'It wakes up the very spirit. Önd flows deeply there. You two should get out there and try it.'

For a moment the three men sat in silence, taking in the majesty of the rain, the wind, and the beautiful green that surrounded them.

At last Björn was up on his feet again and went rummaging in his pack. A minute later he came back with a small canvas bag from which he extracted a flat tin container with a slip-on lid. He poured some of the contents of the small container into the third metal cup by the fire, and poured some still-hot water inside of it. After a second or so he took a small twig from the ground nearby and used it to stir the contents of the cup.

'That smells amazing,' Wulfgar said. 'What is it?'

Indeed, the brew that Björn had put together did smell quite delicious. As he has added the hot water to the cup a powerful nutty-spicy aroma had filled the air.

'Have I not given you any of this before?' Björn asked, raising a bushy eyebrow.

When Wulfgar shook his head, Björn set the small can down on the sand near where his student was seated.

'Well, when you are finished having your tea and biscuits like the Queen, give some of this a try. You won't need much so take it easy on how much you use.'

'Yeah, but what is it?'

'It's a special mix of herbs,' Björn replied. 'Mostly chicory and dandelion root.'

'Dandelion root? Really?'

'Dandelion is a powerful plant helper,' Björn said. 'Our friends in the First Nations know that there are a lot of things you can do with it, from medicines to things like this camp coffee. Ask Qorvas here; his grandfather and his uncle used to make some pretty fantastic dandelion wine.'

'Actually that was my uncle,' Qorvas said with a grin. 'But my grandpa was pretty good at making other things out of dandelion. Coffee was one of these things.'

'You have much to learn, Wulfgar, but don't worry. You will learn in time,' Björn said, taking a tentative sip of his brew. Since Qorvas had taken the pot off the flames earlier, it had cooled down considerably and Björn did not have to wait so long for his drink to be ready. 'Very good,' he said.

'I know what you are going to say,' Qorvas prompted.

'What might that be?' Björn asked, again with the quizzical raised eyebrow.

'You were going to say 'a Warrior's drink!' ' Qorvas said, doing a fairly good approximation of his brother's voice.

Now Björn smiled craftily

'You never know,' he purred. 'That may have been exactly what I was going to say and it would have been true too!'

The three laughed. It was good to be with brothers, out in the wild places.

Finally, Björn turned to his student. 'So, are you ready for our adventure tomorrow?' he asked.

Wulfgar looked over at him and the smile faded from his face. It was replaced by a serious, attentive look.

'Yes, I am,' he replied. 'Ready whenever you are.'

'Good. We will need to get up early and not sleep in like I know my brother Qorvas probably will.'

'If you call getting up shortly after the sun rises 'sleeping in,' then yeah, sure, that's me,' Qorvas said with a shrug and a half smile. 'If I recall correctly, though, it is the Bear who loves to sleep in.'

'Ha!' Björn countered. 'That's only on the weekends when I am in the city. Not when I am out here in the clean air and the magic of the woods.'

Qorvas turned to look at Wulfgar. He still had the sarcastic half smile on his face.

'Feel free to give your Wataan a kick in the ass if he is not up by about 6am, will you? I certainly won't hold it against you.'

Björn laughed again, slapping his knee.

'Don't even think about it, wishae. I'll be up before you are!'

Björn took a deep drink of his camp coffee.

'So, when I was coming back to camp I heard my name being spoken,' he said. 'Were you two ladies conspiring behind my back or were you praising my glorious legend?'

Qorvas finished his tea and sat the cup down. 'Do you have any more of that green stuff or do I have to go looking in my pack for something to drink?' he asked.

Björn passed him the brown bottle and Qorvas poured a healthy splash in his cup.

'Actually we were talking about Master Tiva and the state of the world,' Qorvas replied.

Now Björn's face took on a kind of hushed, introspective look. It was as though for a moment he was looking at something within his mind's eye.

'A man of legend, that one,' Björn said at last. 'Did Qorvas ever tell you about the last days, when Tiva simply disappeared?'

'That is exactly the thing we were talking about,' Wulfgar replied.

'A powerful story to be sure,' Björn said. 'Just goes to show you that the world that most see is not the real world. Vir as gar'a, eh brother?'

Wulfgar raised his eyebrows. 'Thornish?' he asked.

'Yes,' Qorvas replied. 'You must have heard bits and pieces by now.'

Thornish as a tongue, or way-of-speaking, is not a true language in the sense but is a relatively small collection of words and phrases used exclusively by Thornish people. It lacks the complexity and size of lexicon that a fully formed language might have and was originally created for ritual purposes such as ceremony and certain aspects of the Thornish oral tradition. However, over time, the Thornish tongue, known also as Tornaas Voxa, had grown somewhat organically and, as some said, had at times developed a life of its own.

'Yes, I have,' Wulfgar said. 'But just in bits and pieces. So what did Björn just say?'

Qorvas sounded the phrase out for Wulfgar. 'Veer ash gar…a,' he said. 'that means *We are spears*'.'

'We are spears,' Björn repeated. 'It's something we say to remind ourselves of a number of things, first of all that we as Thornish folk are sharpened implements of the Elder Kin, of the First Law; of nature. Secondly, it's to remind us that what you see here,' Björn plucked at his shirt sleeve with a dramatic gesture, 'is but the tiniest tip of the actual being behind it.'

'Think of it like a great steel-headed spear set on a polished black ash-wood shaft,' Qorvas said. 'This is a great battle spear I am talking about here, a spear of the war-field with a very long shaft. Now imagine the tip of this great, long spear pushing through a barrier, like a hide stretched on a frame. Imagine the smallest portion of that razor edged spearhead poking through the other side, less than half the length of your finger or less.'

'Okay, I am imagining that,' Wulfgar said.

Björn grinned once again.

'Now imagine that the tiny little tip that is poking through the hide is a person, the consciousness of the person and the person that anyone can see. You, me, Qorvas...anybody. That tiny little tip, barely noticeable on this great big bull hide, is how each of us manifests here in the Middle-World. All the while the REAL us, the rest of the spear-head, the rest of the spear on the other side of that hide: That is the rest of you, the full you, the you that extends into the spirit world and beyond. What we see here, this physical stuff? This is just for show.'

'Some say it is mere illusion, but it's an illusion that we have to deal with in this physical incarnation,' Qorvas added.

'The rest of what we are is massive, huge, way beyond the ability of these little brains in these frail bodies to comprehend. What we see here in the Middle-World is but a snowflake on the tip of an iceberg,' Björn said. 'So when we say Vîr as gar'a; we are spears, that is what we are referring to.'

Wulfgar nodded.

'Veer Ash Gara. You are right, I know very little,' he said humbly.

To this the great bear of a man, Björn, laughed once more. It was an honest, hearty laugh that held no malice in it at all.

'Compared to the Great Essence, that intelligent energy field of the multiverse and even compared to our true, higher selves, none of us know anything! I am surprised we are as awake as we are and not stumbling about covered in our own shit. But the Old Ones have given us at least a glimpse of the spark and it is the job of re-awakened ones like ourselves to rekindle the sacred sparks and grow stronger!'

'And for those who honor the teachings of Qor there is a third meaning to Vîr as gar'a,' Qorvas said. 'To be of the spears is to be a particularly focused instrument. It is to walk a way of deep honor and commitment and to understand that most of modern society is a fabric of lies .and weakness. It is to constantly strive to bring more wood to the great bonfire of the reawakening.'

'Qor is the primal hunter, the primal bear-warrior.' Björn said. 'We

Thornsmen have known about him for a long, long time. He is the primal spearman among other things, so the idea that we are all spears…it makes good sense.'

'And it was Qor who spoke of the need for the *Rekindling* of pagan hearts and spirits to save the world.' Qorvas added. 'According to the stories our elders have told us, anyway…'

'Yes! That is true too,' Björn said. 'We are but the tip of a great spear. And it is men like Master Tiva who knew how to access the rest of that spear…or in his case a two-pronged stang, as it pushed through the fabric of time and space. He knew things and could do things that normal men could not.'

'I think he had an advantage over us with that two-pronged stang of the Farers,' Qorvas said. 'Where the scarlet branch of the Warriors gets a single-tipped spear, the Farers often go about with a forked stang so there is more of them poking through.'

Björn chuckled at his friend's somewhat humorous analogy. 'Yes, they are cheaters!' He laughed. 'This is why they amass so much more magic than we Warriors do!'

'I think they cheat at cards too,' Qorvas said with a deadpan face, one which shifted back to jocularity after a mere moment or two.

Qorvas laughed and Wulfgar, seeing the point of the joke, now laughed also.

'Seriously though,' Björn said at last, 'There are many things that we don't understand and that is why we go out into the wild places, the sacred places, to try to understand. It makes us stronger, wiser and indeed craftier as a result.'

'It's a continuous process,' Qorvas said. 'In this life at least, there is no end to it. We grow in wisdom and in our skills, we try to find others who think like we do and we strive to forge a new tribal way. We are the Rekindling, as I said to you earlier. We are but the first few sparks in the fire-pit, trying to re-illuminate the tribal soul of men.'

'We are stewards who have been handed a burned-out forest, so to speak,' Björn grumbled. 'In this rotting carcass of a world that is being killed day by day, we work to clean up a camp left filthy by drunken fools; a planet killed by the unworthy who take and take, caring nothing for the sacred gift of life or of freedom or of the world. The Old Ones have awakened us for a reason and that reason is to awaken, arise, and do battle with the scum who have been killing our sacred world for far too long.'

'Do battle?' Wulfgar asked.

'Lady Battle has many faces, my young friend.' Qorvas said with a gleam in his eye.

There was a fire there in the Shar Master's green eyes now, something that Wulfgar had not seen before. 'You are young but you have some experience already, growing up as you did in a tough part of the city. You know what it is to fight, to be beaten down and also to taste victory. Yet physical conflict is only one flavor of battle. One can fight a battle of words, speaking to people, encouraging them to wake up and smell the carnage of greed that is all around them. You can engage in debates with the servants of the world-killers and you can go face-to-face with the herd dogs if necessary. But there are many ways to do battle and in this age of information one of the best ways is to see to it that people are informed. Those who are given true information, not the filth of government or corporate propaganda, have the opportunity to awaken. When people awaken they see the damage that has been done.'

'And usually when people awaken the first three things that come to them are sorrow, pain and then anger when they suddenly see what is about them,' Björn growled. Wulfgar looked at his teacher and realized that the same smoldering fire that he had seen in Qorvas' eyes was now there too. Wulfgar himself felt it beginning to rise up from the base of his spine towards his face.

It was, without a doubt, the sacred Bloodfire, that sacred flame that is given by the Old Ones into the blood, liver and bones of Warriors alone; that mighty molten current of passion and honor that drives certain folk not along the sedate trails of the herd but instead up the rock-strewn, danger-filled slopes of hardship and pain, the only true road of glory.

Wulfgar remembered well his own awakening, not all that many years ago when he had been attending college back in the east. One day over his morning coffee, before his classes, he had been looking out over the many other fellow students that had gathered in a large cafeteria. As he sat there he had overheard many voices speaking. It was the usual great murmur of information exchange that one hears in a large crowd and yet although one tries to mind one's own business it is difficult not to overhear the conversations of others.

Suddenly something in his mind began to focus on snippets of conversation here and there. Not far from where he sat there were a group of rather big fellows all gathered around a table, drinking coffee and piling down something that had been advertised as 'scrambled eggs.' By the looks of them and the school jerseys and paraphernalia they were likely members of one of the university's varsity sports teams. One of the fellows was complaining of a massive hangover he had from drinking the night before. Another complained that the girl he was trying to date was continuously refusing his invites for dinner.

At another table one fellow was complaining about how his student loans were going to leave him in a huge debt after he had graduated; that even if he found a good job right away he would be working like a slave for years to pay off the debt. His friend quietly nodded and tried to be sympathetic to his friend's situation.

Another fellow student, this time a young woman, told her two friends that she wasn't sure if she would be able to afford another year at college. Her expenses were already too high.

Yet another, a young man not far from where Wulfgar was sitting, was telling his friend how anxious he was to be finished, to be 'free of this place' so he could go off and start making some 'real money.'

And still another, a fellow off to the other side of Wulfgar, was saying that he was going to try to change his major so that he could get into pharmacy studies. Pharmacy was far more profitable and people could get quite wealthy doing that, the young man said to his friends.

Wulfgar had drifted along for some moments, absently listening here and there and at the same time trying not to listen. He felt for a time as though he was caught up in some kind of surreal dream.

At last a sudden movement brought Wulfgar out of his reverie and he noticed that there was a man asking if he could sit at the table Wulfgar was occupying. The man was considerably older than Wulfgar and he appeared as though he might be a junior professor of some kind. He wore a brown tweed sport coat and wool slacks but no tie. He stood there smiling from behind round gold wire-framed glasses and holding his breakfast tray.

As unusual as it was to see faculty in this cafeteria Wulfgar supposed that its proximity to the center of campus might occasion a few to drop in. Wulfgar had found himself seated at a table with three chairs and yet despite the crowd no one had, as yet, asked to take a seat.

'Not much room in here,' the man said. 'Is it okay if I join you?'

Wulfgar, by now jolted back to wakefulness, nodded and said, 'Sure, no problem.' And the man had gratefully sat himself down.

'You were kind of lost in thought,' the newcomer told him. 'I was hesitant to disturb you.'

And so for awhile, after having exchanged the usual polite pleasantries, Wulfgar drifted back to his coffee cup and the man who had joined him set into his eggs and toast while looking over what appeared to be student papers.

Wulfgar found himself drifting again, in and out of various conversations, when the man across from him said something to him. What he said shocked Wulfgar back into consciousness and indeed ignited the fuse of deep change within his mind.

'I probably shouldn't be saying this, you know, but you seem like a decent enough fellow,' the man said. 'But you don't look like you belong here. You look like you came to college with expectations of another decade and found...well, something that you didn't really expect or like.'

At first Wulfgar said nothing but simply looked at the man. What he had said was almost exactly in tune with what he himself had been thinking over the past three years on campus; that he had come hoping to have a traditional collegiate experience and had found instead something...else.

'I know that look you had on your face,' the man said after a moment more. 'I know it because I had it on my own face once, long ago. But the only difference between you and me is that I didn't realize I had that look until I was starting my doctorate. By then I was so much in debt I had to finish and try to get a job teaching. I was lucky and managed to get in before the shit really hit the fan jobs-wise. But that was a long time ago. This is now.'

'Yeah, you are right,' Wulfgar told the man. 'I came here expecting all of the school pride and the social fun as well as the classes in the ivy-covered buildings. What I found instead were lots of people in deep debt and not so much school pride as I had hoped.'

'They are no longer the aspiring professors or community leaders we had when I was an undergrad,' the man said. 'They are mostly a big group of scared young folks who have no idea about the future. Some more than others. Now there seem to be two kinds of students: the ones who try to drown it all out with drinking and partying and the kinds who drive themselves relentlessly, brutally, all with the hope of good grades and a high paying cubicle on the other and of graduation day.'

'So what does it all mean?' Wulfgar found himself asking and at the same time marveling in the weirdness of this entire situation.

To this the man leaned closer across the table and said in a very serious, conspiratorial tone, 'The world is not what most think it is. The world the herd-people see is mostly illusion. We are living in a modern day version of the Middle Ages, only now it is elite corporate interests occupying the place that royalty formally did. The few are still rulers of a vast serfdom and only those who properly re-awaken themselves have any hope of breaking free of this great deception. What you see around you, largely, are herd people training to be more efficient chattel. They have no chains about their necks or ankles yet the result is the same. Freedom is never free, my young friend. and I sense that you are well aware of that.'

The cryptic bespectacled man leaned back, stopped speaking for a moment, and took a considered sip of his coffee.

'Yet a great change is coming,' he continued. 'In this change many will die. Warriors will rise to battle and cowards will flee from it. The old ways will emerge to fight the sickness of two millennia or more that has infected the world. Many ideas will die in this conflict but from the ashes a new world will be born.'

The man paused for a moment and then added, 'Lions kill sheep, not the other way around, and the unworthy will exclude themselves.'

Suddenly the man straightened up, looked at his watch as if he had some pressing engagement, and took one last sip of his coffee.

'You look like you might be one of those lions I was speaking about,' he said. 'That is why what I have said to you I say only to about one in a thousand.'

After this the man stood up, and gathered his things and his tray. He smiled at Wulfgar as he turned to make his way back through the crowd.

'Good luck to you in the times to come,' he said, 'Sharpen your claws, young lion!' And then he was gone.

After that strange meeting Wulfgar's attitudes about things had begin to change. He began to question everything and the more he questioned the more a single realization grew in his mind; that the mysterious professor had been right. The world was sick, twisted and run by a relatively small cabal of people who were either seriously mentally ill or supremely evil. Wulfgar began to understand that the world was certainly what the mainstream world and the mainstream media wanted him to believe it was…and with that, slowly, painfully, sorrowfully, had come the beginnings of his full awakening.

Wulfgar never saw that mysterious professor again although he spent considerable time trying to relocate him. Finally, he realized that some things are meant to happen one time only in a person's life and he accepted it for what it was.

Not wanting to leave unfinished business behind him Wulfgar had stuck it out and at last, a year later, he finally graduated from college. As the professor had suggested there was little out there for a person with a mere undergraduate degree other than a dim, cloudy horizon. Wulfgar decided to take to the road and travel while he still could. In the west, finally, after months of wandering, he chanced across a small neighborhood pub. And there, in that dimly lit place of Irish music and merriment, he made the acquaintance of the man called Björn Hammarson, a Thornsman and Shar Master.

'And now, here you are, almost two years later, in a cave by a river…with two Thornish Warriors,' Björn said suddenly.

Wulfgar snapped out of his immersion in memory and looked at his teacher in surprise.

Björn spread his hands apart and shrugged his shoulders.

'There are no psychic powers involved,' he said plainly. 'I know that look you had there on your face. I've worn it on my own face from time to time as I pondered the path from there to here. Everyone has come here of their own unique trail, my friend. And everyone's story is interesting and worth listening to.'

'In essence all we really are, after the deeds are done, is our stories,' Qorvas added.

'Yeah, I did get a little lost in memory there,' Wulfgar admitted. 'I was thinking about college and how one conversation with one man really got me thinking….and how that thinking started to wake me up and that waking up eventually brought me here.'

'Ah, the Professor,' Björn said. 'I have heard that story from you. It is a good story.'

'And a true one too.'

Björn clapped his student on the back. 'Of that I have no doubt,' he said.

'We were speaking about battles, though,' Wulfgar prompted, looking at Qorvas.

'Yes we were,' the older man replied. 'I was saying that not all battles are moments of physical conflict and this is true. Some are battles of words or of influence or of information or even of the spirit. It is up to the wise individual to decide when to fight in which particular way.'

'And when to decide when actual combat is warranted,' Björn said. 'And believe me, more and more in these times you will find that society is spiraling towards physical combat. For too long the social scientists and other cowardly manipulators have tried to turn the people of this world into spineless docile creatures. It sickens me more than you can know. However, try as they might to re-make humanity into a single gray, passionless mass, they will never truly be able to succeed.'

'Because of the Elder Kin?' Wulfgar asked.

'Because of many things, not the least of which are the Elder Kin,' Qorvas answered. 'The Old Ones, the spirit people who are all around us, the elemental beings of the world and the planet herself strain against this artificial behavior. It's not the destiny of humankind to become tamed cattle and as more and more people wake up and realize this the more resistance there will be to the political correctness experiment.'

'It is a disease,' Björn growled. 'And awakened, intelligent people who are not afraid to fight, are the cure. It does not matter if these people are Thornish or even Pagan. What matters is that many people are coming to the truth, a truth that has been hidden for a very long time.'

'And what we do as tribal people is a part of that truth,' Wulfgar said.

'Part of that truth, certainly,' Björn replied. 'And I will tell you that there can be no compromise on the truth of balance in nature, the balance of the First Law, the law of the cosmos. A clean, balanced planet where everyone has enough to eat and clean water to drink and where people can truly embrace freedom; that is the truth we strive for. Human beings who act as instruments of nature, as stewards of the land and not parasites upon her, that too is a truth we strive for. Individual perspectives or not, there can be no sane point of view that involves doing what so many of these governments and companies are doing to this world.'

'And we bide our time,' Qorvas said. 'We learn and train and grow and pass along what we know to those who are worthy. We try to live by example and we hold our tribal relations, friends, family and allies close. We do this so that we do our part in the great re-awakening and if we are called upon to fight – in any of the ways we have described – we will do so without hesitation.'

Björn raised his cup high. 'Without hesitation,' he echoed.

The next morning saw Björn and Wulfgar off on their quest as planned. They took with them small backpacks and left the main cache of their gear and supplies with Qorvas, who remained in the camp. They also took with them their Frith-knives and ceremonial spears as they headed off down the northbound trail.

Qorvas wished them well and settled into the peace of the camp. He would spend the next three days largely in meditation and silent contemplation. On one of the evenings, as a brilliant full autumn moon rose in pale orange above the camp, Qorvas chose to consult his runes. He performed a general cast, which involved scattering all thirty-three rune-staves upon the cloth, and spent a good deal of time pondering what they had to say to him.

On another day a small, shy black bear wandered through the perimeter of the camp. Qorvas was pleased to see this little brother and spoke friendly words to him but the bear, unused to humans, quickly took his leave. Other than these two things the time that Qorvas spent on his own was quite uneventful, which was exactly as he had hoped it would be.

The morning of the fourth day saw the return of the two brothers to the camp. Indeed, the sun had barely begun its rise above the local mountains to the east when Wulfgar and his teacher came walking into camp. As they had expected, Qorvas was waiting for them there, sitting by the fire with a cup of camp coffee in hand.

There was absolutely no surprise in the actions of Björn. Almost as soon as he got back into camp he greeted his brother, dropped his pack, set his spear down respectfully against the shelter and trotted off toward the river. Björn carefully cultivated his image as a fearsome Nordic Warrior and as such he was also fastidiously clean. It was quite obvious to Qorvas that his Oath-Brother had not found any other streams or lakes along his way that had been suitable for bathing. He had probably been dreaming of returning to the river for some time now.

Qorvas smiled at that and also smiled at seeing the return of their younger brother, Wulfgar. 'How did it go?' he asked, simply enough.

'Very well, I think,' Wulfgar replied.

And yet there was something different about the young blonde-haired man that Qorvas detected but had a hard time nailing down. There was something in his demeanor, his attitude; perhaps the way he carried himself that was not the same as before.

Wulfgar set his spear down in the same place as Björn had and then sat down across the small fire from Qorvas. The Warrior offered him a cup of the camp coffee and he gratefully accepted.

'You went to that peak that Björn had been talking about?' Qorvas asked as he handed the cup to Wulfgar.

'Yes, we did,' Wulfgar replied. 'But it was way harder than we thought. A big part of the south face was sheer cliff so we had to make our way around. We stopped about three quarters of the way up. You should have come with us. It was amazing.'

Qorvas shrugged and took a drink from his tea cup. 'I've had my share of adventures with Björn Hammarson,' he smiled. 'And besides I really enjoyed the peace and quiet. I did some meditating and wandering around. I even took a dip in the river.'

'Oh, that,' Wulfgar said, grinning. 'About halfway back Björn started telling me about how much he missed that river and what he was going to do the minute he got back here. At one point there was a pair of big bears down the trail from us and when I suggested we wait for them to leave or go around Björn wanted to just walk right past them. I guess he was very eager to get his dip in the river.'

'What did he do?'

'I convinced him to wait. Sure enough, the bears left after a while.'

Qorvas smiled and ran his fingers through his goatee.

'By now I am sure you are aware that Björn Hammarson is essentially fearless?'

Wulfgar nodded.

'He is a true Warrior,' Qorvas said. 'His greatest desire is to one day die a glorious death in battle. I am really serious about this. It is his true nature. Hopefully he will get his wish but hopefully this will be many years from now because I am fond of my brother and want to have him around.'

Wulfgar nodded again.

'I myself have seen him fight.' Qorvas said. 'Once, in fact, we fought a fierce battle with some troublemakers in the downtown area of the city. We were walking to the car after a night of enjoying ourselves and these three scum dared to try robbing us. To my brother's credit he did try to talk his way out of the situation, but the three who set themselves against us did not realize that Björn was talking because he wanted to preserve *their* safety, not ours.'

'And they still fought?'

'Yes. It was their big mistake,' Qorvas said. 'I barely had to do any work. I fought one who was not a very skilled fighter, I must say. He did get one or two good hits in on me before I put him on the ground. Björn, however, took on the other two and well... there was no contest. A bit of blood, but no contest. One ran away screaming insults and the other two, quite wisely, remained down.'

'Done like Warriors!' Wulfgar said, smiling.

Qorvas shook his head.

'They were no real match for us,' he said. 'Had there been another one or maybe two it was possible that WE would have been beaten. But I will tell you about a true Warrior act: When the two who remained on the ground began to plead that Björn not hit them anymore, he stood over them, gave them each a $20 bill from his wallet and said, 'If you are in need then ask. There are plenty of people who will help you if you just ask. The next time I see either of you I will kill you though, do you understand?' And my brother was being 100% honest when he said that too. He meant what he said and the two on the ground believed him. Lucky for those two guys we have never seen them again.'

Wulfgar said nothing but the look in his eyes, of the rising tendril of Bloodfire there, spoke volumes.

'There were a few other scrapes we got in, but the result was the same. Björn is a true Warrior and you are very lucky to have him teaching you. He is the kind of guy they wrote songs about back in the day.'

'I know that very well,' Wulfgar said. 'He has regaled me with tales of his service in the Armed Forces and of the many battles he has fought even as a civilian and emerged victorious. I can tell from the look in his eyes he is not bullshitting me.'

'My spear-brother does indeed tell some interesting tales. He is a good storyteller and a fine entertainer too. But he is not lying when he tells those tales. It would not be honorable for him to deceive another Thornish person by telling tall tales about such things.'

'Only Thornish people?'

'Well, Thornish people and others who are worthy of being treated respectfully,' Qorvas said. 'Never forget what you have, I am sure, been taught about honor and dishonorable people.'

'Do not waste honor upon the dishonorable,' Wulfgar quoted.

'Good,' Qorvas said. 'It is important to remember that. It was not always that way. There were times when it was thought a true Warrior was respectful and even-handed to almost everyone. However, there were times when this kind of thing was taken advantage of and used to make certain Warriors weak. Now a Warrior peers very carefully beneath the veneer of everyone he meets, ever cautious of those who would deceive and manipulate. As such now only the worthy are accorded honor and respect by Thornish people. There are indeed many people in the world worthy of our respect and courtesy, but not all. The unworthy reveal themselves quite easily most of the time.'

'I hear that,' Wulfgar said. 'Since Björn has started teaching me I have had my eyes opened up to a great many things, some pretty mind blowing things actually.'

'I think I am experiencing some déjà 'vu here!' Björn said, this time swaggering back from the riverside completely naked. 'Just like last time I hear my name being spoken around the fire and I wonder...are you two planning my assassination?'

'Well, if we were you are an easy target with your white skin in the morning sun,' Qorvas joked. 'Or perhaps we will wait until you are at ease and jump on you with knives.'

Björn walked past Qorvas chuckling, just as he had done days earlier, and went in to the back of his shelter to find more clothes.

'I doubt that either of you would jump on a naked man...and that I would use to my advantage in the battle!'

'Of that my friend, I have absolutely zero doubt,' Qorvas replied. 'I assume you had a good trip?'

'Did this wet behind the ears pup tell you that he experienced a Vision up there in those peaks?' Björn said dryly from his location behind them. 'After only a couple of days in the heights? I must say I am quite jealous! I had to work much harder on that kind of thing than this guy.'

Qorvas looked at Wulfgar. 'No, he did not,' Qorvas said.

'Over the past few days I think our young friend here has learned much about the ways of the Warrior,' Björn added. 'Much indeed.'

Qorvas did not ask Wulfgar about the Vision he was said to have experienced. In Thornish culture such a question would have been considered intrusive or rude. In such cases, should the recipient of such things choose to speak about it they could do so. If not, it was considered to be a private matter and left at that.

Björn, as Wulfgar's mentor, was perfectly within his rights to speak about the occurrence of the Vision, though he did not and would not speak of the details. That would be Wulfgar's privilege or not, as he chose.

'I made a place for myself on a ledge with an amazing view,' Wulfgar said quietly. 'And I settled myself in there to meditate and become one with the land, just as Björn instructed me. I stayed there all day and all night taking only water. The next day came and I sat through it as well. I got up a few time to stretch but other than that I stayed where I was.'

'You know it is not our way to lock ourselves into any particular place for such exercises,' Björn said. 'Had you wished to move around I would have followed you at a discreet distance.'

'I know that, Wataan,' Wulfgar said, addressing Björn respectfully. 'But it felt right to stay where I was. Besides that, I felt a really strong connection to the mountain and even, I think, to the People-of-the-Deep-Earth.'

'Ah, the Deep Earth Folk. Dwarves. That is a good thing. It's good to have them as teachers,' Qorvas commented.

'I left offerings for them,' Wulfgar said. 'Nine copper pennies and an old silver dime I had, from back in the days when there was more silver in dimes. So I left that for them. After that I stayed where I was. Time seemed to blend in on itself, if that makes any sense. I didn't have the same anxiety, the wanting to just get up and leave kind of thing that I had during my deepening. I was exactly where I was supposed to be and I stayed there.'

By this time Björn had returned to the fire and seated himself next to his student. He nodded at what Wulfgar had said, as did Qorvas. Neither said anything at that point.

After a time of silence, Qorvas said, 'There is no need to continue. If the rest is your private matter, then we'll leave it that way.'

Wulfgar shook his head.

'I can go for a bit more,' he said. 'As I said, time started to blend in on itself. It had lost meaning for me. I forgot what day it was and at one point was glad I had Björn with me as a Watcher because I thought maybe I might forget to eat or drink water or something.'

'I was always there, little brother,' Björn said calmly. 'Though you didn't see me for what seemed like a long time I was always close enough, in case anything might have happened.'

'After a time I let go of that worry and began to drift. At one point I thought I was sinking into the Earth herself and though maybe the Deep-Earth folk were inviting me to their homes. But this passed as well and for a long time I just sat there, shaded by that little tree, and waited.'

'Hmm,' Qorvas said after a moment. 'Sounds to me like you were indeed meant to go there to that place. Not everyone can do that. They get impatient or curious about what's over the next ridge.'

'He is really good at this, bro,' Björn said. 'He has some deep talent there.'

'It was then that I saw Qor, son of the Mountain,' Wulfgar said suddenly. 'He was there, that primal hunter, right across from me, sitting cross-legged in the same tribal style as I was. It was like he was looking at me across fifty thousand years of time and space. He spoke to me while I sat there and I will tell you that I felt a very powerful connection with him, like he was my older brother. His power was very dark and earthy but it held no danger for me at all.'

Now Qorvas put up his hand to halt Wulfgar from saying any more. 'Little brother, I want to say something now. It sounds like you have had a very powerful Vision and if it is Qor who has visited you then you are really fortunate indeed. I am sure that Björn is very proud of your achievement as you are too, but I should ask you to tell me no more about it, at least until you have had time to rest and think about your experience. It is a good custom to take time before you reveal all of the details, if that's what you want to do, because in these things there is power. The power was meant for you and you need time to learn from that on your own.'

'I agree with this,' Björn said, 'Even though he was so excited in the end there, after it was over, he insisted on telling me everything.'

'Well, telling your mentor is no great crime,' Qorvas said. 'But I ask you take some time before telling anyone else.'

Wulfgar looked at Qorvas for a moment, not sure how to respond and then said, 'That sounds like a great idea. And you know what? Even though it's daytime I have some sleep to catch up on.'

And with that he got up and went to the back where his blanket and sleeping bag were stored.

'You should sleep naked, so no one will attack you with knives,' Björn joked.

'Not funny,' came Wulfgar's light-hearted reply.

Qorvas waited for a time before speaking. They wanted to give Wulfgar a chance to relax and fully go to sleep.

After a suitable time had passed Qorvas turned to his friend. 'A good experience eh?'

'He is quite gifted,' Björn replied. 'He did not have nearly the trouble he had with his Deepening. He has learned from the experience and had no trouble this time around at all.'

'That's really good. Sounds like a potent Vision.'

'He earned it,' Björn said. 'I was getting concerned and wanted to step in to get him to take more water. He turned out to be okay though.'

The two brothers changed the subject and talked about other things. After a time, they both went back down to the river and sat by the water before returning later to cook food. They noticed that Wulfgar was deeply asleep and did not disturb him. As it was young Wulfgar would sleep all through the night and into a portion of the next day.

A week passed before Qorvas again saw the young Warrior known as Wulfgar. He had been invited over to Björn's home for a weekend barbecue and when he had arrived he found a note from his host stuck to the door with tape that read: 'Gone to the store for more beer. Back shortly. You know where the key is. – B'

And indeed Qorvas knew exactly where the hidden spare key was located. Moments later he was relaxing on Björn's comfortable leather sofa, cold beverage in hand, waiting for his friend to return.

Qorvas was somewhat surprised to hear a knock at the door and find Wulfgar waiting there when he opened it. Qorvas found it somewhat unusual that Björn hadn't told him of anyone else coming over. It was quite a common thing for Qorvas and Björn to simply hang out together on a Friday or Saturday night, but if anyone else had been invited Björn was usually very up front about that. Still it was very good to see the young Seeker again so soon and Qorvas invited him in.

Once Wulfgar was told that Björn was not around his face suddenly took on a rather grim expression. The young man suddenly appeared to have a sense of urgency about him and told the older Thornsman that he had something he needed to talk about with him.

'Can it not wait until Björn comes back?' he asked. 'I have no doubt he will be back very soon.'

'I have already spoken to him about it,' Wulfgar said. 'He was completely unfazed and actually laughed when I finished talking.'

'A joke?'

'No joke,' came the reply. 'What I had to say to him was really serious and his response was totally the opposite of what I expected. At first I thought he wasn't taking me seriously, that somehow he was mocking me and I fought hard not to get angry…but I got angry anyway.'

Qorvas sat back in his seat and looked at Wulfgar seriously. 'Okay, tell me,' he said.

'What you said about sharing the details of my Vision…I am glad that you did that because once I had thought about it for a while I realized that some of it was really personal …in ways I can't even begin to understand. Other than Björn I have told no one the entire story about what happened and I probably never will. I share some of it with you though and you can share it if you want…to teach others.'

'That, my friend, is precisely why we have the custom the way that it is.' Qorvas said. 'People need time to process things like that before they go sharing the power of it. Indeed, some people aren't even worthy to be told about such things and others…well, others don't need to know.'

Wulfgar leaned forward toward Qorvas. 'I learned a lot,' he said. 'It triggered something deep inside of me. It erased a large block of general fear from me that I have been living with my whole life. Nothing serious but just general things that in the past have kept me from doing things as boldly as I would have liked. But in those moments the fear was lifted from me like a dark cloud that had been there seemingly forever. For that I am so grateful, and for a lot of other things. I had my experience with the red-bearded one and it was a very powerful thing. Even if I never have anything like that ever again, this was enough for one lifetime.'

'I too had an experience something like what you describe,' Qorvas said. 'Some time ago I went on a meditative retreat, a sojourn of sorts, along the cliffs by the sea. A strong voice came to me, just popped into my head and told me some powerful things and like you, I felt a sudden weight of what you might call residual life-fear removed from me.'

Wulfgar nodded.

'Yes, it was something like that,' he replied. 'But it was not Qor who told me what disturbed me. Somewhere in there, between the end of my time with the son-of-the-mountain and the time my experience came to an end a little brown-skinned man appeared. He seemed to come right out of the ground, just like that. And do you know what he said? He told me that he was sad because Björn would not get his Warrior's death.'

'Did he say anything else you want to share?' Qorvas asked.

'Nothing that I can remember clearly, but there was this deep sadness to the little man as he stood there. It was like he was hoping I would somehow be able to do something about the situation. I could do nothing but sit there and look at him. Finally, he went back into the ground and that was all I saw.'

Qorvas sat back further in his seat.

'This kind of thing is not unprecedented in my experience,' he said finally. 'My grandfather knew of his end, and he knew about the end of my brother Russell almost a year before it happened. Master Raven received a Vision of his demise as well, though there was no specific timeline attached. So the spirit person did not say when he thought Björn's end might come?'

'No.'

'And he didn't say anything about a dishonorable death?'

'No, nothing like that. Only that it would not be the Warrior's death that Björn has always hoped for.'

'And you told Björn this?' Qorvas asked.

'I didn't want to keep it from him,' Wulfgar replied.

'And he laughed?'

'Yes,' Wulfgar said with a frown. 'I would have thought he would have taken it more seriously.'

'Oh, I think he does take it seriously,' Qorvas replied. 'Only I think you and he have different ideas about what the message means. There can be many honorable ways of passing besides the death of charging into battle against one's foes. I know Björn quite well and I can tell you that while he takes honor very seriously he does not seem overly concerned with what-ifs, if you get my meaning.'

Wulfgar raised his eyebrow questioningly so Qorvas continued. 'A man's destiny is not set in stone,' he explained. 'Certainly we believe that persons of value, of worth to the Elder Kin can have a path which they must take by the end of their material lives; however, this is not considered to be a fatalistic thing. It is not strictly locked in, so to speak, so while a man's destiny might have a path to follow there can be many side-trails, choices that he might make along the way.'

'I think I understand you,' Wulfgar said. 'It's just that I had the impression that Björn was going to die and that when he did it might not be in the manner that he would have wanted.'

Qorvas grinned slightly now.

'The material body, this wolf-robe we have with us here, is a mere conveyance to get us around here in the Middle-World,' he said. 'These wolf-robes have a shelf life and when that is expired they die. We don't die; not the thing that truly makes us…us. We continue on as it always has been and it said that some of us come back over and over again since they like the Middle-World so much. Our friend Björn has an unusually powerful lust for life, as you know, so it seems to me that whatever end befalls him he will be back to have at it again.'

'And this is why he laughed?' Wulfgar asked, somewhat incredulously.

'Very likely, yes, I think so,' Qorvas said. 'I am sure he appreciates your concern but he also knows that a man has to walk his own path and live his own destiny. If Björn Hammarson has anything to say about it he will manage an honorable passing when the time comes.'

'I hope that is true, bro,' Wulfgar said after a moment. 'I care about him. He is a good man.'

Qorvas smiled.

'I know you do, and he is a good man – a great man, actually. I am sure you two will have many adventures together yet before the Dark Mother comes calling for him.'

And just then, at that very moment, Björn came walking through the door with a bag of groceries in each hand and a case of beer under each arm.

'What's this?' he exclaimed in a mock theatrical voice. 'You guys are talking about me yet again? It's a conspiracy, I tell ya!'

Björn set his bags and cases down and began putting things away in the kitchen.

'Our little bro was just informing me of your reaction to the information he got from the spirit people,' Qorvas said.

And now, finally, a look of serious concern fell into place on Björn's strong face. He stopped what he was doing and walked straight over to Wulfgar and took his hand.

'A powerful lesson in being Thornish is that we work to live as well as we hope to die; bravely, openly and without fear,' Björn said, shaking Wulfgar's hand and clapping him on the shoulder in a brotherly way.

'I am sorry if I threw you off when I laughed earlier,' he continued. 'But you see I try to live life according to my own interpretation of the Warrior way. You know the Dark Mother who guides us really gives us three gifts: The passing into the world here with our birth, the potential to live as best we can and finally, when the old wolf-hide is worn out, the chance at a half-decent death. Part of the way I walk is couched in a certain amount of bravado. It's just the way I am and when my time comes I will embrace it with a song in my heart, just as I expect you will. We are not sheep, we are wolves! We live largely and hope to die that way too.'

'I am no longer afraid of death as I once was,' Wulfgar said. 'When I was younger I was terrified of it. It was this great, black unknown. Nowadays I have little fear of it. It's a gateway, nothing more.'

'Good!' Björn exclaimed. 'Sheep fear the great unknown while wolves charge right out there to see what they can see. We are not sheep, little brother. We are something a little more dangerous.'

'My experience up on the mountain took what little fear I had left away,' Wulfgar added. 'It was a burden that was taken away.'

'And yet you feared for my death?' asked Björn.

'Not the idea that you would die,' Wulfgar said. 'I know the Thornish way well enough. We do not hold on to our loved ones selfishly when their time has come. Instead we celebrate them and honor their stories. No, I was worried about the idea that you might not die well.'

Now it was Qorvas' turn to slap Wulfgar good naturedly on the back. 'Well said!'

'Oh, have no worry about that, my good friend,' Björn said. 'I will do what needs to be done, and having said that let's move on to other talk, shall we?'

'There is a reason that the founders of the Thornish tradition left us with the phrase *Todah Miyosh*, little brother,' Qorvas said, not quite finished with this train of thought. 'True, it is the desire of every Warrior to have a good death and this does not mean that we get to go out guns blazing, so to speak. It means that we hope it to be noteworthy, just as we hope our lives will be noteworthy and of some use to the sacred balance.'

Todah Miyosh: the words of the Thornish Warrior. *Die powerfully; die well.*

'Sometimes one has to not be too greedy or arrogant and just be happy with a powerful life lived well,' Björn said. 'Sometimes we need to be happy with what we have right now and not worry overly much about the ultimate fate the Elder Kin and the ancestors hold for us.'

Björn took three cans of dark German beer from the counter where he had just placed them. He handed one each to his guests and cracked his open with a resounding hiss. He raised his beverage in a toast to his guests, his friends; his oath-sworn Thornish brothers.

'Let's keep the Rekindling going, brothers! Let's continue to learn, grow and teach others what we have discovered…until the day when our ancestors take us home again. Todah Miyosh!'

Qorvas raised his beer high, as did Wulfgar, and he saw that all of the earlier apprehension had faded from the younger man's face.

'Todah Miyosh!' he said at almost exactly the same time as Qorvas. 'Die well, but live well too!'

'I will drink to that yet again!' Björn said in a powerful tone, raising his drink high.

And drink he did.

A note on people and places...

Throughout this book there are a good many names to be found, both of people and places as well as other things. As the reader may have gathered from this or other works I have authored on the subject, the Thornish way is about respect, among other things; respect and balance. As such I thought it prudent to mention that while I have kept as true to the original tales as I could I have also made a few changes in order to protect both the personal privacy of some of the individuals mentioned. In many cases, with regard to the human beings in the stories, their tribal names or kennings for their names are used, and believe me these are as accurate (if not more so) descriptions of these individuals as their mundane names are.

Recall that names hold power and names that are earned hold even more power.

As well, I have remained deliberately vague about certain locations and places mentioned in the book and this is out of respect for the power of these locations and the spirit folk that dwell there.

Those who have become acquainted with Thornish culture will understand that knowledge is earned and wisdom is the clear comprehension of knowledge gathered through various acts over time. Respect is key to this process: Respect for the subject matter and respect for the self.

The knowledge contained here is intended to inspire and, to some degree, to educate. It is intended that it should help forge a key to a door, not to hand over everything which lies beyond that door. To simply hand it over would not be prudent or respectful. It would indeed rob the searcher of the delights of their own journey.

In order for one to truly gain power and wisdom in the world they must seek out their own trails of knowledge and cultivate their own wisdom based on their own experiences.

Let me add that hidden knowledge is a repository of power. Secret things hold a special kind of energy that retain their potency only when kept private. Thornish people know that those things which are hidden are of equal or greater power as those things which are fully exposed to the light. Only the unenlightened imagine that they should have the right to the secrets of others. Such assumptions are ignorant, at best, and woefully disrespectful as well.

As with any esoteric body of learning one of the most important lessons is that knowledge is earned and secrets are revealed only to the worthy. In the context of the Thornish way and many other such societies this is heady food for thought.

And finally, for those who have come this far and wish to continue along the Thornish Path, I wish you a most hale journey.

Regards,
Jack

Afterword

The Thornish tradition which I have described in the preceding pages has been in existence since November of 1958 when it was founded by a group of primally-focused yet forward-thinking men. These fellows saw the need for the creation of a society which would serve the awakened few who sought the roads of wisdom and power which was once the heritage of all human beings. In their quest to re-create a tribal circle of Earth and freedom-focused people they also worked to infuse their creation with considerations for flexibility and a mastery of adaptation which they hoped would see their creation forward into the decades beyond their own.

They succeeded in this even though at times the road was not easy. It seems that in the world of the modern human being there is resistance to those who have awakened. There are many obstructions placed in the path of those who have come to reclaim their birthright and who seek to re-establish themselves as stewards of the land. Strength and perseverance was required in order to overcome these hurdles. Wisdom and insight were the guiding implements of continuance.

During the nearly sixty years since those original six stood around a ritual fire and swore oaths of brotherhood, the tribal entity which they created has evolved, bent like a willow in the winds of time and, rather than break, it has grown stronger for the experience. In the early years, during the times of the society that was the progenitor of the Thornish tradition, a wise and gifted man predicted that there would be three 'fires' or manifestations of the tribal experience that we have shared.

The First Fire was found in the highly secretive form of the original Black Talon Society, a mutual protection order which sought to simply keep what few pagan and Native traditions that remained safe from the clutches of the overwhelming christianisation of those times. The Second Fire, so the prophecy has now proven, emerged in the form of the first Thornish lodge in the winter of 1958. Still somewhat secretive and exclusive in many ways, the Thornish tradition took on a special life of its own and while it evolved and became different from the Old Lodges, it still held proudly to the core principles and ideas which had been at the heart of its own creation.

The manifestation of our tribal spirit continued in the mode which we call the Second Fire for many years, yet with changing times eventually it was seen that a further evolution was required in order to adapt to the world of the 21st century. The heavy bonds of secrecy which had been the hallmark of both the First and Second Fire traditions were seen as needing to be lightened. The manner by which our tradition was communicated to the world needed to be altered if we were to utilize the amazing opportunities offered by modern technology. In nature, survival requires change and for the Thornish ways this change has gradually occurred.

In the winter of 2015 a gathering of Thornish initiates was held to discuss the changes which were needed if our tradition was to do well in the modern world. Though our numbers have never been overly large, we hoped that by adopting a more open approach we might get our particular message out so that other reawakened people might benefit from what we have come to know. Thus, by the end of this gathering, known by us as the Winter Council, the way of the Thornish tradition entered into what is now known as the *Third Fire*, an adapted, somewhat more modern form of the tribal culture which we have held since the middle of the 20th century.

This rekindled form of Thornish culture definitely contains the magic and the power of its predecessors, possibly more so, as it is the end result of decades of work and dedication. We have continually learned from those who have gone before us. We hope to kindle our fires even brighter and more profoundly than before and offer our teachings to those who might find them of interest.

We have believed for many years now that an awakening of the human spirit is upon the world and as Thornish tribal folk we know that more and more Earth-oriented tribal folk will arise to take up the defense of freedom, magic and life on our sacred home world. While we are but a single manifestation of such a spirit, we hope to play our part in the changing times ahead.

For more information on the Thornish tradition:

http://www.thornwoodpress.com/

https://thornwoodpress.wordpress.com/

Appendix:
The Black Spiral Prophecy

The Black Spiral Prophecy is the result of a powerful Vision experienced by Thornish Master and Elder Raven, known also as Ari Torinsson, during the autumn of 1957. The words of the prophecy are contained in three parts.

1. It was here in this place that I sat in silence and eventually was permitted to enter the realm of the spirit-world. For long hours I sat in that wild place, that place of deep history and in that place I had more history, that of the world not yet born, thrust into my hands.

It was here in this place, though still in the deeps of night that the land suddenly glowed as though dawn had arrived, yet I knew that it had not…and I saw in this dream that I was standing in the center of a grove of ancient trees. It was autumn and colored leaves were blowing everywhere on the wind. I looked down and I saw a piece of flat stone near my feet, barely pushing up above the ground.

As I watched, the stone grew in size, breaking free of the soil and rising before me until a dark menhir, some ten feet high, stood at the center of the grove. Suddenly it was as though I was above it, a raven on the wind and I could see that the dark menhir was but one of a band of brother-stones spread across the world in an immense, ancient spiral. Each Brother-stone represented a clan of sacred warriors who would come into being to protect the Lore and the sacred places in the world from the coming storm.

2. From the shadows of the earth far below I saw the flicker of light and I, in my raven-form, returned to the earth. When I landed there in a clearing near the stones, becoming a man again, a figure approached from the black beneath the trees. He was hooded and his face, other than a shaggy grey beard which hung below, could not be seen.

He spoke with authority in a voice which rolled like honeyed thunder over his grey beard.

He told me that in a time not my own yet a time of men I would teach, the cult of the bringers of the mind-death would at last begin to die. Their two equally destructive brothers would as well begin the slow fall to obscurity and fight it though they would, they would become extinct in the face of the great winter.

He told me that a sign to look for was the sign when even their greatest leaders became hunted and the folk of the world would believe less and less of their lies.

A great winter would eventually come, said the hooded one; a time of ice and cleansing. It would follow the false-summer which so many people would believe to be happening, for the warming would be the key which unlocked the door to the ice.

There would be a great cleansing and many wrongs would be righted.

The Elder Ones, he told me, were not pleased with what the desert-spawned ones had done to the realm of Midgard. He told me that he was disappointed in the ancestors of my own folk who had not risen against their filth sooner, yet he was glad it was finally happening.

The hooded one spoke of the milling throngs, folk of the world who had become no better than slaves or herd animals. He spoke of them with disgust and said that he would rejoice at the death of so many of them – something which would not be long in the coming. He also said that he would especially delight in the deaths of the ones who had led so many to their doom.

He said: 'They fathom that they might, by use of their riches, survive, yet their own, those closest in kin, will eventually turn on them.'

The hooded one told me that there would be years to come when much grimness would prevail in the world and this was a sign that the ice was creeping closer. He told me that I was to prepare by teaching the way of the sacred balance to those who were worthy.

3. The grim, hooded one faded from my sight and I was removed to another place, still in my human form.

I looked down on a vast plain and saw what appeared to me to be space-ships or planes leaping off of the ground and into the blackness above the world. There were long rows of people down on the plain and more arriving in various vehicles. The people were boarding these craft and they too were departing.

Others however, warded the perimeter of the field. They did not leave the world in the space-ships as the others did, but set about ever-widening the perimeter, pushing back those who were unworthy and who tried to force their way to the ships.

A soft presence made me turn and I looked upon a small, balding man in a green coat that looked as though it might have been made in the Indian-buckskin style. His head, I reckoned, was roughly at the height of my mid chest. He was quite short and though short, quite average-seeming in build otherwise.

His skin was very wrinkled with age and the weather, it seemed, and the color of his complexion was a dark, tanned brown.

The strange little man held a cane and he looked upon me with deep wisdom- filled eyes of dark grey. I knew without asking that I could not determine the species of this small person for there was a strong instinct telling me that he was not a human man. He was certainly not a white man and I did not think he was an Indian or any other kind of human race I had ever before seen. I reflected that perhaps he might be a form of elf, or perhaps of some spirit realm with which I was unfamiliar.

The little man spoke and he told me that I needed to be mindful of my duty: That I needed to pass on what I knew and what I would be taught, and that if I was successful some of my students would be on those ships going to the other worlds. In this way what we stood for would go out among the stars with the blessing of the Grey Farer.

The little man, with his strange speech, told me further that while some of our folk would fare to space, others would remain here as the ice approached, so that they could continue their duty to the Black Root and to the teachings of the Elder Kin. They would stay in the hope that the ice would not completely engulf the world.

The little man warned me that there would be a dire time coming and that my students would be the first to weather the onslaught of the storm; that I needed to teach them well. I was told that there would be few in the beginning, yet the number would grow and one day many would wear the sacred Raven-Sign. I was told that there was hope for humankind yet, because though the storm was now unavoidable, the spark of nobility among men had come out from the shadow of pestilence and many more each day were awakening from the lies of the mad.

At last the small man bade me heed my dreams and my instincts, and to 'seek always the Black Root' for in those things my greatest understandings would arise.

And with that the small man was gone, the scene of the space-ships was gone, and again I found myself floating in raven-form upon the wind. The great black spiral spread across the land before me and as I lofted higher and higher I could see that it was yet a small island of land in an approaching sea of ice.

As I rose toward the stars the voice of the hooded one rang loud and clearly in my mind. 'Seek your folk; seek your kin and never forget what you are.'

* * *

So ends the description of the Vision.

List of Illustrations

Fig. 10: Chapter Eight - **Crossings**
Representative of the mysteries of initiation

Fig. 11: Chapter Nine - **Mastery**
A Thornish symbol denoting traditional mastery

Index

CPSIA information can be obtained
at www.ICGtesting.com
Printed in the USA
BVHW041542080620
581024BV00007B/397